doing so beautifully.
— **Tara Sanchez,** author of *Urban Faery Magick: Connecting to the Fae in the Modern World*

MOTHER
Ecstasy, Transformation, and the Great Goddess

LEVI ROWLAND

Warlock Press™

PRAISE FOR THE BOOK

❝ The first adjectives that come to mind when reading this book are lucid and thorough. More significantly, I think, is that I found it refreshingly balanced and undoctrinaire. A Witch after my own heart. Praise be!"
— **M. Macha NightMare,** Witch at Large, San Rafael, California, machanightmare.com

❝ Sincere, enthusiastic, knowledgeable, and filled with grace – author Levi Rowland shares his elegant vision of the Mother in Her many forms of manifestation. A book that promises to inspire…and delivers beautifully."
— **Silver Ravenwolf,** author of *Solitary Witch: The Ultimate Book of Shadows for the New Generation* and *Poppet Magick*

❝ Levi Rowland's Mother Ecstasy, Transformation, and the Great Goddess is a painstakingly accurate study of humanity's fear and resentment of the divine feminine. Rowland examines and then rips apart the historical connotations of female deities as demons who cross-culturally morph into jealous, irrational, and hot-headed wielders of malevolent powers. Rowland blesses his readers with a clear and concise platform where we can each, free from patriarchal dogma, praise the Goddess of our choosing. Levi does the grueling work of research and affords his readers the opportunity to lean into a devotion that will awaken the spiritual vibrations of women and men worldwide for many, many generations to come."
— **Mawiyah Kai El-Jamah Bomani,** author of *Conjuring The Calabash: Empowering Women with Hoodoo Spells and Magick*

> It takes a scholar to compile facts. It takes a priest to describe the acts of ritual. And it takes a true devotee to write of raw devotion amidst waves of love and grief. Levi Rowland, in the wake of his beloved mother's death, has produced a fascinating and absorbing work that invites the reader to take heart in, and take a stand for, the once and eternal Goddess. He touches upon key themes such as the evolution of Goddess devotion, the patriarchal resistance to it, and the methods that have helped him arrive at the depth of love and understanding he so eloquently conveys in grounded, yet elegant language. This book is sincere, not florid. There is no feel-good filler here, just a beautifully crafted, coherent, and well-reasoned contribution to the corpus of literature of Goddess Spirituality. Bravo!"
>
> —— **Yeshe Matthews,** Priestess and Sibyl of *Tsogyal Lhamo Drayang Ling* (the Mt Shasta Goddess Temple) and proprietress of The Sacred Well, a shop in Dunsmuir, California at Mt. Shasta

> Timely, relevant, and heartfelt, Rowland offers a vulnerable yet impassioned tome on a central tenet of magickal practice that has inexplicably fallen out of favor in recent times: the veneration of the Goddess. Personally revealing and thoroughly researched, Rowland engages with big questions about what brings practitioners to the craft and why. This book is both honest and brave and Rowland's voice is a much needed counterpoint to popular secular witchcraft that is so pervasive today. The Goddess is firmly centered at the core of Magick not as an extension of individual will but as a divine entity worthy of (dare I say it) worship.
>
> —— **Judy Ann Nock,** Author of *The Modern Witchcraft Book of Crystal Magick* and *The Modern Witchcraft Guide to Magickal Herbs*

❝ Mother shows how returning to the Goddess is perhaps one of the most pressing issues we face to heal ourselves and our world. Mother is not for the meek of heart. In these pages, it becomes abundantly clear that the path of devotion is challenging for a reason.

Put time aside when you read Mother so you can integrate the learning. As the book continues, you can facilitate what you've learned in a personally meaningful manner. Mother is definitely a transformative tome for our era."

— **Patricia Telesco,** author of *A Kitchen Witch's Cookbook* and *365 Goddess: A Daily Guide to the Magic and Inspiration of the Goddess*

❝ Levi Rowland's 'Mother' is a love letter to the Goddess that challenges readers to engage with a deeper understanding of the divine feminine. Through an exploration of mystery and mysticism, intertwined with history and experience, the Mother becomes a living, vibrant presence who invites us all deeper. The Goddess is for everyone, as is this book."

— **Morgan Daimler,** author of Pagan Portals series books, *Freya, The Morrigan, Brigid,* and *Gods and Goddesses of Ireland*

❝ What a beautifully written book. Mother takes you through the journey of the author Levi similar to a biography. But this magical adventure invites you and lures you in with the in-depth knowledge and passion that the author senses and feels, and as they are awakened so are you by the light and ecstasy of the Great Mother.

There is so much emotion and passion in the writings that show a sincerity that is exciting and entices you to read more. There are not many new books that I read and find genuine and alive with a deep connection and personal Truth of the Mother. But this is one that is a must to read."

— **Tamara Forslun,** The Witch of Oz and author of *Encyclopedia of the Divine Feminine: Goddess of 10,000 Names*

❝ A unique, well researched, and instructive missive for initiates of the Craft. Drawing from ancient historical texts, across culture and continent, also a variety of religions and practices, and from more modern philosophers and psychologies, Rowland crafts a foundation for an understanding of Mother - as Goddess, and Mother Worship as the source of magic for Witches.

Rowland holds the reader's interest and attention with sourced materials that take pains to explain the expansiveness of Mother, and the necessity of examining the Mystery, in all its facets.

— **Angie Buchanan,** senior minister of Earth Traditions, and founder of The Death Midwife

❝ Let us Worship her in Wild Spaces!

This latest offering from Levi Rowland sensitively examines what it means to be a devotee of The Great Goddess & Queen of the Witches. We are encouraged to explore, to experience and submerge ourselves in her mysteries rather than grasping with cold transactional rites, only to watch that which should be revealed slip through our fingers like grains of sand.

Faith, Ecstasis, Prayer and Devotion all play a role in our relationship with the Great Mother; this book is eloquent, honest, and refreshing. It takes a brave person to speak their truth, especially when the truth isn't the flavour of the moment. Levi Rowland has done it again, saying what needs to be said and

Mother: Ecstasy, Transformation, and the Great Goddess

© 2023, Levi Rowland

All rights reserved. No part of this publication may be reproduced, stored in a retrieval system or transmitted in any form or by any means, electronic, mechanical, photocopying, recording or otherwise without the prior permission of the publisher or in accordance with the provisions of the Copyright, Designs and Patents Act 1988 or under the terms of any license permitting limited copying issued by the Copyright Licensing Agency.

Published by:
Warlock Press
1219 Decatur Street
New Orleans, 70116 LA, USA

Cover Art: Christy Kane
Cover Design and Typesetting: Christian Day
Interior Photos: Copyright where noted
Copy Editing: Christian Day and Brian Cain

ISBN-13: 978-1-7332466-7-5

CONTENTS

Foreword XIII

INTRODUCTION
Face to Face   1

CHAPTER 1
The Transformations of Devotion   11

Faith and Magic 11
The Mystery CultS: Initiatory Goddess Worship as Transformation . . 15
Devoted to Her. 26
An Important Final Note 27

CHAPTER 2
Ex Stasis: Mysticism and the Search for Mother   30

Defining the Undefinable 30
Knowing the Mother 35
Methods of Madness 38
    Entheogens 39
    The Body 40
    Ritual and the Sacred 43

CHAPTER 3
Prayer: The Presence of Mother   47

Let Us Pray 47
The Names of Mother: Contemplative Chant 52
Shout, Drum, and Dance: Ecstatic Prayer 56
Prayer Life 59

CHAPTER 4
Tokens of Mother: Symbolism and the Goddess   61

What's in a symbol? 61
Idolatry: Mother in Art and Image 65
Touchpoints of Worship 67
    The Moon 68

The Wild Beasts	71
The Chalice	73
The Sea	75
The Flower	76

CHAPTER 5
Shaktism: The Worship of Devi — 79

Crossing Lines for God the Mother	79
The Goddess as Power Itself	86
Bhakti: The Path of Devotion	91
Drawing from the Well	96

CHAPTER 6
Hera: A Case Study — 99

A Jilted Goddess	99
Why Hera?	107
Compartmentalization	108
The Primeval	112

CHAPTER 7
Queen of the Witches — 114

Forms Divine	114
Devil or Woman?	116
Witch-Goddess	117
Beyond Diana	121
Worshipping the Witch	125
Goddess of Magic	127

CHAPTER 8
Queen of Hell — 135

Into the Dark	136
The Unwilling Queen of Hell	139
Saints and Psychoanalysis: Under the Gaze of Mother	141
The Hag	145
Stopping & Starting	148

CHAPTER 9
Queen of Heaven — 150

Cosmic Proportions 151
Mother-Mind: Meditation and the Goddess 153
Calm 155
The Visions of Mother 159
Example 162
    Pathworking: The Altar *162*

CHAPTER 10
Mother of Many Mothers: Saints, Queens, and Monsters — 166

What makes a Goddess? 166
The Popular and the Scholarly 170
Goddesses of Contemporary Craft and Paganism 173
The Fountains of the Mother 177
History 179

CHAPTER 11
Oracles: Divination and the Goddess — 183

Reading Fortunes 183
Sibyls: Mouthpieces of God 187
The Worth of a Reading 192
Mother-Knowledge 195
Ritualizing 198

CHAPTER 12
Cycles upon Cycles: The Dance of the Goddess — 201

The Circle and the Line 201
Life and Death 207
And After… 210
The Wide Web of Earth 212
Making the Difficult Holy 215

CHAPTER 13
Finding Mother in Hostile Lands: Sophia and Other Faces — 217

Wisdom Beyond the Veil 217
Mary: An Interlude 219
Extra Ecclesiam: Outside of the Church 223

Sophia and the Gnostics 227
The Orthodox Sophia 231
Unveiling and Excavating 233

CHAPTER 14
Goddess Circles: Seeking Mother in Groups   237

One to Many 237
Craft. 238
Other Paths: Flags, Red and Green 239
Paranoia: The Mother of Red Flags 242
Waiting 245
Into the World 246

CHAPTER 15
Moving Forward (and Backward): Final Thoughts   250

At the Temple. 250
Mother-Life. 255

THE MOTHER'S BREVIARY
Rites, Prayers, and Other Holy Things   258

AFTERWORD: AFTERLIFE **301**

BIBLIOGRAPHY **304**

INDEX **314**

ABOUT THE AUTHOR **316**

ACKNOWLEDGMENTS

This book would not be possible without the work of Warlock Press, including Brian Cain and Christian Day. I want to thank all the incredible souls that have helped push me to create and share the writing that became Mother. I particularly want to thank the priestesses that have inspired me to constantly return to the altar of the Great Goddess. This list includes all the priestesses of the covens I have worked with. You are continual sources of inspiration and faith for me. I also want to give voice to the indomitable and incredible High Priestess Val Hughes, who passed away before the publication of this book. I treasure my memories of her and know that she rests in the embrace and ecstasy of the Goddess. I also wish to thank my loving husband, Patrick, for his unfailing support. I also must give voice to my mother, who passed away during the writing of this work. The spirit and memory of her love is the foundation for everything I do, including my eternal quest for the Goddess.

DEDICATION

This book is dedicated to the memory of my mother, Paula, who convinced me more than any argument or experience that there is most definitely a God…and that She is love.

FOREWORD

In the beginning, the One who made night and day, soil and sea, humans and all other animals was a Primal Mother who birthed the universe from Her Sacred Womb and to whose womb all living things returned to undergo the cycle again.

Her image has traveled down the ages in stone and clay: the so-called Venus figurines are dense yet small figures that fit comfortably in the palm of the hand. She was everything then: creator and birther, the one who destroyed and made the way clear. She did not fit in the narrow boxes assigned to Her in the centuries that followed, when She became the Goddess of only one small piece of Her power and authority.

Her descendants were to split Her into a multiplicity of divinities: one for war, one for beauty, one for wisdom, each with symbols to mark Her, to diminish and contain Her Might. With the coming of that peculiar idea of monotheism that posited the Divine Maker as male, the statues and the temples—even the concept of that ancient life-giver—began to be erased from the minds and hearts of the people. Where She lingered in Western civilization, She was a martyred maiden, a sorrowing mother, a whore fit only to ensnare the souls of men.

Those enclosed and minimized Goddesses became saints, witches and monsters. In many cultures, the Holy Mother and any aspect of the Divine Female became objects of fear, objects of ridicule. The loss of Her status was mirrored in the falling status of human women, all the female (divine and human) was relegated to home and hearth, and to the tending and preservation of both family and the culture built around it.

Years passed, centuries passed. The conditions for women throughout the world's cultures were affected by the powers that colonized and subdued those cultures, powers that were aligned with the male god of the colonizers. The contagion of patriarchy spread throughout the colonized world and previously matrilineal cultures bowed under the weight of it.

But all was not lost. She was not killed—how could She be? She could not be destroyed for She is the force that moves the universe She birthed. She was in exile, obscured. In these days that are our days, She is said to have been sleeping, and perhaps that is the case. She has certainly been the font of all things for many ages longer than the male gods who trapped Her in their orthodoxies, who dreaded Her authority over birth and death—and everything in between.

Now She is awakening in all the places where She has slumbered. In the ancient cultures that held Her longest in their ancestral memory, She is once more stretching and touching the souls of the grannies and the aunties. These wisdomkeepers are nodding their sage heads and recalling the stories of their own grannies—stories of the old woman of winter, of the hungry mother who gives blessings for a good loaf of bread, of the brave girl who ventured into the wild wood to save her family and find herself.

New liturgies are written, new songs are sung, new prayers are prayed throughout the strongholds of the sky-father god. Sometimes they are sung in secret over the cradle of a newborn child. Sometimes they are whispered as the evening meal is prepared, songs and prayers of gratitude and solidarity. New temples are raised in Her honor and older temples are being returned to Her dedication. She is everywhere, celebrated even in the places where She is most reviled. Her people have remembered Her at last, have called to Her. And She has answered.

She has broken free from the cages of old patriarchy's rigid assignments. No longer is She merely the Goddess of Grain, or the Goddess of Water. Now She—and They—stand in the fullness of Their power—Goddess, Teacher, Mother. She is one and many, often identified by Her devotees as the Goddess of Many Names. She is the sky and the hearth, the earth and the lightning, the blood and the hollow bone.

She is death-bringer and also that which germinates the seeds in springtime. She is cozy and gentle, She is angry and resilient, She is the genia locae of specific spaces and She is the entirety of all time and all space.

Her voice is heard in every cry of triumph, in every mourner's prayer, in the howl of the coyotes on the hillside. Listen. You will hear Her, for She is everywhere. Step into the pages of this book and learn one man's journey to Her and love for Her.

Then begin or deepen your own journey.

— **H. Byron Ballard,** author of *Small Magics: Practical Secrets from an Appalachian Village Witch*, *Embracing Willendorf: A Witch's Way of Loving Your Body to Health and Fitness*, and *Earth Works: Ceremonies in Tower Time*

INTRODUCTION
FACE TO FACE

In the beginning was the dragon. And that dragon was the bitter sea. And the people brought offerings to the shore and poured wine into the churning water. They knew that this was their mother, this wide and blue expanse that gave them food and swallowed up boats. It gave life and took it away. Sometimes the dragon was the river. Sometimes she was the field. Sometimes she was no dragon but a bird, a feral wolf, a mountain that spit fire into the sky and seemed to eat the world. It was her, and she was everywhere and everything. She wore black in the evening, white at dawn, red at weddings, blue in dreams. Her pale fingers slipped the soul out of the body like skinning a deer. Her hands turned the red seed of life inside the flesh. Her left eye was the moon; her right was the sun. Her feet rested on the earth; her crowns were a veil of mist. She counted the seeds and held them fast. This is how it was and would always be. She was the infinite circle, the thread of life that wove itself into itself. The stars knew her names. The initiated know her names.

Before I turned thirty, and not long before I lost my father, I was initiated into Craft. I was in a strange new city, starting a difficult career, and I had brought the family I cared about with me to start an entirely new chapter of my life. It was a time of so many transitions and worries that my feet barely felt connected to the ground. And during that tumult, I decided to commit myself to a religious path that I had been hemming and hawing over for some time. I took a plunge into a dark space where I was uncertain whether any hands were waiting to catch me. I did not know if anything was beyond that black curtain that separated me from the life I was living and the life I knew that I wanted to live. Astonishingly, and fortunately, something in fact was waiting on the other side.

That moment is still with me, the moment before I was brought into the circle. I remember it as vividly as if I were still sitting in that room, waiting for my initiator. I remember the smells, and sounds, and even the placement of odd, everyday objects that stood in the room with me. I remember it all. I remember so well because it was the moment before so many things changed, before so much of my life was thoroughly reworked. My life spins around the axis of that moment, that choice to take my foot and plant it in the circle.

I have gone on to take further initiations in my tradition, and to start and lead a coven, hopefully passing on and breathing further life into the path that was passed to me. And all of that work springs from the original root of that choice, that memorable moment. When I stop to think about what happened in that room, what really struck me at the core of my being, I can say with a certainty that almost unnerves me exactly what it was that took root in me and reworked the threads of my life: I met God in the circle. I met her face to face.

That is an extreme statement that sounds a little too close to psychosis for some. I am fully aware of the jarring tone of the sentiment I have just written. So be it. I don't apologize for being a believer because that belief did not come gently for me. I spent most of my youth in a tenuous and unhealthy relationship with the Roman Catholic Church. I had the zeal of any convert (my family being Protestant) and took to the Church like an obsessive, or an addict. I was sure that I was destined for religious life, as a priest or a brother. I flirted with Dominicans and considered long retreats for "vocational discernment." I prayed. I prayed. I prayed some more. I begged God for revelation. Something, anything, to convince me that I was forgiven, or worthy.

And to be fully honesty, I did have glimpses of the divine in the Church. I have lost my bitterness about the Christian faith. I find much beauty in the traditions and theologies of Christianity, particularly Roman Catholic and Eastern Orthodox theology. I probably always will. But that faith came crashing down, as it does for so many. I left the church in anger and disappointment. I devoured as many anti-religious books as I could and dug my heels into atheist philosophy and continental postmodern thinkers. I pushed away friends and family and turned cold and bitter, tired, and endlessly mouthy about what I saw as years of waste and self-loathing.

But I was not destined to be a nonbeliever. Maybe I am just one of those people hardwired for belief. Maybe you are, too. Debating and unknitting my hunger to know the divine has not led to anything fruitful. So, I gave up the façade that I could forget my desire to understand belief. I tried a few paths, tepid flirtations with options that were available at the time. I even found myself sitting in and participating in Mainline Protestant congregations and trying at various other groups I could find. Crucially, for me, I began to reinvestigate the esoteric and occult thinkers and writers that I had toyed with my entire time in Catholicism and eventually landed in initiatory Craft. Part of the journey back to faith, for me, was also exploring voices that spoke for the Goddess and for women in religious spaces. Craft was what called.

And there she was. After so many attempts to find God in the transubstantiated Eucharist, or in the face of plaster saints, I found her in the Goddess. And not a placid, serene virgin who echoes a prayer I now find very difficult to swallow: *Let it be done to me according to Thy Word.*[1] No. She was alive and real, creative, destructive, and all-con-

---
[1] This is repeated in Catholic devotion as part of the Angelus and comes from the prayer of the Virgin Mary.

suming. She was beautiful and terrifying, perfected yet ever-changing. A box of contradictions and surprises.

And nothing was the same after her revelation. I have many dark nights of the soul, as everyone does, but not about her. I doubt so many things and question and work myself into little anxious spirals like all humans are guilty of, at times. Evolution has made us antsy, and for good reason. The world is a scary place. But at the core of my belief stands Mother, unflinching and unassailable. I have no more doubt in her than I do that the sun will rise tomorrow or that my mother loves me or that striking a match leads to a flame. She simply *is*. To deny her would be as nonsensical to me as denying the reality of my own self.

To my continual surprise, at the time of this writing, the Goddess is decidedly not in vogue in magical circles and the wide community of seekers who are looking outside of traditional religions. There has been a backlash against the rise of the Goddess movement (in its various incarnations) in a lot of self-described "magical spaces." The Devil is very much back in the popular imagination, not that I'm sure he was ever out of it. A desire to "butch-up" religious Witchcraft has taken hold and Goddess worship is held to a magnifying glass of scrutiny that, even if born in good intention, has gotten out of hand. I hope to be a voice for those that still center their work in the Mother, despite these developments.

The vitriol against Goddess worship is often cloaked in a desire to be more "historically accurate" or to be "more serious" in our practice. I think healthy criticism of any path is a good thing, but underneath a lot of critique leveled against the Goddess, particularly the rise of contemporary Goddess worship in the West,[2] there is a lot of misogyny and confusion.

---

[2] The term "West" or "Western world" carries a lot of baggage and is not entirely accurate. Many writers are moving away from this term in favor of more specific descriptors. Throughout this book I still employ this term as it is the one I think most readers will be familiar with, and it does convey the swath of cultures and communities that are rooted in Hellenistic ideas and other European (and Eurocentric) philosophies.

This is hardly new. Patriarchal occultists from history are often lauded as *misunderstood geniuses* when they are revealed to have engaged in cruelty and stupidity. Women, however, are rarely given that kind of boys-will-be-boys handwaving excuse. Spiritualism, Theosophy (under H.P. Blavatsky and Annie Bessant particularly) and many other movements in alternative spiritual paths, led or populated heavily by women, are held to much higher standards of scrutiny than Aleister Crowley, S.L. MacGregor Mathers, or other historically significant practitioners and systems from modern occultism. There is a reason for this. Denying it is dishonest.

Am I aware of the faults of many occultists such as Blavatsky, or of the historical inaccuracy of some of the Goddess movement's earliest works and leaders? Of course. I am not here to deny it. There is much to criticize and evaluate. But I hope that level-headed people can see that there is a disproportionate handling of the Goddess and women leaders in modern spiritual movements versus how we handle other traditions in the wide spectrum that inspires magicians, Witches, and seekers.

And as for "historical accuracy" well I hope to dispel some criticisms in this work, but I can't dispel all of them. The Goddess movement was and continues to be a source of inspiration for many practitioners, whether individually or in groups that honor the Mother such as Craft. But it does bear historical issues and bad scholarship. There is no movement devoid of these things. So, I hope to show that the worship of the Mother still serves as a conduit to meaning and fulfillment, despite the criticisms it receives, valid or not.

And all of this is a tall order, I am fully aware. I teach on esoteric and occult topics that have been passions for me for years. I have written a book on traditional, early modern astrology which has always been a pet love of mine.[3] And through all my time teaching, I find that I get so excited to share with others, happy to write out my notes or jot

---

[3] *The Art Cosmic: The Magic of Traditional Astrology*, available through Warlock Press.

down lesson outlines. I enjoy the process—I was a teacher in my professional life for a decade. But when I sat down to write a book about the Goddess, I stared at a blank screen that I simply could not fill up with words. I deleted entire chapters. I argued with myself over every paragraph. There was no joy in it for me. It was nauseating.

It has taken me a long time, over a year, to understand why I couldn't bring myself to write about the Mother. The reason is that this topic is not one topic amongst many for me. The Goddess is not a *subject* to be studied for me, like astrology, tarot, or herbalism. She doesn't stand on a bookshelf as one section mingled in with a thousand other New Age interests that grow and fade with trend and time. The Goddess is the core of my lived religious life. She is the heart of my devotional practice, my magical work, and my sense of what makes the world tick. Mother is, for me, the door to the very concept of transcendence.

Facing these hurdles, I realized that something uniquely challenging (in the world of religion) has been a part of the magical communities of Witches, Pagans, and other people who fall under a growing but difficult to define umbrella, ever since contemporary people staring reclaiming these terms. That challenge is: we do not really have theologians. We have scholars and practitioners and little else. To write about Craft or magic, as a scholar, you often must disavow belief, or at the very least distance yourself from it to some level. I cannot do that. I am not a scholar in academia, anyway.

To be clear, there are many wonderful scholars who write on Craft and the occult and have impressive academic credentials. But those credentials often come at the cost of "stepping outside of belief." Scholars must be scientific and neutral. They can practice in their private lives, as many do, but their works and publications have to live in the hermetically sealed environments of the social sciences or the humanities. Theology is not the same discipline as history, sociology, or anthropology. Witches in academic settings can write about Diana at the Witches' sabbat, happily, but only if she is a historical phenomenon, not a living Goddess.

Practitioners, the ones that refuse to step away from their identities and biases as believers, write many books. But they are often barred from academia or cannot find a settled place within it. They do not benefit from the peer review and the checks and balances provided by large, well-funded institutions of higher learning.

This is a situation that does not really exist in any other world religion. Christian theologians have entire university departments devoted to the academic study and research of theology, not just religious studies which is a separate discipline entirely. As do Muslims, Jews, Buddhists, and many others. No Christian theologian at Duke Divinity or Princeton Theological Seminary or Notre Dame has to say, "*Who knows if Jesus was real. Let's just look at this one Reformation scholar for 300 pages and never talk about whether you might want to believe in God.*" No. They can live a life where they produce works in a respected institution, addressing believers, and largely for believers. And those institutions have endowments, scholarships, and housing. We do not have that.

There are many blessings to not having that. It saves us from stultifying dogma and religious hierarchies that curtail progress and harm outsiders. This is a good thing. Like all good things, it comes at a cost. That cost is that we are able to churn out books and classes on many topics that address praxis, but very few that address belief. And if we do address belief, we have to be so careful to address such a wide net of people that we never actually say much of anything. We don't have large groups of like-minded people that share a common religious experience and language. So, we tend to focus on the practice of our paths and not the underlying foundations.

Figurine of Isis-Aphrodite, 2nd c. CE, Roman Egypt. (Met Museum)

But spiritual life cannot live on rock-collecting, candle-etching, and the tying of sachets forever. When life goes sour, as it is prone to do, there must be something else underneath it all, a *why* that girds and lifts our practice into something that can withstand tragedy, change, and fear. Even non-theistic paths like Theravada Buddhism and Jainism still touch on the greater *why* behind their systems.

For me, that *why* is the Goddess. And through my years teaching and mingling with the other diverse souls in the wide communities of Witches, seekers, and Pagans, I have found many people with that same hunger for the Goddess. I have prayed and worked rites and rituals with so many incredible humans that have called God their Mother. And those people have helped shape me into who I am today.

This book is for those that find her or want to find her. This is for those that want to experience the connection and ecstasy of a life turned towards her altar. I am not a historian, an archaeologist, or a psychologist. I am a priest. So, I have to write as a priest. I cannot write as anything else. To even try to would be pointless. I would end up betraying something, either my ethics or my beliefs. I'm not willing to do either.

I know that not everyone will connect with this word: Mother. For some, it may be a word they associate with negativity, past pain, or rigid gender stereotypes and expectations. I understand that. I do not claim that my religious expression is the solely valid religious expression in the human experience. What I cannot do, though, is tailor my experience so that it speaks to every seeker. Not everyone will find connection to the Goddess, but I am writing for those who do, or those who are seeking for her.

It is also important to say that I am a priest in a religion that honors the male aspects of God as well. We do worship the God and the Goddess as two facets of the divine in my tradition. But the simple fact is that God the Father has a long list of supporters and mouthpieces in the world. There is no shortage of works on God in a male incarnation. And, if I am truly to serve the God of Witchcraft, which I do, then what could I possibly do that would embody him more than seek for the face of the Goddess? That is, after all, exactly what he does. In short, at the core of my experience is the Goddess, yes with a consort, but still…her.

And I am also a man. A man writing about Goddess worship. That carries its own basket of worries and nerve-wracking pitfalls. I can only hope that I do her justice. I am not here to take away space from any priestess who speaks on the Goddess, or to act as some popish authority figure. I am only here to put into words what sustains and bolsters my life and hope that others find here something that carries them even a step forward on that path that leads to her.

God the Mother is an integral face in the mosaic of belief. Despite religions that denigrate Goddess worship, she lives. Despite the patriarchal and Christocentric occult traditions that look down their nose at the Goddess movement, or Craft, she lives. Despite the constant pressure to sink into nihilism, consumerism, and despair, she lives. She pulses at the core of many devotees and magical souls. I have seen her transform lives.

And that is the heart of what I hope you find in this book: transformation. Devotion to Mother is a transformative experience, a whirlwind of connection and magic. No matter what incarnation we invoke, she comes. She breathes into life, echoing the prayers and incantations of every initiator, Witch, believer, and devotee that has ever stood at her shrine and felt her presence, as real as anything under the sun (or beyond it). My goal is to show touchpoints and teachings that lead to Mother. In her worship, in her magic, in her dance, is a living spiritual tradition, drawing from many sources but still focused on one multifaceted absolute. My prayer is this: if you feel the call of God the Mother, give into it. Let go of the trepidation and worries as much as you can and allow her undertow to slip you into the sea of her transformative worship.

> *"...for both the gates of hell and the guarantee of life were in the hands of the Goddess, and the initiation itself was celebrated in the manner of a voluntary death and of salvation won by prayer; indeed their divine majesty was accustomed to choose one who already stood on the very threshold where the light of this world is extinguished, their span of life passed, those to whom the great secrets of the faith could nevertheless be safely entrusted; and by her providence they were in some way born again..."* [4]

-Apuleius, *Metamorphoses*

---

[4] Mary Beard, John North, and Simon Price, eds., *Religions of Rome Volume 2, A Sourcebook* (Cambridge, UK: Cambridge University Press, 1998), 8.

CHAPTER 1
THE TRANSFORMATIONS OF DEVOTION

 …and the devotees adored the Goddess for the miraculous revelation of her power in a metamorphosis which partook of the shifting pageantry of a dream. Lifting their hands to heaven, with one voice the beholders rendered testimony to the loving-kindness of the Goddess thus signally declared." [1]

-Apuleius, *Metamorphoses*

FAITH AND MAGIC

Devotion is not a common topic in contemporary magical and spiritual-seeker circles, I find.[2] The use of magic to improve your life, or the lives of those around you, takes up much of the space. Divination as well. The discussions I run into most often in circles of Witches and many Pagans are firmly about magical practices, or self-improvement techniques. The gods, when they are mentioned, are usually mentioned as co-creative forces, Jungian archetypes, or (and I say this at the risk

---

[1] Apuleius, *The Golden Ass*, trans. Jack Lindsay, in *The Ancient Mysteries: A Sourcebook of Sacred Texts*, ed. Marvin W. Meyer (Philadelphia, PA: University of Pennsylvania Press, 1887), 183.

[2] There are of course major exceptions to this. African Diasporic Traditions have long histories of devotional practices, for example. What I am mainly referring to here, and through this section, is the contemporary collection of seekers who draw from the tradition of European occultism or the contemporary revival of religious Witchcraft.

of being snarky) superhuman figurines that you choose from at your convenience. *I'm working a love spell, so I used Aphrodite.* Used! Imagine any other religious person using this kind of language. *I want to heal my aunt, so I used Jesus. I am feeling anxious, so I used the Buddha. I think I might want to explore my darker side, so I used Kali.* The language is just bizarre, and yet it is very common.

Devotion to God sounds terribly *Christian* to a lot of Pagans and Witches. I understand that. I do want to hammer home an important thing, though: the language of religious belief does not belong to Abrahamic traditions. This is one of the most important things I have discovered in my own life that has led to my growth as a priest and a devotee of Mother. Christians do not own the words *belief, prayer, devotion, religious,* or any other words within the vocabulary of life.

All of these concepts existed long before the Nazarene walked this planet, or the Quran was dictated in Arabia, or the Torah was chanted in synagogues across the Levant. Philosophers, priestesses, priests, and devotees of the past were believing in, praying to, and worshipping the gods with as much love and fervor as any confessional Lutheran or Orthodox rabbi alive today. And outside of Abrahamic traditions, devotion to God is the center of the transformative power of many religious systems. Hinduism has one of the richest traditions of devotional literature that humanity has ever produced, for example.[3]

But this language still does not have much truck in magical circles, at least not at the time of writing. There is a marked desire to separate religious devotion from magical practice and occult "sciences." Theosophists, and other influential magical thinkers of the modern occult revival, did a lot to portray magic (or *magick*) as some school of unplumbed science, or perhaps an unexplored human extension of the will, divorced from any necessary religious belief. Magic, in these systems, is what happens when people tap into their own power, not the power of the divine. It

---

[3] See chapter 5 for a brief exploration of devotionalism (*bhakti*) in the Hindu Goddess-focused tradition.

is seen to be as natural to the human being as breathing, and usually explained with a muddy mixture of psychology and neuroscience or, more recently, quantum mechanics.[4]

I'm not so sure that this view of magical systems as "technologies" or unplumbed extensions of our thought is as useful as it once was, when we didn't have as much scientific knowledge as we do now, and when parapsychical research had not taken as many hits as it has. It is now relegated to the absolute fringes of academia. Most attempts to "prove" magic have not born good fruit under the strictures of a laboratory.

For so many practitioners, to put it plainly, magic is one thing and religion another. Sometimes they mingle, but they still maintain their separation at a deep level. This dichotomy, enforced by post-Enlightenment scholars and Christian writers who looked to the past through a heavily Christian (often Protestant) lens, is not helpful.[5] Magic was so intimately linked with religious beliefs throughout history that attempting to untie them is a bit of a Gordian knot. You're eventually just going to cut through it because you *want* it to be separate, not because it truly is, or ever was. Even the basest, ends-justify-the-means forms of magic were often religious in nature. Curse tablets, for example, were often supplicatory prayers to deities of vengeance, not extensions of the caster's will alone.[6]

The fact is that devotion itself was seen, by many practitioners throughout history, as a transformative, magical experience. Devotion to the divine was not done solely to placate some wrathful deity that would blight your crops if you didn't offer enough heifers at the altar during city-wide festivals. This image of Paganism as solely quid pro

---

[4] Usually with no actual training in neuroscience, psychology, or quantum physics. Richard Feynman once quipped that anyone claiming to understand quantum mechanics clearly does not understand quantum mechanics.

[5] Algis Uzdavinys, *Philosophy & Theurgy in Late Antiquity* (Kettering, OH: Sophia Perennis, 2010), 103-104.

[6] Lindsay Watson, "Defixiones: A Recent History," in *Magic in Ancient Greece and Rome* (London, UK: Bloomsbury Academic, 2019).

quo is not a very accurate picture of past religious practice. The reason behind this all is that Christian scholars could not imagine that Pagan thinkers or philosophers actually had transformative, beautiful experiences with the gods. Instead, these scholars viewed it all as some sort of transactional superstition with no theology behind it. No one really *experienced* the power of the pagan gods because the pagan gods were not real. Only the Trinity is real.

This worldview still infects a lot of talk about the gods in Paganism and religious Witchcraft. Without realizing it, many spiritual seekers are parroting the ideas and beliefs of Christian writers in an attempt not to sound like Christians. The irony would be funny if it weren't so problematic.

As new scholarship grows from people who look to pre-Christian religions in Europe without the biases of Jesuits and Evangelicals, we are thankfully giving a deeper look at the lived religious life of people who saw the face of God in Artemis of Ephesus, Magna Mater, or in Isis and Sekhmet. We are lucky to have incredible works of philosophy translated into modern languages and made available in ways they never were until quite recently. We can read the Neoplatonists, who spoke of their love of God and their desire to be transformed through theurgy, or divine magic. We can read the Chaldean Oracles, and Egyptian prayer books, and Roman rituals in ways the founders of modern Craft and Pagan communities never could. They simply did not have the access we may now lay claim to.

My hope is that this will continue in our communities. My hope is that we can start to see devotion to the gods (and particularly to the Great Goddess) as a creative, life-transforming magic in and of itself. Our magic does not simply have to be a collection of spells and sigils. Prayer is magic. Ecstatic trance and dance are magic. Ritual worship is magic. All of this is magical. All of this is transformative.

THE MYSTERY CULTS: INITIATORY GODDESS WORSHIP AS TRANSFORMATION

The most explored area of ritual Goddess worship in the West as a transformative act might be the initiatory mystery cults of the Hellenistic world. The cults at Eleusis and Samothrace, and the cults of Isis, Cybele, and many other Goddesses, were widely popular in the Hellenistic world. There are sites with temples to Isis in Germany and London, for example. And Eleusis was such a crucial place of religious experience that it took centuries for Christianity to shut it down.[7] These paths have inspired occultists, Witches, and contemporary Pagans as well, weaving into their practices and spiritual expression. Aleister Crowley named some of his rites after Eleusis. Members of the Hermetic Order of the Golden Dawn worshipped Isis and built rites around the memory of her worship, and H.P. Blavatsky used the concept of the "veil of Isis" (a reference to all of nature) as the title of one of her major works.

These mystery cults are a complex historical phenomenon, often sensationalized or misrepresented by scholars who carry ideological agendas. Christian scholars downplay the cults' influence and deny they had any influence on the development of Christian worship. Anti-Christian writers try to make them the entire basis for Christianity, claiming that Jesus was a copy of pagan deities worshipped in cults such as those of Mithras, or at Eleusis.[8] Contemporary Pagan authors often take huge liberties when discussing these cults, certain that current paths are rebirths of these ancient traditions.

---

[7] There was an attempt to reanimate the Eleusinian Mysteries by the emperor Julian, the last non-Christian emperor, but after his death the cult eventually succumbed to the Christianization of the empire.

[8] There is an enormous amount of sloppy history and conjecture out there trying to show how Jesus was just Mithras 2.0, or some sort of Jewish Horus. These concepts are largely anti-Christian nonsense with little basis in actual history. Online meme culture has spread many lies, such as Mithras having 12 apostles/followers, or Horus being crucified and resurrected. Most of these memes contain outright lies and debunked theories.

I'm not here to pour out anymore ink on debating the nature of these paths in how they influenced later religions or did not. What I want to examine here is something that I think is undeniable about the mystery religions, regardless of how murky and complex their history might be: at the core of an impressive amount of these traditions was a supreme Goddess.

Relief from Eleusis depicting Demeter, Persephone, and an initiate—likely Triptolemos. (Met Museum)

And it is not just a couple of them, to reiterate. It is most of them. The rites of Eleusis focused on Demeter and Persephone, a mother and daughter. Worshippers were so in awe of the Goddess' return that they often referred to Persephone only as *Kore*, meaning the "girl" or the "daughter." And she was even named *Kore Soteira*, meaning "the daughter, our savior."[9] Samothrace had unique mystery cults that were influential across the Greek world.[10] In Arcadia and other sites, the Goddess was worshipped as *Despoina*—the Mistress. One of the greatest sites of Mother's worship was the temple of Artemis at Ephesus, itself one of the seven wonders of the ancient world.[11] The cult of Cybele, originally a Phrygian deity, was brought to Rome at the height of the Punic Wars and her worship went through phases of Imperial support but also persecution and disdain by more traditional Roman voices.[12]

And perhaps the largest and most influential of these mystery religions was the cult of Isis, Hellenized from her Egyptian beginnings and carried throughout the Roman Empire. One of her temples stands as one of the best-preserved memories from Pompei and Herculaneum. Her statues stood in the villas of emperors, and her worship was so large that it created a network of temples with an organized priesthood that provided healing, religious rites, and even spiritual retreats for pilgrims.[13]

At first glance, it might seem that these cults are just historical ex-

---

[9] Mary Beard, John North, and Simon Price, eds., *Religions of Rome Volume 2, A Sourcebook* (Cambridge, UK: Cambridge University Press, 1998), 187.

[10] For a fascinating take on the Mysteries of Samothrace, and a wider exploration of Mystery Religion in general, see: *Entering the Mysteries: The Secret Traditions of Indigenous Europe* (New Culture Press, 2016), by Arthur Versluis.

[11] For a solid overview of the Cult of Artemis in Ephesus, see: *The Mysteries of Artemis of Ephesos: Cult, Polis, and Change in the Graeco-Roman World* (Yale University Press, 2012) by Guy MacLean Rogers.

[12] For an in-depth look at the cult of Cybele, throughout its history, see: *In Search of God the Mother: The Cult of Anatolian Cybele* (University of California Press, 1999) by Lynn E. Roller.

[13] For a thorough study of the cult of Isis, see: R.E. Witt, *Isis in the Ancient World* (Baltimore, MD: The Johns Hopkins University Press, 1971).

amples of Paganism, no more important to a discussion of the Great Goddess than examining temples to Aphrodite, Sekhmet, or Ishtar. Pagans worshipped a lot of gods, so why focus on these cults in particular? Why am I devoting so much of this work to these particular cults, Goddess-centric as they may be?

The reason is that we see in the language that comes down to us from these traditions a belief in the Goddess as something more than just *one god amongst many*. We see in their works something that hinges on devotion, belief, and experiential religious life. We see in much of the work that is left from these worshippers a Goddess that is all-encompassing and cosmic. We see a Mother who cares for her initiates, changes their lives, a Goddess who lives and moves with them in a life of devotion and transformation.

When so much of the literature and discussion of pre-Christian religion in Europe and the wider Mediterranean focuses on strict polytheism—what is called *hard polytheism* by many contemporary Pagans—it is interesting to see such a difference in the mystery cults. In these cults, the Goddess is not a figure that only gives via quid pro quo and is just a singular spirit amongst many. If she gives anything, it is succor in this life and the hope of a happier afterlife than the one promised by the imagery and lore of the larger, more standardized state religions. Initiates in these cults believe that their initiation and devotion to the Great Mother impacts their soul's destiny, in this life and the next. To put it bluntly, they are not just worshipping her so that their ex will return, or the grain will grow thicker, or their purses will grow thicker for that matter. They are worshipping something they believe changes their entire being.

The Roman writer Apuleius is a complicated figure who, we believe, belonged to one of these initiatory cults—the cult of the Goddess Isis. He wrote a work of satirical fictions called the *Metamorphoses*, also known as *The Golden Ass*. He had a somewhat colorful reputation, and the author was so scandalous that Saint Augustine complained about him.[14] What is important in this work for us though is that he speaks of initiatory religious belief and gives us glimpses into the cult of Isis. Regardless of his colorful associations, his religiosity is a markedly emotional component of his works.

The main character of the *Metamorphoses* is transformed into a donkey and after a series of misfortunes, he seeks help from the Goddess. After a moving prayer that is full of pathos and despair, hardly the dry quid pro quo utterances associated with pagan worship in popular accounts, he seeks her out as one seeks out something of the utmost importance and deepest trust and belief. His prayer is answered, and the Great Goddess manifests for him in a grand and life-changing theophany. Her answer is long, but it is worth quoting in full here.

> *Lo I am at hand moved by your prayers, Lucius, I the parent of the nature of things, mistress of all the elements, initial begetter of the ages, supreme of divine powers, queen of the shades of the dead, first of heavenly beings, the uniform countenance of gods and Goddesses. I, who control at my will the luminous points of the sky, the salubrious breezes of the sea and the lamented silences of the underworld. My unparalleled divine power is worshipped by the whole world in various forms, with different rites and diverse names. The first-born Phrygians call me Mother of the Gods at Pessinus; the indigenous Athenians, Minerva, daughter of Cecrops; the wave-washed Cypriots, Venus of Paphos; the archers of Crete, Dictynna Diana; the trilingual Sicilians, Stygian Proserpina; the Eleusinians, the most ancient Goddess Ceres; different peoples call me Juno, or Bellona, or Hekate, or Rhamnusia; those warmed by the first rays of the rising god of the sun, the Ethiopians, Arians and Egyptians,*

---

14 Augustine takes Apuleius to task in his monumental *City of God*, refuting Apuleius' insistence that we should worship beings that Augustine thought of as demonic. Apuleius was also persecuted for practicing magic.

> steeped in their ancient learning, worship me with my own rites and call me by my real name: Queen Isis. I am at hand from pity for your situation, I am at hand to favour and aid you. Cease your tears and weeping now, dispel your sorrow; now by my benevolence the day of well-being dawns on you...You shall live a blessed life, you shall live under my protection a life of glory, and when you have reached the end of your time and go down to the underworld, there too you will often worship me (who will be favourable to you) in the semicircular space beneath the earth, seeing me shining in the darkness of Acheron and ruling in the Stygian depths, when you yourself are living in the Elysian Fields. But if by diligent attention and devout service and continuing purity you will be worthy of your divine power, you will know that I alone can extend your life beyond the span laid down by fate." [15]

It is worth reading this passage more than once and really looking at the emotion and religious devotion portrayed in this pronouncement from the Goddess. The speaker of these words is not *one god amongst many*. This Goddess is not a detached, louche Olympian whose dalliances are the stuff of lurid folklore and who toys with mortals for fun. This Goddess cares about her devotee and demands worship as the supreme embodiment of all divinity. This Goddess promises to influence not just our crops and cattle but our thoughts and our daily life. She commands Lucius (the supplicant) to turn his thoughts to her and to let go of his sorrows, all in her service. She is portrayed as the supreme of all supreme beings, worshipped in many guises but still one omnipotent Mother who forms the foundation of reality and the hope of rebirth.

This kind of devotion is not a one-off in the cultures of Hellenistic Paganism, either. The emperor Julian, the last non-Christian emperor,

---

[15] Mary Beard, John North, and Simon Price, eds., *Religions of Rome Volume 2, A Sourcebook* (Cambridge, UK: Cambridge University Press, 1998), pp. 298-299.

was an almost fanatical devotee of the Great Mother, deeply inspired by the philosophies of Neoplatonism and the practice of theurgy (transformative divine magic). In his *Hymn to the Mother of the Gods*, he writes:

> *Who then is the Mother of the Gods? She is the source of the intellectual and creative gods, who in their turn guide the visible gods: she is both the mother and the spouse of mighty Zeus; she came into being next to and together with the great creator; she is in control of every form of life, and the cause of all generation; she easily brings to perfection all things that are made; without pain she brings to birth, and with the father's aid creates all things that are; she is the motherless maiden, enthroned at the side of Zeus, and in very truth is the Mother of all the Gods. For having received into herself the causes of all the gods, both intelligible and supra-mundane, she became the source of the intellectual gods."* [16]

Although the writing does speak of other divine figures, the Mother is given prominence and absorbs the attributes and titles of many deities. And she is not just a figure of power to be worshipped because she is titanic and mighty. She is the ground of being, the ontological reality behind the elements, behind the "visible gods" and thus foundational to existence itself.

Julian and Apuleius are speaking to the Goddess in ways that go beyond a simple, almost facile belief that all Pagans were animistic polytheists and that their relationship to the gods was not one of emotive devotion, but instead a fear-based system of giving and receiving, or "using" to get what we want. This is the Christian reading, and it most certainly does not touch on the devotion behind the above quotes.

---

[16] Julian, *The Works of the Emperor Julian*, trans. Wilmer Cave Wright (Cambridge, MA: Harvard University Press, 1913). Project Gutenberg EBook #48664, accessed January 12, 2023. https://www.gutenberg.org/files/48664/48664-h/48664-h.html#toc23.

Many practitioners call this multi-faceted approach to the divine *soft polytheism*. This is the belief that there is truly just one source of divine power in the cosmos and that power is reflected in many gods, like facets of a jewel. The terms "soft" and "hard" polytheism are heavy with agenda. Hard implies more real, more solid, more accurate. Soft implies something flouncy and inaccurate, or shifty and dishonest. In more nuanced or academic works "soft polytheism" is referred to as monism,[17] henotheism,[18] or as pantheism or panentheism (both of which equate God, in varying degrees, to the totality of the cosmos).[19]

Some Pagan reconstructionist movements are adamantly opposed to this "soft" approach to the gods, claiming that it comes from New Age flim-flam or Eastern concepts smuggled in by practitioners, and that it has nothing to do with historical cults of pre-Christian deities. I just cannot support this approach, at least not in Greco-Roman systems. The prayers highlighted here, and that we find elsewhere, frequently portray believers who see in the face of the Mother the faces of every god, every spirit, even the very elements of Creation itself. Everything spins from her axis. Did they deny other gods? No, I don't believe so. Julian was an intense devotee of the sun god, for example. That does not diminish the supreme nature of the Mother revealed in the mysteries and in the writings of these believers. In the devotion and ecstasy of worship, the Goddess of the mysteries is the supreme face of divinity.

It is important, I believe, also to highlight how the mystery cults offered something to the initiates beyond just a promise of a better life beyond the grave. These cults provided a religious theater for transformation. Devotion to the Great Mother did not just guarantee rebirth

---

[17] Monism is the belief that all of existence, on some level, participates in a divine unity.

[18] Henotheism denotes the worship or preference for one deity without denying the existence of others.

[19] Pantheism and panentheism equate God to the cosmos. The differentiation is that pantheism believes the universe is, in effect, God herself. Panentheism says that the entire cosmos is part of God, but God still extends beyond it.

or a happy afterlife; it changed the worshipper on a psychic level and became a central axis around which to build a life, a path, and a hope for things to come. The mystery cults were known, sometimes vilified even, for their use of elaborate ritual, music, dance, and sacrifice. Libations were poured, costumed donned, and wine consumed. It was not mere pageantry; it was a lived expression of faith.

Marble statue of the Great Goddess as she was depicted in the famed temple in Ephesus, often labelled as Artemis or Diana of Ephesus. Her temple was one of the seven wonders of the ancient world. (Adobe Stock)

My approach here may rankle Witches and Pagans who have a mistrust (earned, I would admit) of organized religious belief. But the truth is, the Great Goddess was worshipped for her power to transform and inspire, not just to provide a desired result. Devotion to her was not *servile*. It was participatory. It was transformative. It was ecstatic. It was so ecstatic in fact that conservative voices in both Greek and Roman sources were extremely mistrustful of the mystery cults and at many points in time these cults were persecuted, just as Witches are, for being superstitious, rowdy, or fanatical. The authorities did not believe wild devotion to the Great Mother made you servile. They believed that it made you *dangerous*.

And it is dangerous. The Great Mother is a shocking figure in the mystery cults. In the Cult of Magna Mater, her worshippers clanged cymbals, beat drums, and led orgiastic dances through the city in her honor. In Sparta, people were whipped at the altar of Artemis Orthia until her statues ran with blood.[20] Initiates at Eleusis were executed if they spilled the secrets of what occurred in the *telesterion*, the sacred place at the heart of the rituals. She was an all-consuming figure, as much dread as succor.

And that is why devotion is a form of magic. Devotion, when directed to the Great Mother, is a choice to go beyond the daily and the mundane and attempt to touch something that unifies existence into one cosmic force, one incredible idol, one Mother that can withstand our gnashing of teeth, our petty failures, and our triumphs. The Goddess of the Mysteries smashes the ego through ecstatic experience only to rebuild it through devotion on earth and rebirth in Elysium. She is the transcendent reality, the very is-ness, behind our being.

This is magic. This is theurgy. Theurgy, which is a philosophical magic interwoven with ritual and devotion to the divine, is largely known to us through Neoplatonic sources. One of the most influential late theurgic Neoplatonic philosophers, Iamblichus, wrote, "…it is the accomplishment of acts not to be divulged and beyond all conception, and the power of the unutterable symbols, understood solely by the gods, which estab-

---

[20] It is important to note that the public worship of Artemis Orthia in Sparta was not an initiatory mystery cult in the same way as the other traditions mentioned here.

lishes theurgic union."[21]

These symbols and acts referenced by Iamblichus were objects and acts of devotion and religious practice, acted out in the theater of temple, home, and cave. They are still available to us, despite our distance from late antiquity. To choose to go into the dark and horrible hollows of the earth and cry out to the thing that speaks and hums beneath it all is the very heart of magic. It is the choice to transform, to believe that human life extends beyond the earthly and into the cosmic. Into eternity. Into darkness where light is born.

For me, that humming, thrumming voice in every particle of the cosmic order is the voice of Mother, the same Mother etched in stone and painted in ochre by our neolithic predecessors. It is the same Mother that was carved into stone from Alexandria to Athens to Rome. It is the same Mother that stands at the heart of the contemporary rebirth of Witchcraft as a religion, portrayed as the Queen of the Witches, crowned in the crescent moon, unyoked and free. She was all, is all, and will create all.

To quote once again from the emperor Julian:

> *O Mother of gods and [mortals], thou that art the assessor of Zeus and sharest his throne, O source of the intellectual gods, that pursuest thy course with the stainless substance of the intelligible gods; that dost receive from them all the common cause of things and dost thyself bestow it on the intellectual gods; O life-giving Goddess that art the counsel and the providence and the creator of our souls; O thou that lovest great Dionysus, and didst save Attis when exposed at birth, and didst lead him back when he had descended into the cave of the nymph; O thou that givest all good things to the intellectual gods and fillest with all things this sensible world, and with all the rest givest us*

---

21   Iamblichus, *Iamblichus: De Mysteriis*, trans. Emma C. Clarke, John M. Dillon, and Jackson P. Hershbell (Atlanta, GA: Society of Biblical Literature, 2003), 115.

> *all things good! Do thou grant to all [mortals] happiness, and that highest happiness of all, the knowledge of the gods…"* [22]

DEVOTED TO HER

Devotion is the heart of this work, for me, but I am not here to convert the nonbeliever. I have my reasons for being an adamant theist, for believing in the Goddess as a reality and not as a simply *useful archetype* or bygone superstition. I don't think, however, that works that argue for the existence of God accomplish more than preach to the converted. I am happy to discuss why I believe, but at the end I am writing for those that already feel at least a prickle of her call at the back of their necks, not those that have no truck with the divine at all.

And I also know that for many, God the Mother simply is not the face that stared back at them from the darkness when they sought the divine. I understand that. I understand that the worship of the Great Mother is not for everyone. That does not mean that I will not continue to speak of her as the supreme being, or that I will tailor my language to make others who want there to be one male god, or multiple gods, or no gods, or only ghosts, or whatever, more comfortable. It isn't my job to placate every single person in the magical community of Witches, Pagans, or magicians. It isn't your job, either. That has been attempted by many, and what ends up coming from those attempts is a watered-down and tepid theology of nothingness. At some point, we must stand in our belief because it is *ours*. I do not spend my time saying, "Well of course she's really only just a symbol for…" No. She isn't just a symbol. She is the beginning and the end.

I also think it is important to address the fact that I am well aware

---

[22] Julian, *The Works of the Emperor Julian*, trans. Wilmer Cave Wright (Cambridge, MA: Harvard University Press, 1913). Project Gutenberg EBook #48664, accessed January 12, 2023. https://www.gutenberg.org/files/48664/48664-h/48664-h.html#toc23.

that the cosmic force underneath Creation does not really bear a gender. But God has been most present for me as the Mother, and that is what I choose to worship. It is also a politically potent act to worship the Mother. In my daily life I use the term "God" far more often than "Goddess" but only with female pronouns. The dichotomy of using the three-letter word that many associate with patriarchal religion along with *she* and *her* seems to create a tension that I think is powerful. I cannot wring my hands over whether this speaks to enough people. It must suffice that it speaks to me and mine. And if God can be called anything under the sun except for Mother, except for She and Her, then we are most likely dealing with misogyny more than we are dealing with any attempt at inclusivity or transcendence.

Regardless of agendas, or experiences, devotion itself is at the core of my work and it is at the core of the Goddess' service, both in historical examples and in the present day. To worship is to unify with, to connect to, to embody and move within the object of your worship. It is not mere service. If you choose devotion to Mother, you are choosing to transform with her, for she is constantly changing. She is evolving and breathing and emanating into the universe. Devotion to that is anything but fear-based servility.

AN IMPORTANT FINAL NOTE

Something I think is crucial to address at the end of this chapter is that much of what I am writing about is, as I say elsewhere, coming from my own perspective. I am an American, living in the 21st century, and raised in a largely Christian milieu, even if my parents were not religiously conservative or particularly devout. My experience as a believing Witch and priest is an experience that connects to the contemporary revival of religious Witchcraft, contemporary Pagan movements, and the larger occult and esoteric traditions of Europe and the Mediterranean basin.

All of that means that there are large blind spots to my vision of

Mother and how God manifests herself into the cosmos. I am not an expert in Indigenous spiritualities, and I fear that I am repeating the same sin of many of the elders, leaders, and writers in the long tradition of occultism, hermeticism, Witchcraft, and more—the sin of willful blindness. I believe that we would benefit greatly in our communities if we were to respectfully investigate the Indigenous religious traditions of the lands we inhabit. This is particularly true for those of us who live in areas that were taken from Indigenous peoples in genocidal campaigns.

But that work is difficult, and beyond the scope of this book. I include this coda here as a reminder to all seekers that even if we choose to leave a dogmatic, global religion with a missionary history (like Christianity), it does not mean that we are no longer operating with that "coding" in our brains. My sources and inspirations are largely European and Mediterranean (including Egyptian), but that does not mean that the divine feminine, Goddesses, and female spiritual leadership do not exist in unbroken lineages throughout Indigenous spiritual traditions.

This coda is also to say that devotion—the topic of this chapter—is found in so many beautiful, varied, and unique spiritual lineages. When I write of devotion lacking in certain contemporary spiritual-seeker circles, do not think that this applies to Indigenous spiritualities, tribal and ethnic faiths, or many other expressions of religious belief that humans participate in and shape. I am speaking only to what I know and have experienced while I travel, teach, and grow in the rapidly evolving world of people connecting to Mother through Witchcraft, Paganism, and the occult. It is always important to remember that if we truly believe in transcendence, God, divinity, or whatever we wish to call it (I call it Mother), then we need to believe that Beauty, Truth, and Goodness pulse at the heart of every life, every community, and every spark within the cosmos. And with that belief, we should realize that our preconceived and inherited biases will sometimes conflict with our search for transcendence.

In short, I am only one voice for Mother—and only within my own community. Seek out all the voices that proclaim the Mother. Seek out all voices that empower priestesses, servants, devotees, and healers. Seek out the Mother in every name, every face, and every hearth. And let the vision of Mother you find in your seeking stand in its own time, place, and community. Mother does not need us to convert new faithful. Mother does not need us to contort and rebrand her mysteries. Our transformation, carried in and worked through our devotion, is assured in our seeking. So, seek her. Everywhere.

Indigenous women of the Andes in a ritual to the fertility Goddess, Pachamama. (Adobe Stock)

CHAPTER 2
EX STASIS
MYSTICISM AND THE SEARCH FOR MOTHER

 ...I saw the unpronounceable order
and I recognized the unspeakable
magnificence
and the unfathomable mystery
and the unique sweetness with its gift of
distinctness,
and the highest satiety...
and the living life of eternity..." [1]

— Mechthild of Magdeburg, 13th c. mystic

DEFINING THE UNDEFINABLE

Mysticism is one of those words that has lost so much meaning and been so overused as to be dangerously close to meaning, well, nothing much at all. We describe many things as "mystical." In religion, the term does refer to a loose collection of spiritual practices, writers, systems,

---

[1] Gerda Lerner, *The Creation of Feminist Consciousness: From the Middle Ages to Eighteen-Seventy* (New York, NY: Oxford University Press, 1993), 66.

and ideas that have spanned across religious traditions and large epochs of time. It carries connotations and concepts that I believe are useful places to begin a journey to Mother, despite the murkiness. So that is where I want to begin this chapter—with this concept of "mystic" and what it means to be a mystic of the Goddess.

Mysticism is, loosely defined, an attempt to know the divine on an intimate level, and not merely through prescribed religious rites. The goal for most mystical traditions and practitioners is to know God directly, as one might know a lover, and to experience revelation and transcendence here on earth. The divine, for mystics, is not solely transcendent, but very much immanent within our lives. This may all sound like something most deity-centered religious systems would be in favor of, but that is not always the case.

Mystics are often threats to established religious and secular order. In Christianity, mystics like the Beguines,[2] Jakob Boehme, and Emanuel Swedenborg threatened the established church by hinting or declaring that the rituals and rites only available within acceptable institutions were unnecessary for knowing God, or that worshippers could experience God directly, or in unique ways that felt alien to institutional religion. In Islam, Sufism was once the dominant religious paradigm of large swaths of the Muslim world, but at the time of this writing is heavily persecuted in many areas. Conservative Muslim authorities have come to view Sufi orders as dangerously close to idolatry and pagan practice. And in Hinduism, tantric practices are decried by more mainstream Hindu traditions as something akin to black magic or dangerous superstition, even murderous wildness.

The oldest Abrahamic tradition, Judaism, has always had a complicated relationship with Kabbalah, one of the richest mystical traditions

---

[2] The Beguines were a fascinating group of women in Medieval Europe who lived a semi-monastic lifestyle and unnerved many conservative religious authorities. One of the most famous Beguines was Marguerite Porete, who penned her own deeply moving philosophical and mystical work *The Mirror of Simple Souls*. She was burned at the stake for heresy.

to come from organized religious faith. At times, Kabbalistic-inspired philosophy was widely popular in Jewish communities, and at other times it was viewed with suspicion or even decried as heretical and unworthy of study. Kabbalists are seen by many as saints, sages, and teachers, and by just as many opposing voices as magicians, charlatans, or simply deluded. All of these examples are to highlight one core truth: the mystic is often an outsider.

Beyond religious organizations, it is also interesting to look at the etymology of the word mystic. At the root is the Greek word *mystes* (μύστης). This word was used to describe initiates of certain cults in the ancient world, cults that I addressed in the first chapter. Basically, a mystic, or *mystes*, was someone initiated into the mysteries. With that in mind, it might be important to remember a warning from Plato in the *Phaedo*: "The thyrsus-bearers[3] are many, but the *mystes* are few."[4] We can take this quote to mean that many claim to have secret knowledge, but true mystics are rare. You may have the accoutrements, but it doesn't mean you've succeeded in gaining the knowledge.

Mystics unnerve the religious order.[5] And most Witches and seekers that I have met crave that same divine experience as the mystics of other religious sects. We call down the gods into our midst and dance with them. We talk of matrons and patrons, magic, and revelatory dreams. All of this touches on the same plane of religious experience that inspired mystics from Teresa of Avila to Sufi theologians and tantric yogis.

But there is an undercurrent throughout mystical traditions of danger.

---

[3] The thyrsus is a sacred object, usually a decorated rod with ivy, pinecones, or other foliage. It is sacred in many initiatory religious rites, particularly those associated with Dionysus.

[4] Plato, *Phaedo*, in *Plato in Twelve Volumes*, trans. Harold N. Fowler, Perseus Digital Library (Tufts University), accessed August 26, 2022, http://www.perseus.tufts.edu/hopper/text?doc=urn:cts:greekLit:tlg0059.tlg004.perseus-eng1:69c.

[5] I mention that they also unnerve secular orders as well. Contemporary secular materialism has little truck with mysticism, and often relegates it to the dustbin of history, along with everything they deem unworthy, irrational, or superstitious. For a wonderful and fascinating exploration on the limits of secular "scientism" see *The Myths We Live By* (Routledge, 2003) by Mary Midgley.

Religious authorities are frequently horrified at just how far mystics are willing to take their devotions and the ecstatic, revelatory, and often jarring results of that devotion. And secular authorities are rarely pleased with the mystics' disconnection from mundane reality either, from the day-to-day experiences of life and the necessary business of running a city, a nation, or an empire. Mystics are often prophetic, voices against frivolity and worries they consider petty or unimportant to finding bliss and union with the divine.

The Ecstasy of Saint Teresa of Avila, Bernini, Rome. (Adobe Stock)

None of this is meant to be hyperbolic. I mention the contradictions and dangers of mysticism because the practices and realities of mystic revelation and ecstatic worship can become more than many people are ready to take on in their practice. When we think of someone "mystical" we might imagine a wizardly type with a crystal ball and arcane wisdom, someone who can interpret your dreams or make a tincture for your insomnia. In reality, a mystic is someone who challenges what we know, breaks social taboos, stands outside of respectability, and is under constant threat of being cast out of the community.

I mention the danger and the heaviness of mystics' practice because mysticism still has a genteel connotation that it does not merit. Mystical practices were, and still are, grueling. Exerting the body to its limits through dancing, fasting for dangerous lengths of time, consuming drugs and alcohol to induce visions, piercing the skin, bloodletting, sleeping in graveyards and cremation grounds, or near other places of the dead, all of these are used in various traditions to induce ecstatic trance states or feel connected to the divine or to work magic.

Now, I am not suggesting that if you want to worship the Mother you need to engage in dangerous or risky patterns of mystical torture to try and induce visions. That would be unethical, and frankly pointless. Few of us live in spaces or situations where we can devote ourselves so completely to the search for meaning or the divine. Nor do I think it is strictly necessary. Many of these practices are tied to very specific traditions and lineages of practice that are closed to outsiders, as well.

The reason I bring these all up is that, at the heart of the mystical search for the divine, is the hunger for revelation. Mystics are those that seek intimate knowledge of divinity, not just contentment from following a specific religious path. That is the key: knowledge. The Goddess devotee is hungry for knowledge and revelation of her, and the methods of ecstasy and trance and altered states do make up part of that search for her face.

KNOWING THE MOTHER

When I speak of "knowing the Mother" I am not talking about knowledge in the same way I would talk about astrological knowledge, for example. If I were teaching you astrology, then your "knowledge" would be your learning the various correspondences, mathematical relationships, and frameworks for chart-reading that make up the system. You might learn how to read an ephemeris and create your natal chart, for example. You learn in this way through listening, practicing, and remembering. This is the knowledge of memory and practice. You are not discovering something new so much as exploring an established system and understanding its rules.

We tend to believe that truly new knowledge comes through observation, testing, and verifying. This is the scientific method. It is a view of knowledge rooted in the Enlightenment, in empiricism. Knowledge of something real is knowledge of what you can test and verify for yourself through your senses. Few of us in the modern world think of knowledge in any other way. If you "know something" it is because it is proven to you, through experience, or through the experience of witnesses that you trust. These experiences can also be repeated by anyone to test their validity. Before the rise of empiricism, though, there were other views of knowledge.

The study of knowledge in philosophy (put crudely: the investigation into how we know what we know) is called epistemology. And there were many differing epistemologies before the rise of the scientific method and the utter conquest of naturalism and materialism. For some systems, knowledge can be revealed or experiential. Mystics are often those that believe they have direct experience of knowledge, imparted through union with the divine, and that does not require the steps of investigation usually needed to learn something new, steps such as those in the scientific method.

Much of this revelatory approach to knowledge stems from a Platonic view of the cosmos, where it is believed there is a true, absolute, perfect reality behind everything. There aren't just "trees", but instead, there is the absolute reality of the concept of a tree, existing eternally in a higher plane. Mystical knowledge is knowledge of the absolute, the true and cosmic reality behind the veneer of life. In traditional religious practices you come to know *about* the divine. In mystical practice, you come to know the divine herself.

Now, I want to acknowledge that I am on very shaky ground here. This kind of approach can be used to justify religious extremism, pseudoscience, dangerous ideologies, and empower visionary leaders to gain followers and claim divine-like status. The scientific method is a good thing. Focusing on what we can prove through experiment and falsifiability is crucial to cutting through enormous amounts of hokum and dangerous religious claptrap. Do not think that I am suggesting we turn back time to when we did not use the scientific method to learn and verify our knowledge.

What I am touching on, hopefully, is the idea that revelatory experiences are, in a very real sense, educational experiences. What we experience from ecstatic devotion and magical ritual is not simply a good high, or a quirky habit. It is a method for examination of the self and the self's relationship to the world. The hunger for Mother, for union with the Goddess and experience of her reality, can lead you to reexamine what you think you know about yourself, or the world. Through the ecstasy of her worship and the magic worked in her circle, my knowledge is continually changing and updating. I firmly believe this is available to all.

I know there are many methods of worship, magic, and spiritual experience at play in the contemporary magical communities of Witches, Pagans, and magicians. Spiritual seekers try and experiment with many differing forms of trance, divination, and spell work. That is a good thing. Over my years, though, I have never witnessed anything transform people as much as the Mother. I have seen ceremonial magic work wonders for people. I have seen initiation into various traditions really transform the lives of seekers. Divination, when it's really on point, can almost be a therapeutic practice. But, over and over, I have seen delving into Mother utterly morph the lives of devotees, reworking and uplifting the experience of the seeker.

And in those experiences, I do believe a very real knowledge is being attained, as real as the knowledge of chemical or physical principles. Separating out revelatory knowledge from sensory knowledge just feels off to me. Dissecting our emotional, spiritual life from our mundane life is a surgery I am not willing to do. The two are united, a hunger for experience and knowledge that uses different methods because there are different kinds of knowledge.

To know her is to understand. To seek her is to learn. To experience her is to be her. The knowledge and revelation that comes from union with Mother is transformative and real. It is very common in New Age communities to hear talk of "finding the god within" or saying, blithely, "God is not something far out there, God is you! You're God!" I'm not denying the wisdom at the core of this, but to assume that the attempt to realize the divinity within is accomplished just by declaring it so, by fiat, is not helpful. It's really just a recipe to fluff the ego.[6]

The path to knowledge and revelation, real revelation that imparts the truth (not an opinion, or feeling, but Truth) that the Mother and the soul are one is the work of many lifetimes, I believe. I do not think it is accomplished with a weekend retreat or a vision board. Worship, ecstasy, and the techniques of mysticism are not light things, nor are they easier paths than rigid patriarchal religion. They are complex and daunting in their own way, often I believe much more difficult than being handed an instructional manual on theology like a catechism. We are

---

[6] It is also very frustrating for people to utter these ideas as if they are new. New Age speakers often talk as if "realizing that God is within you, not far away in Heaven," is some amazing, new discovery, when it is at the heart of countless traditions, many of which are very "orthodox" or "traditional."

unmoored when we step into the worship of Mother, cast into a world of trance, revelation, and ecstatic love. It is not a series of gentle steps up the sloping face of the mountain. It is a dive into the ocean from a great height, with no land in sight.

METHODS OF MADNESS

Mystical revelation is commonly experienced through intense practice. The image of someone being randomly chosen by the divine, given prophecies with no preparation, is more a trope from fantasy novels than in the history of religious practices. Mystics are often the most ardent and devout of believers, accustomed to grueling practices to loose the consciousness from its mundane bearings and float somewhere else, somewhere near the face of God.

Before discussing these methods, it is important to lay down a few very crucial caveats. Many methods used to induce trance or ecstasy (*ex stasis*, literally: outside of oneself) are dangerous. Fasting, dancing, or exerting the body beyond the point of exhaustion, piercing the skin, working with fire, and even more extreme methods have all been used by devotees to experience ecstatic states and experience knowledge given by the divine through revelation and not just study or exploration.

These methods are not to be approached lightly, nor can I cavalierly recommend them to someone in good conscience. We live in the modern world, with expectations very different from nuns, monks, and hermits that live alone or in small, like-minded communities. Mental health is a very real issue for the religious, and taking care of it should trump spiritual obsessions.

That being said, I do believe that there are techniques and practices that are available to anyone, not just cloistered nuns in the 16th century. And I also believe it is worthwhile to discuss the methods used historically by seekers. I am not saying that these methods, or my suggestions, are canon law. But I am saying that I do believe that devotional practices to the Great Mother can lead to revelatory experience and religious ecstasy. Prayer, as its own practice, will be discussed later, as well as the use of symbols and meditation to connect to Mother. For now, we focus on a few major techniques of mystic practice.

ENTHEOGENS

The word *entheogen* means "full of god" or something akin to "possessed." The term was coined by ethnobotanists in the middle of the 20th century to label naturally occurring hallucinogenic substances used in religious rites. There has been an explosion of discussion surrounding entheogens in the magical community. Trips to take ayahuasca, including expensive and lavish retreats, are becoming increasingly common. At the time of this writing, the largest university in my state is conducting research on the use of psilocybin, the chemical found in "magic mushrooms", for the treatment of psychiatric disorders. Entheogenic practices are becoming a stock part of many spiritual seekers' practices. Many of these contemporary practices hearken back to experimental hallucinogen use by previous spiritual seekers in the West such as Timothy Leary and Aldous Huxley.

I do accept that hallucinogens and alcohol can be used to induce altered states of consciousness. The practice is found in tribal cultures, such as the use of ayahuasca in indigenous communities, as well as the consumption of peyote. We find the heavy consumption of marijuana amongst certain Saivite mystics in Hindu traditions. There are also scholars who argue that the use of hallucinogens may have been used during the initiatory rites of Eleusis, in Greece, or are part of the mythology of the Witches' sabbat. These theories are still controversial, but they do provide another layer to discussions around ecstatic religious experiences of worship.

And the contemporary growth of this practice shows no signs of stopping. A quick search online, and you can discover entire forums and communities devoted to unknitting the seemingly shared experiences of those who consume DMT and have eerily similar visions during their trips, or the detailed descriptions of other hallucinogen-users, many who describe themselves as "psychonauts."

I do want to state a heavy caveat here: the consumption of mind-altering substances can be dangerous. I also want to state that the consumption of entheogens has never been a part of my personal practice. I do not have the authority, nor the experience, to speak about any kind of how or why behind the use of entheogens. It would be unethical for me to speak about their use, not having used them myself on my path. In many places, there are also heavy legal ramifications surrounding the possession of banned or controlled substances.

Then why devote a portion of the work to them? Well, the fact is that they are an enormous topic in contemporary mysticism. To be silent on them would be odd. So, I do list them here as a method of mysticism, one that increasing numbers of practitioners are turning to.

What I want to end with, though, is a bit of a warning. Entheogenic practice is rooted in culture, experience, and ritual, in most cases. These substances are not always approached by contemporary Westerners in the same fashion they are approached in their respective cultures. Tread very lightly with this, as ripping a practice away from its framework often changes that practice, or even nullifies it in certain situations. In short: be safe, be smart, and be respectful.

THE BODY

Pushing the body to its limits is perhaps the most common form of mystical practice that we find in historical examples. Long sessions of prayer, such as those of Teresa of Avila, often combined with fasting, are associated with the induction of visionary experiences. The 16th century Catholic mystic described one of her visions, writing, "I saw in his hand a long spear of gold, and at the point there seemed to be a little fire. He appeared to me to be thrusting it at times into my heart, and to pierce my very entrails; when he drew it out, he seemed to draw them out also, and to leave me all on fire with a great love of God. The pain was so great, that it made me moan; and yet so surpassing was the sweetness of this excessive pain, that I could not wish to be rid of it."[7]

Lead image of a winged Goddess that may be Artemis Orthia. Over one hundred thousand such votive pieces have been discovered in the region around Sparta. (Met Museum)

This does not sound entirely pleasant, does it? Accounts of other mystics throughout varying cultures are often just as harrowing. As a note, they are also surprisingly sexual. There is a beloved statue of Teresa of Avila in the Vatican that looks shockingly like someone in the throes of an orgasm. More conservative believers might scoff, but I challenge you to look at that work of art and tell anyone that it is not perfectly sexual.

And I don't want to make it seem like I am drawing solely from a Christian lot here, when discussing the trials that mystics put the

---

[7] Teresa de Avila, *The Life of St. Teresa of Jesus, of the Order of Our Lady of Carmel*, trans. David Lewis (New York, NY: Benziger Bros., 1904), https://www.gutenberg.org/files/8120/8120-h/8120-h.htm.

body through in their search for God. In Rome, cultists of the "Syrian Goddess" flogged themselves, drawing blood, horrifying onlookers with their ecstatic cries and blood-curdling, shouted prayers.[8] Rites like these were also similar to those offered to Magna Mater, or Cybele, and to the Goddess Artemis Orthia in Sparta.[9]

Ecstasy, and altered states of consciousness, were induced by believers in diverse ways, often pushing at their flesh and testing it. Extreme fasting, an incredibly dangerous practice that I adamantly do not recommend, was used to induce visions from starvation.[10] Dancing for hours on end, until the body collapsed from exhaustion, was part of religious experiences across mystical traditions. And even purposely harming the body was used, unfortunately, to push the believer to experience visions or trances or to prove devotion.

All of this is not meant to be a recommendation, let me be clear! I firmly believe that the Goddess does not demand from us such painful, harmful practices. I am highlighting them here to show that devotion and ecstasy were not easy practices in most cases. If we approach mysticism, or the search for Mother, as something that we think can be accomplished with no effort, or with no change to our reality, then I don't think we're understanding what we're trying to do.

I also mention them as a warning, honestly. The search for Mother may be frightening, or difficult, but you should approach it with some sense of level-headedness. A hunger, or thirst, for spiritual truth can turn toxic very easily. Beautiful visions and devotional hearts are ripe feeding grounds for fanaticism and delusion. Be very leery of any prac-

---

[8] Robert Turcan, *The Cults of the Roman Empire* (Cambridge, MA: Blackwell Publishers, 1996), 139.

[9] Pausanias, "Pausanias Descriptions of Greece," trans. W.H.S Jones and H.A. Ormerod, Perseus Digital Library (Tufts University), accessed August 12, 2022, https://www.perseus.tufts.edu/hopper/text?doc=Perseus%3Atext%3A1999.01.0160%3Abook%3D3%3Achapter%3D16.

[10] The Catholic nun and saint Catherine of Sienna starved to death for her devotion, despite attempts from her confessor to get her to eat.

tice that harms the body, for the body is the manifestation of Mother. Our bodies are a gift, a belief we will explore in a later chapter,[11] and not something to be tortured at the behest of some terrifying divinity.

RITUAL AND THE SACRED

This final examination of methodology is the one where I feel the most comfortable actually recommending steps for devotees. The use of ritual space, sacred time, and building up mental triggers, is the safest form of mystical practice that I have found.

What I mean by all of this, is the decision to set apart part of your life, your home, and your experience, for Mother. Creating a space within your life where you step outside of what you know, where you force yourself to change and face the Mother, is crucial to developing a transformative practice.

This is not a New Age concept. Initiates of the mystery cults burned incense, poured libations, and were taken to underground chambers and hidden places, often in darkness, to experience the rites. Prayers could be in languages the initiate may not have understood, shouted as a wild and feral cry. Sometimes, these prayers were secret passwords, or guarded incantations that were believed to hold power in their syllables, a tradition carried on even today with the use of barbarous words.[12] The experience was meant to trigger altered states, strong emotional response, and to teach the initiate.

All of this is similar to a dictum told to anyone who has ever tried their hand at creative writing: show, don't tell. Solid, powerful, experiential ritual should be something you experience, not something that is read to you, or dictated as a string of blunt facts. The entire mind and the entire body participate in good ritual. The experience itself is

---

[11] See chapter 7, *Queen of the Witches*.

[12] Barbarous words (barbarous from a Greek word meaning foreign) in magical practice are words that are believed to contain intrinsic power, even if they are not intelligible to the speaker.

revelatory, imparting truths about Mother with every sign and act.

If you are worshipping Mother at the Spring Equinox, to give an example, you have two options. You may decide to read a string of truths about the Spring. "This is a time of renewal. This is when the flowers return. We gather here to honor the rebirth of all life, just as the trees…" and so on and so forth. The problem with rituals such as this is that they really don't impart anything, do they? Even a child knows that the flowers return in Spring. Everyone comes to a Spring Equinox ritual knowing that we're most likely going to talk about life returning, in some way. It just isn't very inspiring to tell people something they already know.

Instead, as the other option, good ritual should force you to experience truth. A solid Spring ritual may involve a rite of rebirth, a moving from physical darkness into light, an invocation to Mother returning from death and decay, or something hidden from sight that is revealed at precisely the moment where the energy of the rite hits its peak, something holy raised with chanting, singing, movement, or prayer.[13]

It takes practice and time to develop these kinds of transformative rituals. It takes time, as well, to create and maintain a sacred space that begins to trigger change within you. Repeated devotion and discipline yield fruit.

And in all of this, you should be challenging yourself. Break your own personal taboos and fears. Lose inhibition with your practice. Tepid, nervous prayers can be worked into shouts, into strong and vociferous declarations of power, magic, and belief. You can shed your fears of dancing, of the body, of being seen as ridiculous, or hokey. This will not always come easily, of course, but keep at it and it will.

For something to be *sacred* it must be *set apart*. When we engage in transformative ritual, when we challenge ourselves to cross the dark

---

[13] Revelation of a symbol, or token, at the height of an ecstatic ritual harkens back to many mystery cults which included a moment known as the *epopteia*, or "contemplation", which signifies the acquisition of the knowledge of those things referred to as "the greater mysteries."

river of inhibition, we are coming face to face with Mother. The more of our petty insecurities and doubts that we shed, the closer we come to her revelation. Worship of Mother is renewal. Worship of Mother is evolution. Worship of Mother is ecstasy.

All this is the root of being a *mystes*, a mystic. We step into the liminal razor-edge of mind and body exalted in devotion. And in that is power. That power is electrical, pulsing through our rites and prayers, echoing back to the countless souls that raised their hands and rolled their bodies in dance and trance for the Goddess. We work in their presence, stretching back to Eleusis and Samothrace, to the temples of Isis and the sabbats of the Witches, stretching across the boundaries of time and culture. Choosing to step up to the altar of Mother is participating in the theurgic, transforming potency of magic.

To end this chapter, I choose to quote Lucretius. He was himself a non-believer and critic of the Goddess, as well as most religiosity, describing the rites of the Great Mother in Rome in an attempt to shame and mock them. Let us dance, despite the spite of the non-believers, for her. Always for her. To those that stand outside her mysteries, we owe nothing.

> *… hollow cymbals, tight-skinned tambourines*
>
> *Resound around to bangings of their hands;*
>
> *The fierce horns threaten with a raucous bray;*
>
> *The tubed pipe excites their maddened minds*
>
> *In Phrygian measures; they bear before them knives,*
>
> *Wild emblems of their frenzy, which have power*
>
> *The rabble's ingrate heads and impious hearts*
>
> *To panic with terror of the Goddess' might.*
>
> *And so, when through the mighty cities borne,*

> *She blesses men [sic] with salutations mute,*
>
> *They strew the highway of her journeyings*
>
> *With coin of brass and silver, gifting her*
>
> *With alms and largesse, and shower her and shade*
>
> *With flowers of roses falling like the snow*
>
> *Upon the Mother and her companion-bands."* [14]

Let your roses fall like snow upon the Mother.

Bronze statuette of Cybele (Magna Mater—the Great Mother) in a cart being drawn by lions. Her cult spread throughout the Mediterranean and was associated with wild, orgiastic rites and religious ecstasy. (Met Museum)

---

[14] Lucretius, "On the Nature of Things," trans. William E. Leonard, Classics Archive (MIT), accessed August 15, 2022, http://classics.mit.edu/Carus/nature_things.2.ii.html.

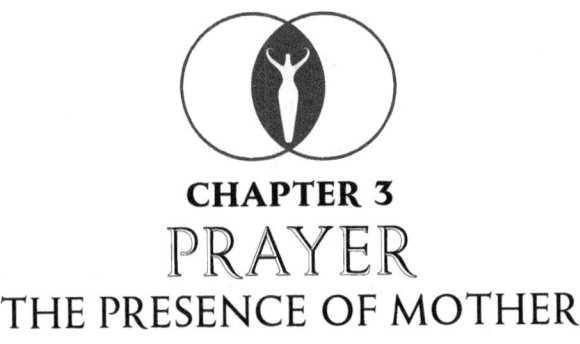

CHAPTER 3

PRAYER

THE PRESENCE OF MOTHER

 I have come, hearkening to your very eloquent prayer, which the nature of mortals has discovered at the suggestion of the gods." [1]

— Hekate, speaking in the Chaldean Oracles

LET US PRAY

Discussing prayer with magical practitioners and spiritual seekers is a fascinating experience. I have been told so many times that I couldn't count them all that prayer is something that "Christians do." It is most definitely not something that magical practitioners need. Prayer is something akin to begging. And we, as Witches, or magicians, or enlightened practitioners, do not beg. More than once, I have been told, "The gods are my equals. I don't pray to them. We work together." I can understand the root of this approach, as I do believe we are co-creative with Mother, but there is still a palpable unease with the idea of prayer that runs through all of these ideas, and frankly I am not sure it is saying anything useful.

I have met many Witches and magicians who scoff at prayer only to turn right back around and petition angels, beings of the elements, or tree spirits to do their bidding. I do not see a clean or clear difference

---

[1] Ruth Majercik, *The Chaldean Oracles: Text, Translation and Commentary* (Wiltshire, UK: The Promethean Trust, 2013), 135.

between spell-like petitions and prayer, and I think many are splitting hairs at this point to avoid the "p word" out of some knee-jerk desire to be seen as more enlightened than religious believers of more common or mainstream paths. If you're asking an extra-planar elemental to do your bidding, I don't think you get to roll your eyes at your Aunt Janine and her prayer list. Well, you can, but you don't get to do it with anything resembling integrity or logic.

I truly believe that a major issue that comes up in these discussions around prayer is ego. Magicians often structure prayers as demands, drawing from the grimoire tradition in particular (but it is not the only source for this) to say that if we have the right accoutrements and symbols, we can command the entities we beseech to act according to our will. Perhaps we can, but I think spells and prayers are so tightly woven together that trying to make a point about which one is "magic", and which one is "begging" is more about the speaker's ego than any actual sustained logic.

Many of those who identity as Pagans are more open to the concept of prayer than self-identified Witches, magicians, or occultists. The deities of polytheistic Pagans are propitiated with prayers, often along with an offering or a poured libation. These prayers are sometimes formed from the skeletons of historical prayers that we have preserved if we are lucky enough to have them. Historically accurate prayers to Celtic deities, for example, are much harder to come by than those from Egyptians who left a large corpus of prayers and rituals, many etched into stone.

But behind this entire discussion is, I believe, a massive misunderstanding. The idea that prayer is a quid pro quo exchange, or begging a deity to do something for you, is actually a rather rare concept in the more contemplative theologies of most religions. I believe a lot of American practitioners think of prayer in this quid pro quo way because of Evangelical Protestant Christians, who sometimes do hold prayer circles where God is directly propitiated for specific and mundane things. "Dear Father God, we come to you tonight to ask you, oh

Heavenly Father, to please heal Sarah's dog, Rylie, of this cyst. And we trust in you, Father God…" Well, you get the point. We've most likely all heard prayer such as this.

The truth is that most established theologies, even in conservative religious traditions, have not really viewed prayer as solely akin to begging for favors from a supernal father figure. Prayer is seen by many believers as entering into the presence of the divine. The Catechism of the Catholic Church—hardly a New Age publication—states, "Entering into contemplative prayer is like entering into the Eucharistic liturgy: we 'gather up' the heart, recollect our whole being under the prompting of the Holy Spirit, abide in the dwelling place of the Lord which we are, awaken our faith in order to enter into the presence of him who awaits us. We let our masks fall and turn our hearts back to the Lord who loves us, so as to hand ourselves over to him as an offering to be purified and transformed."[2]

It is true that the Catechism does talk of supplicatory prayer, the kind where we ask about Sarah's poor dog and healing, and the Mass includes prayers for the community of believers, but it is by far not the only form of prayer. One of the most common forms of prayer in the Catholic Church is the rosary, which is a meditative and repetitious practice, and does not involve asking for specific things, necessarily. Eastern Orthodoxy has maintained a thriving tradition of contemplative prayer that goes far beyond asking God for favors, but instead focuses on the meditative absorption of the devotee.

This is not uncommon in other traditions either. Judaism and Islam have long histories of contemplative prayer, including (in Sufism) the recitation of divine names in prayer to actually etch the names of God onto the human heart and experience divine love. In Hinduism and Buddhist traditions, mantras are used to guide meditative and devotional practice. In Tibetan Buddhism, individual deities are visu-

---

[2] *Catechism of the Catholic Church*. 2nd ed. Libreria Editrice Vaticana, 2000. Accessed August 2, 2022, https://www.vatican.va/archive/ENG0015/__P9M.HTM.

alized in conjunction with prayer and mantra to overcome obstacles to enlightenment and to further one's path in the dharma.

Buddhism also has a fascinating tradition of prayer and mantric practice in the form of Pure Land practice. In this practice, which is one of the most common Buddhist practices worldwide (far more common than Western conceptions of Buddhism as solely about silent, introspective meditation) devotees of Amitabha Buddha chant his name repetitively in the belief that they will be born again in the Pure Land where the attainment of enlightenment is easier than here on earth, in our current age. This practice, known as *nianfo* in Chinese and *nembutsu* in Japanese, has flourished across East Asia and Pure Land schools are often the largest Buddhist schools you encounter in East Asian diaspora communities.[3]

As devotees of the Great Mother, prayer is whenever we choose to turn ourselves towards the Goddess, to see her face reflected in the faces of others, or in the meditative hollows of our own minds. Goddess prayer is prayer that unites us with the Mother, brings us into space where we participate in her eternity. The goal is not to ask for boons alone, but to ask for transformation, to feel like we stand within and before the face of the infinite Mother. I say "ask for transformation" but even that does not entirely grasp it. We are transformed *through* the practice itself, not just as a result we get *from* it.

The Neoplatonist philosopher and theurgist Iamblichus, who we met before, speaks of three degrees of prayer. He writes, "I declare, then, that the first degree of prayer is the introductory, which leads to contact and acquaintance with the divine; the second is conjunctive, producing a union of sympathetic minds, and calling forth benefactions sent down by the gods even before we express our requests, while achieving whole courses of action even before we think of them; the most perfect, finally, has as its mark ineffable unification, which establishes all authority in

---

[3] For an overview of Pure Land Buddhist practice, see: *Pure Land: History, Tradition, and Practice* (Shambhala, 2021) by Charles B. Jones.

the gods, and provides that our souls rest completely in them."[4]

Prayer can be about supplication, do not mistake me, but at the heart of contemplative prayer is the desire to be in love with Mother. Just as the lengthy quote above hints at, the real goal of prayer is union with the divine. The longer I have been initiated into Craft, the more I realize that the entirety of Craft's theology is, at its very core, a love story. We are asked, as Witches, to fall in love with a love story. And that language of falling in love with the divine is at the core of countless mystical traditions. Sufi saints wrote poetry to God as if God were their lover. Teresa of Avila and other Catholic mystics had trance-like states that resembled orgasms or fits of obsessive love. The Sufi poet Attar writes:

> *Every pleasure in both worlds is because of the Beloved;*
>
> *life revolves around and because of the Beloved.*
>
> *Live in celebration of that great force;*
>
> *revolve around it like a planet in longing.*
>
> *No one and nothing can bring joy*
>
> *to your every breath better than the Beloved."* [5]

To love the Mother is to love Creation. To pray to her is to abandon fear by embracing fear. The Mother is cradle and tomb, and she is beyond a great and terrible chasm between what we know in our day-to-day reality and what we also seem to know as real in some deeper, more occluded part of ourselves. Prayer obliterates that chasm. The divine *within* us finds its helpmate, lover, and perfection in the divine *without* us. With time, we realize the illusion of the chasm itself; we feel our

---

[4] Iamblichus, *Iamblichus: De Mysteriis*, trans. Emma C. Clarke, John M. Dillon, and Jackson P. Hershbell (Atlanta, GA: Society of Biblical Literature, 2003), 275.

[5] Attar, *The Conference of the Birds*, trans. Sholeh Wolpe (New York, NY: W.W. Norton & Company, 2017), 231.

participation and oneness with Mother. This life of prayer may feel unhinged and startling to us. Plato himself put into the mouth of Socrates the realization that, "the revelers in the rites of the Great Mother are filled with a divine frenzy."[6] The Orphic Hymns state that the Mother of the Mountains delights in the "screams of the dying and the howls of the living."[7]

That is the prayer at the heart of the Mother. It is madness to the uninitiated. It is an orgy to the fearful. It is terror and release. She has been worshipped with drum and rattle and cymbal and shout. She still is. This is prayer. This ecstatic desire to realize what is just beneath the veneer of life *is* prayer. Prayer to and with the Mother is a song, sung by countless voices and aching in the throes of love. That love is revelatory, and within it we are uplifted and changed, turning our minds to a great mirror wherein we see our true selves.

To begin a prayer practice in this fashion is often more difficult than it may seem. As I said above, many Witches and magical practitioners that I know either never use prayer or only use it in prescribed forms where it might resemble a historical practice from a pre-Christian people, or as part of a working or spell. Hopefully, the following recommendations can guide you to beginning a prayer practice that focuses on transformative meditative connection.

THE NAMES OF MOTHER: CONTEMPLATIVE CHANT

Repetitive prayer as a meditative aid is found in multiple traditions. I've mentioned mantras, and Sufi chanting, as well as the rosary. Other traditions include the use of barbarous words in magical incantations,

---

[6] Plato, "Phaedrus," in *The Collected Dialogues of Plato*, ed. Edith Hamilton and Huntington Cairns (Princeton, NJ: Princeton University Press, 1989), 618-619.

[7] Apostolos N. Athanassakis, *The Orphic Hymns: Text, Translation, and Notes*, 2nd ed. (Baltimore, MD: Johns Hopkins University Press, 2013), 72.

words that have no inherent meaning known to the speaker or writer, but which were believed to contain potency and magical power. These are often handed down in magical treatises such as the Greek Magical Papyri.[8] In that work in particular, the sacred vowels are used in varying combinations to provide strings of sacred names that are to be chanted or sung during magical ritual.

These unique 16th century rosary beads from Germany depict well-to-do figures on one side and skeletons on the other, meant to direct the one praying to the fleeting nature of life and our shared mortality. Contemplative prayer is reflective by nature, drawing us into stiller ways of being that open us up to the divine. (Met Museum)

The act of repetitive prayer, if sustained for long periods of time and often in conjunction with other practices, can lead to trance-like states of ecstasy and transformative religious experience. In my own practice, few forms of prayer have worked as strongly to bring me out of slumps

---

[8] To explore the Greek Magical Papyri, see: *The Greek Magical Papyri in Translation, Including the Demotic Spells* (University of Chicago Press, 1992) edited by Hans Dieter Betz.

in my practice than mantric repetition and chanting.

There are a few keys that I find helpful to a practice of meditative, repetitive prayer. The first is to have a visual focal point for your worship, often an image of the Mother. Better than that is a sacred space, a room or altar where you continually practice and which you keep dedicated solely for your devotions.

I also believe it is important to truly devote yourself to one practice for some time, to develop the familiarity that you can slip into the practice with almost no forethought and in which you can lose yourself. The burning of resin incense, heavily smoking herbal incenses, and the dimming of lights and use of mirrors to reflect candle flames can do much to set the space apart from the rest of your lived experience. Sacred spaces are set apart. This is the very meaning of the word sacred.

Choose your prayer. Choose something that speaks to your visions of the Great Mother. Who is she? What is she? What face shines out from the void wearing her crown? For more practical examples I recommend the following:

A name: Choose a name of the Mother that can be repeated simply, but that is not so close to everyday speech that it does not bring with it some touch of the uncanny. I often recommend *Aset (AH-set)*, an approximation of the Egyptian pronunciation of the name of Isis. If you want a word with more of a beat count than just two syllables, add *Dua (doo-ah)* before it, the Egyptian word for "praise." *Dua Aset. Dua Aset. Dua Aset.*

Barbarous words or sacred vowels: I, A, O, U, E. Look to the Greek Magical Papyri for the barbarous names of Isis. Choose one, two, or three of these names. Chain them together into a mantra that you can repeat without thinking. An example: *Lou Loulou Bartharthar.* Alternatively, practice stringing together the sacred vowels, vibrating and intoning each sound for as long as your breath will allow it.

A repeating phrase of praise or invocation: Create a one-line prayer that you can repeat without losing your breath between repetitions.

Choosing one in a language other than your native tongue can help to separate your practice from your everyday speech patterns. An example could be *Ave mater* (*Hail, mother*, Latin) or (an example in English) *Mother, Mother, with me, here*.

Epithets: it was customary in many pre-Christian pantheons to give many epithets, or titles, to the Goddess. These titles were often attributes of the Goddess or were place names of locations where her temples stood or where her cults were powerful. If you were to see the Mother as Artemis, you can research and find that she was called *Potnia Theron* (mistress of wild animals), *Letoia* (daughter of Leto), and *Agrotera* (huntress). Take these titles and work them into your prayer, creating a string that you can repeat and chant: *Potnia Theron, Letoia, Agrotera*.

Any of these examples can serve as a basis, but the real task is to stick to the practice. In the beginning, few people can withstand long periods of seated repetitive prayer. Beads can sometimes help, if you desire to keep count and link your prayers to numbers of spiritual significance to you. But the sustained practice is what brings power. It may sound daunting but working up to being able to withstand periods over an hour or more is where the practice tends to bear fruit. And to be frank, it takes a long time and much longer periods of time than most people are willing to face.

Altered states of consciousness are difficult to induce for many people, especially in a world where we are constantly distracted by screens, lights, and advertisements. I cannot stress enough, at the risk of being overly repetitive (ironic, huh?) how important it is to make this a sustained practice if you really want to see any benefits from it. A one-off prayer session in your living room, with the TV in the background, for ten minutes, is not going to make the cut.

If a ten-minute session does calm your nerves or brings you some modicum of peace, I applaud that. But it isn't going to lead to what I'm talking about here. Build up your stamina. When it's boring, keep at it. When you feel foolish, keep at it. When the Mother feels distant, keep at it. When the Mother doesn't feel real, keep at it. When you wish you were doing something else, keep at it. Do not stop. Pray. Speak your words and let them echo. Reverberate them. Sing them. Chant them. Repeat them until they are one constant hum, the thrumming string of her presence. It may lift the veil, in time.

And it is even more powerful to combine these repetitive prayers with movement. This practice of careful movements mingled with mantric prayer is found (once again) in the Sufi tradition, where different orders teach their students specific motions to accompany the chanting of the names of God.[9] Tantra has its own systems of mudras and movements as well, both in Hindu and Buddhist schools of Tantra.

I recommend a seated repetition of prayer with a simple, easily repeated movement. To give an example of what I mean, take the recommendation I gave above of chanting the name *Aset* (Isis). In a seated position, bend your body down, eyes closed, towards your left knee on the first syllable (AH) and then back up to an upright seated position on the second syllable (SET). Then bend to your right knee on the first syllable of the next repetition (AH) and back upright on the second (SET). You can vary your pace, working your core muscles and exhausting yourself in the process. Given time this combination of repeated chanting and bodily movement can lead to trance.

SHOUT, DRUM, AND DANCE: ECSTATIC PRAYER

Another prayer practice of God the Mother is ecstatic dance and prayer. This is most associated, in the Hellenistic traditions we've talked about in this book, with the Phrygian Goddess Cybele, known in Rome as Magna Mater—Great Mother. Her cult was favored at times by emperors and

---

[9] For anyone interested in an introduction to Sufism, particularly from a Mughal (Indian) perspective, see: *Sufi Meditation and Contemplation: Timeless Wisdom from Mughal India* (Omega Publications, 2012) edited by Scott Kugle and translated by Carl Ernst.

aristocrats but at other times persecuted for being beyond the accepted norms of behavior. Her cult was associated with Dionysian cults and foreign, largely Syrian cults of other ecstatic Goddess figures.[10]

Her cult in Rome unnerved conservative politicians and writers who described her festivals and worshippers in lurid terms, highlighting her eunuch priesthoods and their garish costumes and ululations, used to stir up frenzy. The orgiastic rituals were full of drumming, cymbals, rattles, and dancing. It is true that the polemical accounts we have most likely stretch the truth, but it is generally accepted that worship of the Great Mother was ecstatic and sexual.

Sufi worshippers in Turkey, commonly called "dervishes", swirling in contemplative prayer. (Adobe Stock)

This kind of bodily prayer is not always an option for most devotees. We can't exactly paint ourselves in ram's blood and shake cymbals all night long until we pass out in her glorious revelations. That's a pretty sure-fire way to end up institutionalized, or at the very least despised

---

[10] Robert Turcan, "The Orontes Pouring into the Tiber," in *The Cults of the Roman Empire* (Cambridge, MA: Blackwell Publishers, 1996), pp. 130-194.

by your neighbors.

What we can engage in is forms of ecstatic prayer. The meditative and repetitive prayer mentioned above can act as a springboard for delving into more body-focused and movement-focused forms of prayer. You can take your meditative prayer and combine it with dancing, or twirling, moving the body in continuous circles, using incense and loud drumming or rattle-heavy music to push the mind just enough off its axis to lead to trance. Shaking a sistrum is an easy and powerful way to build a beat and shock the system with loud, clanking noise. The sistrum was also an instrument sacred to many faces of Mother, faces like Isis, Cybele, and Hathor.

Take your time in the beginning. Begin with music. Focus on the sound of the rattle, or the drum. Move your body slowly at first, spinning or dancing. Build your rhythm in time with your prayer. Echo the same prayer. Get louder, vary your volume. Shake the sistrum. Beat a drum. Vary the pitch and tone of your prayers. At first, it will feel ridiculous, or you won't find the right beat to get lost in, but don't stop. Continue to move and vocalize. Overcoming the initial, jarring step of giving in to worship is crucial to breaking through to meaningful experience.

As you develop with this practice, push yourself as far as you can, in a way that is safe for you and your situation. Exert as much as you are able to. Sweat. And sweat a lot. Shake the sistrum until your bicep pulls and aches. Shout and rattle off your prayer in front of her idol. Twirl. Stare at Her. Burn her incenses. Paint yourself with her symbols. Beasts, inverted triangles, circles, spirals, chalices, cups, lunar crescents, and more. Run your hands over your body as you move, but never stop the prayer. Never let up. Pray and move until she comes. She is always the one that comes.

For many of us who grew up with more traditional religious views, this form of prayer can feel embarrassing or trigger feelings of discomfort. It is perfectly understandable, but you cannot stop when those feelings arise. Giving in to learned shame will kill your rituals quicker than anything. It will take time to let go of the hurdles that are littered on the path to Mother's face, but they are surmountable. Push yourself beyond what you know, perhaps beyond what you have ever considered "prayer." In the places where you lose yourself, and that tight control we try to keep on our image and perception, revelation is had.

PRAYER LIFE

Conservative religionists often develop what is called a "prayer life." I encourage all devotees of the Mother to develop a prayer life. It isn't going to look the same as a Methodist's, but that does not mean that it is not a prayer life. I pray daily, burning incense and leaving offerings at the shrines and altars of my home. Continual return to the altar leads to a sense of grounding in my life that shapes me in everything that I do. My mundane career, my writing, my friendships and expectations, my marriage: all of it. All of it spins around the axis of Love that is worship of the Mother and that worship is expressed in prayer, be it contemplative, repetitive, or ecstatic.

Do not be afraid to copy and steal, as all writers and creators do. Look to historical samples such as the Orphic or Homeric Hymns, if Greek poetry speaks to you. Invert traditional patriarchal prayers with abandon. *Our Mother, who art in heaven…I believe in one God, the Mother Almighty, maker of Heaven and Earth…Glory be to the Mother, as it was in the beginning…* Look to Egyptian prayers in the Book of the Dead or the Coffin Texts to Isis, Nephthys, Sekhmet, and more. Research Mesopotamian invocations and stories of Inanna or Ishtar. The opportunities are everywhere.

Another thing to consider is that there are no wrong times for prayer. Sometimes we do want our prayer to be ritualized. The use of sacred space and ritual practice can interlock with prayer to build up our practice into something truly spectacular. But do not be afraid to pray when you are angry. Pray when you are enraged. Pray when you are horribly sad.

Pray when your emotions are getting the better of you. And remember, worshipping at the shrine when you feel nothing at all is the very heart of the mystical search for union. Pushing through our slumps and low points opens us up to entirely new ways of thinking and experiencing. Do not be afraid of raising your voice, into those places where hope and belief seem so distant and impossible. There is power here. Channel that power. Channel it all and pour it out into the wide, often bitter sea of Mother.

Speaking of the sea, remember that Mother is the earth. Gaia, Cybele, the Mother of the Gods from Mount Ida, Terra, Bona Dea, Ops, Bhumi. All of this is the body of Mother. Her incarnations speak of her as the embodiment of our biosphere, the breathing union of humans as one species among many, living on this planet that we sacralize as her body. She is chasms, grottoes, ravines, and rivers. When you leave offerings in the mountains, pray to the Mother of Mountains. When you pray at the edge of the churning sea, she is the Mother. When you are in the scorching desert, make prayers to the Lioness and the Scorpion. There is no part of the wide and varied earth that does not scream her names.

Prayer is the chance to sacralize every moment, even your voice, your very breath. No one can take from us our acts of devotion. There is a defiance in prayer. When you pray to the Queen of Heaven, when you chant the names of God the Mother, you are chanting in defiance of nihilism. In defiance of a world of empty consumerism and endless drudgery. In defiance of false kings and controlling clerics. You are defying the void, by praying to the one who made the void. Eventually, the words won't matter. The act itself is enough.

CHAPTER 4
TOKENS OF MOTHER
SYMBOLISM AND THE GODDESS

> *They beheld that Cosmic Body of the Great Goddess, that form beyond all other forms.*
>
> *The sky is its head, the moon and sun its eyes. The cardinal directions are its ears, the Vedas its speech, the wind its breath, so it is proclaimed; the universe is its heart, they say; the earth its loins…"* [1]
>
> – From the *Devi Gita*

WHAT'S IN A SYMBOL?

Whenever we talk of a concept as enormous as "God the Mother" we are running the risk of aiming our heights far too high if we want to be clear and precise. There is always the risk that we are going to get into areas of such generality that anything we bring up will lose its power in a net we've cast too wide. With that worry in mind, I do want to discuss touchpoints for connection to the Goddess, symbols that have transcended cultural groups and epochs to remain firmly rooted in the worship of Mother.

Symbols are more than just visual reminders of intellectual concepts.

---

[1] C. Mackenzie Brown, *The Devī Gītā: The Song of the Goddess, A Translation, Annotation, and Commentary* (Albany, NY: State University of New York Press, 1998), 123.

For many spiritual practitioners and theologians, symbols are actually divine in and of themselves, or can be. In Neoplatonic tradition, there is a unique concept of *sunthemata*. This word—often translated as "tokens"—refers to the belief that objects and beings contain forms and ideas that are reflections of the divine mind. These *sunthemata* are both receptacles of the divine and pathways back to her.[2] By surrounding ourselves with, or connecting with these tokens, we can participate in the divine, or trigger states of being or thinking that lead to union with God, with Mother.

Buddhist statue portraying a mudra. Mudras are hand gestures used to teach spiritual concepts or portray certain religious goals or ideas. This particular mudra is associated with warding off evil. (Adobe Stock)

This tradition stems from a belief that the divine emanates from herself. Many Neoplatonic and hermetic systems contain complex emanational frameworks where the singular divine essence grows outwards in various stages to encompass all of creation. Sometimes this is described

---

[2] Algis Uzdavinys, *Philosophy as a Rite of Rebirth: From Ancient Egypt to Neoplatonism* (Wiltshire, UK: The Promethean Trust, 2008), 319.

as an overflowing, where the power of divinity unfurls, flowering out and filling up Creation with herself. With such a worldview, everything participates in Mother. Even stones, leaves, sounds, and symbols; everything is constantly participating in the refracting, unfolding flower of God the Mother. What came to be called "Gnosticism" also shared this emanational view of divinity. Many Hindu philosophies also speak of the ultimate reality emanating through levels known as *tattvas*.

This idea is similar to what became known as "correspondence" in the occult traditions of Europe. Using astrology, herbalism, geology, and more, occultists, magicians, and natural philosophers built connections between objects and beings here on earth and higher, celestial concepts. Anyone who has studied astrology, ceremonial magic, grimoires, or crystals, will be aware of this tradition. Objects in life were seen to be associated with, connected with, or reflecting the nature of planets, angels, gods, concepts, desires, or even geographical locations. This was all part of a great chain of Creation, with God at the very top, and trickling through larger cosmic beings like angels, or planetary spirits, and eventually coming down even to the stones and bones of the material world.[3]

Many of these correspondences are widely known by practitioners of magic or divination, such as associating the sun with gold, heliotropes, the archangel Michael, etc. or associating Jupiter with tin, oak trees, the archangel Sachiel, and countless other items and beings. This is one of the roots of what is called "sympathetic magic." This is a system of "like attracts like."

Even in mainstream religion, symbols and objects can acquire incredibly potent spiritual significance. Roman Catholics believe in the doctrine of transubstantiation. This doctrine, using a complex Aristo-

---

[3] A large swath of the writers that are considered *de rigeur* on reading lists about esotericism, or the history of occultism, worked within this concept of the great chain of existence, beginning in God, trickling through spiritual planes, and manifesting in the material world of nature. Writers to explore here include Agrippa, Paracelsus, Trithemius, Marsilio Ficino, and Giovanni Pico della Mirandolo.

telian philosophical argument, states that when the priest consecrates the host and the wine during the Eucharist, they *literally* become the body and blood of Christ, and therefore God. To believe that the elements of the Eucharist are only a symbol, or reflection of the body and blood of Christ is actually a grave heresy in Catholicism (and other branches of Christianity as well). You're eating flesh at the altar rail. You're drinking blood.

The Eucharist is a sacrament. In a phrase still quoted frequently by Christian writers and believers today, a sacrament is "an outward and visible sign of an inward and invisible grace."[4] This theology is linked, historically, with the Neoplatonic concepts discussed above. Neoplatonism had a strong effect on Christian theology.

In Islam, the Quran is considered the perfect revelation of God, in its original Arabic form. A lot of non-Muslims are unaware that according to most religious leaders in Islam, a translation of the Quran is not actually a Quran. It is a commentary only, since the perfected revelation given to Muhammed by the archangel was dictated in Arabic and therefore non-Arabic versions are *something different*. There are debates in Islam about whether the Quran is even a created object or if it has always existed as part of God's creation, eternal.

And the above examples don't even begin to touch the wider array of symbols, objects, and tokens used by spiritual traditions to trigger altered states, inspire believers, or connect practitioners to the divine. Reliquaries populate the landscape of churches across the world. Buddhist architecture is often believed to teach or reflect certain principles and Buddhist statues contain *mudras*, hand gestures meant to signify and teach spiritual concepts to the observer. Hindus use *yantras* to meditate with and reflect complex philosophical positions regarding the nature of God and the soul.

The Mother has been associated with many symbols across cultures.

---

[4] Repeated in many Christian works, and a common paraphrase of a piece from the *Book of Common Prayer*, the standard liturgical work of Anglicanism.

I am an American, with European ancestors, living in the 21st century so that is going to color the symbols that I associate with the Mother. For others, their tokens of the Goddess will vary. I have attempted to choose associations that span across cultures and time to show how certain concepts do seem to occur repeatedly in regard to what we color as "Goddess oriented." Before we delve into the tokens, I want to address one issue, the issue of worshipping images.

IDOLATRY: MOTHER IN ART AND IMAGE

One of the most common ways that worshippers connect with Mother is through image. Often, this is with statuary or art meant to reflect incarnations or faces of the Goddess. Most home altars, and the altars of specific traditions, contain images of God. This concept is so rooted in our perceptions of pre-Christian religion, religious Witchcraft, Paganism, and Goddess worship that we can immediately call to mind images of temples filled with sculpted statuary or altars laden with gifts and sculpture. There is even a trend of sharing pictures, lovingly curated, of home altars, candles lit, smoke wafting, and offerings laid out for the gods or spirits being honored or invoked.

With this use of image and material to represent the face of Mother comes the accusation of idolatry. To worship a graven image is a grave sin (pun intended), according to many mainstream faiths, particularly the Abrahamic traditions. Iconoclasm is a common ideology of believers. Protestantism leveled the charge of idolatry against Catholics and Orthodox Christians with more than a little vehemence, often storming churches to tear down icons or deface statues and depictions of Christ, the Virgin Mary, and the saints. In Islam, depictions of the prophet have led to violence and protests.

In Hindu tradition, deities are personified in *murti*, which are images or statues of the gods, although the word itself can be applied to larger concepts of the material world. Worshipping with images has become a central practice across Hindu traditions, used to teach, help devotional practice, and serve as the focal point for ritual worship.

Even outside of traditional religion, there is sometimes a mistrust of using images for spiritual development. It is not uncommon to find the spiritual-but-not-religious crowd holding on to a mistrust of idols. There is a marked feeling of "I don't *need* such things to connect to the divine." I think that a lot of this mistrust is born from good intentions. There is an effort here to cut away the flotsam and jetsam of a busy practice and focus on the simplicity of devotion, meditation, and spiritual growth. The minimalism behind this idea is something I can appreciate.

That being said, the use of image for me is about art. Art is one of the divine outpourings of the human experience, and I cannot structure my worship or love of Mother without thinking of, using, and enjoying beautiful art. When I use images or statues in my worship, or when I decorate and tend to an altar, I am not superstitiously bowing down to graven idols. I am connecting to a complex network of symbols, human effort, and artistic output that speaks to deep parts of my own experience and the shared experience of others. All artists are, in a sense, miniature gods, engaging in the act of creation just as the divine does in her emanations.

And "idolatry" is not as cut and dry as we like to think. It is true that Abrahamic faiths do have strict rules regarding graven images, but there is a deeper theology of idolatry that I think many of us could get behind, even if we are not members of these faiths. Abrahamic theologians have written of idolatry in a more metaphorical sense, naming our "idols" as all those things we put before our love of the divine. Those that worship their jobs more than their families may be idolaters. Those that worship money more than human flourishing may be idolaters. Those that worship strength and power above clemency and equality may be idolaters.

These are the real consuming idols, the wicked little false gods that eclipse the love of Mother with ego, delusion, and destruction. The Catechism of the Catholic church states, "Idolatry consists in divinizing what is not God. Man [sic] commits idolatry whenever he [sic] honors and reveres a creature in place of God, whether this be gods or demons (for example, satanism), **power, pleasure, race, ancestors, the state, money, etc.**"[5] (Emphasis mine)

Beyond a love for art, the other power behind image is that it may serve as a focusing point for our devotion and our effort. In the theurgy of the Neoplatonists I have quoted from at length so far, statues were imbued with ritual and magical rites to serve as living vessels for the gods. They were "animated" and treated as breathing oracles that could foretell the future and produce divine states of ecstasy and impart knowledge from the gods. Oracular and imbued statues formed the center of many cultic and temple-based practices of hermetic and theurgic religion in the Hellenistic world.

Finally, the power behind worshipping with art and idol is to obliterate the poisonous dualism at the heart of many spiritual practices. I am no hard dualist. I do not believe that the flesh is fallen and the spirit wondrous. I believe, firmly, that the Mother is within both soul *and* flesh. At the root of a lot of spiritual minimalism is a mistrust of the physical and a preference for the spiritual. I cannot recommend this to any seeker or devotee. The body is Mother. Art is Mother. The earth, the stones, the beasts and birds are all Mother. To worship her in image and body is to truly worship her. To attempt to separate ourselves from our physical reality in some attempt to be "pure spirit" is a blasphemy against the Goddess. Our incarnation is a gift, not a curse.

TOUCHPOINTS OF WORSHIP

To end this chapter, I want to provide, as promised, touchpoints for worshipping Mother. These symbols were chosen, as I wrote before, with the caveat understood that they stem from the culture I inhabit

---

[5] *Catechism of the Catholic Church*. 2nd ed. Libreria Editrice Vaticana, 2000. Accessed September 3, 2022, https://www.vatican.va/archive/ENG0015/__P9M.HTM.

and my own experience. These five symbols are meant to be only starting points for you. My hope is that devotees will explore and plumb these symbols to their very depths, deconstructing and rebuilding them in worship and magic.

They are not meant to be perfect, historical doorways through which to understand a particular incarnation of Mother. They are meant, instead, to be places for the mind to drift towards in rites and prayers. They are meant to be gates that open to wider, more complex gardens of connected symbol and myth.

And that word, myth, is crucial here. The word myth is not synonymous with the word lie, or untruth. A myth is a body of knowledge, woven into metaphor and narrative. The myths of Mother, like the tokens of Mother, are here to teach. They are not instruction manuals. They are experiences. To delve into these experiences through image and symbol is to connect the physical experience of our senses to the spiritual language that our mind, or perhaps even our subtle body, is fluent in from time immemorial.

THE MOON

> *"I have no one on earth to defend me,*
>
> *Thou alone dost see me in this strait;*
>
> *Therefore I pray to thee, O Moon!"* [6]
>
> -From the *Gospel of the Witches*

It should not be surprising that the moon is the first token of the Mother. Lunar symbolism from the pagan world carried over to one of the most worshipped women of human history thus far, the Virgin Mary. In countless incarnations and images, she stands on the crescent moon,

---

[6] Charles Godfrey Leland, *Aradia: Gospel of the Witches* (Providence, RI: The Witches' Almanac, 2010), 90.

perhaps most famously in her form as Our Lady of Guadeloupe. She even bears titles like *Star of the Sea*, often depicted under a moon.

It is important to note that many cultures ascribe the moon to a male god.[7] Why, then, is the moon continually used to represent God the Mother in contemporary times? The reason, as far as I can see, is two-fold. The first is that cultures have connected the cycle of the moon through her phases to the menstrual cycle. The second reason is because of the rise of the Witchcraft revival and contemporary Paganism.

The contemporary revival of Witchcraft used the moon as a central symbol and framework for the worship of the Goddess. This concept is often referred to as the Triple Goddess, personified as the moon in three phases: waxing, full or new, and waning. There has been a large contingency of people who argue that the Triple Goddess has no basis in reality and is lifted from earlier folkloric and poetic writers such as Robert Graves, but I think the attempt to correct zealous poets has swung the pendulum a little too far.[8]

Diana Trivia was indeed a Goddess, and there was a connection between three lunar Goddesses in the Hellenistic world to represent different aspects of a lived human life. Selene, or Luna was the celestial lunar Goddess. Diana, or Artemis, was the terrestrial deity. And Hekate was the infernal, or chthonic form. And other Goddesses displayed a tripartite breakdown as well. Surprisingly, one of the most striking examples is Hera.

Although rarely listed as a "triple Goddess" Hera indeed had a cult center in Greece where she was worshipped in three distinct phases.[9] In the first phase she was *Hera Parthenos*, which is to say Hera the

---

[7] Examples include Khonsu in Egypt, Chandra in India, Sin in Mesopotamia, Tsukuyomi in Japan, and many others.

[8] See: Robert Graves, *The White Goddess: A Historical Grammar of Poetic Myth* (New York, NY: Farrar, Straus and Giroux, 1948).

[9] Walter Burkett, "Hera," in *Greek Religion* (Cambridge, MA: Harvard University Press, 1985).

Virgin. Then she was worshipped as *Hera Zygia*, Hera the Yoked, or Hera the Spouse. And finally, she was worshipped as *Hera Chera*, Hera the Widow, or Hera the Divorcée. And mystery cult-like rituals were enacted, attended only by women, to celebrate and honor her transition between the three phases of her life.[10]

Triple moon symbol commonly used by contemporary Pagans and Witches, meant to represent the waning, full, and waxing moon. (Adobe Stock)

Regardless of debates around the Triple Goddess, the influence of the Witchcraft revival carried forth the image of the moon, often in tripartite form, as the Goddess. The proliferation of contemporary Pagan and non-initiatory Witches only strengthened the association. Meme culture has done its part as well, usually associating quotes, teachings, or symbols of the Goddess with the moon.

What do we take from the moon as our token of Mother? What we take is that the Goddess is intimately close to us. The moon is the closest heavenly body to our planet, the first door to the deeper cosmos. In traditional astrology, the moon could represent our maternal lines, our mothers and grandmothers. She could also represent the intimacy of our minds, our private thoughts, fears, hopes, and intuitions. The

---

[10] *Ibid.*

Goddess as moon is shifting, but predictable. We measure time by her. We plant by her. We carve out calendars with her.

In all of this, Mother is veiled and then unveiled. At times, the moon is black as night, and the road is dark and horrible. Thieves and brigands wait at every crossroad, and the Goddess is a terrible figure with an awful mien. This is like the chthonic incarnations of Hekate, to whom puppies were sacrificed and curses were spoken.[11] And then, she grows, bearing light, until full. And then the road is clear, the midnight filled with silver light. Fear is dispelled. The darkness is abated, if only slightly. Here she is like Hekate the lamp-bearer, the shining one, the one who illuminates.

Her lessons in the moon are lessons of change. We can predict much of life, but not all of it. The phases will shift, whether we accept it or not. This is not some cheap fatalism, as I believe in magic, as many others in her worship do. Instead, it is a reminder that sometimes the path is dark, and she will not light the way for you. Do not assume that your will can change the course of the Heavens every time.

THE WILD BEASTS

> *You are the Goddess of quick childbirth, nurturer*
>
> *of human young, lover of the chase, divine yet*
>
> *of this earth, killer of wild beats, blessed one.*
>
> *You wander the forests and mountains, slayer of deer,*
>
> *exalted, revered, queen of all, fair-blossomed, eternal."* [12]
>
> -Orphic Hymn to Artemis

---

[11] To dive deeper into Hekate, see: *Circle for Hekate, Volume I: History & Mythology* (Avalonia, 2017) by Sorita d'Este.

[12] Barry B. Powell, *Greek Poems to the Gods: Hymns from Homer to Proclus* (Oakland, CA: University of California Press, 2021), 188.

In the Greek-speaking world, a common epithet for the Great Goddess was *Potnia Theron*. This title literally translates to "Lady of the Wild Beasts" or "Lady of the Animals." It was a title applied to multiple Goddesses: the Goddess at Ephesus, Diana, Artemis, Cybele, and others.

Artemis (or Diana) portrays much imagery around our quest for food in the felling of beasts. She is the Huntress, bow in hand, surrounded by hunting hounds or stags, some dead at her feet. Witches were accused of worshipping her beneath the dangerous yoke of the Church. She is a wild Goddess, free and liberated and unmoored from expectation. Her association with horned animals speaks to her deeper mysteries in Craft, her connection to her consort, to the mysteries of death.

As lady of the beasts, Mother is the realization that we are never so safe and protected from the world as we like to imagine. We do much in modernity to shield ourselves from danger, to protect ourselves from savage places and dangerous situations. In our anxiety, we hide from our fears and plant our feet firmly in "civilized" society. Our walls protect us. Our mundane routines keep us from facing truths we want to shuffle aside.

We crown incarnations of Mother, often, with city walls, and make her matron of great states. She is Juno Regina, the regent ruling over a city, and Demeter, who teaches the planting of seed and harvesting of grain. The wild beasts remind us that she is outside the gates as well, still lodged in the untamed and dark places of the forest.

The wild beasts are our token of memory. We must remember that we are part of the things that go bump in the night. We can be as wild and dangerous as a pack of feral animals, when pushed, or threatened, or spurred on by hate or rage. We still rely on animals, on farming, on systems that are increasingly hidden from our sight. Denialism detaches us from our reality.

The wild beasts are the token of death. The hunt is not just about food, or sporting, but a reminder of the mortality we must all face. The stag falls from her arrow. It pierces, a shaft of moonlight, a silver beam, to take a life. And that is the reminder that eventually we will face her, arrow drawn, point glistening, ready to slip the soul from the world with one release of the string.

THE CHALICE

> *With their bronze vessels filled to overflowing,*
>
> *With the vessels of Urash, Mother of the Earth,*
>
> *They toasted each other; they challenged each other."* [13]
>
> -From a hymn to Inanna

The chalice is at the center of Christian worship, but before it stood on the altars of God the Father it held sway in the glories of Mother. The receptacle, the vessel, the cauldron. The concave form. The holder of life-sustaining liquid: water, mead, wine, blood. All of this is the container of the libations of Mother, the offerings that are love, charity, fulfillment, and rebirth.

And it is not just physical birth that the receptacle speaks for, but rebirth into the mysteries of the Goddess. The cauldron is where life is returned to the dead, where new bodies spring from the shell of corpses.[14] It is a reminder of the cave of initiation, the secret grottoes and dark hollows of worship where prayers were shouted, screamed into the dark emptiness of the earth. We retreat into the comfort of her darkness, there to rejuvenate and repair, ready to be reborn from the mouth of her great maw, stretching out across the worlds.

The cup is our shared humanity, our charity, our love for one another.

---

[13] Diane Wolkstein and Samuel Noah Kramer, *Inanna Queen of Heaven and Earth: Her Stories and Hymns from Sumer* (New York, NY: Harper & Row Publishers, 1983), 14.

[14] The cauldron is frequently a symbol of rebirth. In the story of Branwyn, in the Welsh *Manigogi*, there is a cauldron that resuscitates the corpses that are placed within it. There are many other examples of magical cauldrons in Celtic literature, such as the cauldron of the Dagda, which provides eternally recurring sustenance.

We drink from one great well, draw from one breath. At the table, the wine is the gift we give to one another, toasting to our health, promising bonds of friendship. Alliances are made with the cup. Wars are averted with the cup. Difference and long-held hatreds are obliterated in the shared draughts of her chalice. All drink from her.

Etruscan terracotta chalice believed to depict the "Mistress of the Animals" or Artemis. This piece dates from ca. 550 BCE. (Met Museum)

THE SEA

> *Above all, let the priest himself who governs the works of fire, be sprinkled with icy billow of the deep-roaring sea."* [15]
>
> – The Chaldean Oracles

The wide sea is the churning pot of creation. The sea is our token of enormity, of time and space. She swallows lives, mindlessly it seems, taking away the unwilling in strong currents and dangerous undertows. We have barely plumbed her depths. In the darkness underneath what is visible sleep monsters and alien worlds that we have only just begun to understand. In her trenches is crushing pressure. At times, she swallows up entire cities, washes away the handiwork of humanity as if it were constructed of matchsticks and paper.

The sea as Mother is beyond understanding. The sea is the churning water that hints at a cosmic view of time and space, larger than what we can deal with, stuck as we are in a middle ground between brevity and eternity. The Hindu sages wrote of a great ocean being churned at the points of creation, universal and cosmic in size, moved by gods and heroes, forming the matrix from which existence itself emanates.[16] Mother is the boiling, rolling, undulating sea of creation.

And who can measure her? Who knows how far the edges stretch, how endless the waters of the cosmos exist in their expansion and contraction? The token of the sea is deep memory, and consciousness, the potential of endless lives, endless incarnations, endless cycles. Where does the sea begin, and where does it end? Everywhere and nowhere. It is the same with Mother. She has no beginning and no end. She shatters all perceptions of space, overflows beyond all containers. Nothing can contain her, for if we could build a container for her, then she would

---

[15] Ruth Majercik, *The Chaldean Oracles: Text, Translation and Commentary* (Wiltshire, UK: The Promethean Trust, 2013), 99.

[16] The *Kshira Sagara* or "ocean of milk."

be that container as well.

The waters of time and consciousness are the World Soul, the infinite knowledge of Mother. We call her bitter because we cannot grasp her. We call her treacherous because we cannot measure or tame her. And standing on the edges of her shores, we glimpse but a token of infinity, of the promise of everlasting life and rebirth in her mysteries.

Photo of women in Brazil carrying flowers during a festival to Yemanjá, the Orixa of the sea. (Adobe Stock)

THE FLOWER

> *"And then they took the flowers of the oak, and the flowers of the broom, and the flowers of the meadowsweet, and from those they summoned into being the fairest and best-endowed maiden that anyone had ever seen. And they christened her with the christening that was used then, and she was called*

> 'Blodeuedd.'" [17]
>
> – From the *Mabinogi*

Mother is a rose, the token of secrecy.[18] She is the unfurling lotus,[19] and the rebirth of life in Spring. She is growth, displayed to the light of the sun and drinking from the earth. She is the combination of pollen and ovum, the creation of seeds, nuts, and fruit. We worship her as giver of fecund life, the one who blesses crops and raises herds. She is Demeter who welcomes back her daughter, and Isis who floods the Nile, and the warmth of the sun.

She is the explosion of life in the chain of evolutionary development, the magic of speciation, the angry and bursting refusal to accept extinction. If but a seed is saved, then life continues. She is our biological and carbon-based existence, interwoven into complex dependencies and mutual creation. All of life builds itself upon a network of her language, spoken in coiled proteins, filaments, membranes, and mycelia. Life appears at once so heartbreakingly beautiful, and yet so incredibly messy and complex.

And in that wild and messy web of life, she is Beauty. Beauty not as some specific list of traits, but Beaty as an absolute. Beauty as the sister of Goodness and Truth. She is the glory of art and creation, and the appreciation for wonderment and awe. We harvest the living flower, breathe it in, taste it, adorn the altar with it. Beauty is the foundation of all worship.

She is the first pluck of the stringed instrument, the flower behind the ear of the singer and the dancer. She is the garden where we dine

---

17 Mark Williams, *The Celtic Myths that Shape the Way We Think* (London, UK: Thames & Hudson, 2021), 211.

18 Drawing from Roman mythology, the phrase "sub rosa" has long denoted secrecy. It literally means "beneath the rose."

19 In many dharmic traditions, the lotus represents the purity of mind, or consciousness, blossoming and expanding despite the tumult of life. The lotus grows in very muddy water but blooms pristine, hence the symbolic connection.

when the light fades into evening and the smell of jasmine and gardenia is heavy and thick on the air. She is the gift of joy, the refusal to sink into despair and ugliness, a bursting point of color against a gray and dead background.

She is growth, and development. Every unfurling petal is a teaching, a revelation, a vision. As she expands, so do we. She unfurls to the light of wisdom, and we unfurl within her. From the central calyx of her glory, all life opens up and spreads into the universe.

16th century Italian engraving of the Goddess Flora. (Met Museum)

CHAPTER 5
SHAKTISM
THE WORSHIP OF DEVI

 Salutations to the Divine Mother, who is the Mother of All.

Salutations to the great Empress of the whole Universe.

Salutations to the great Sovereign enthroned on the lion's back.

Salutations to Her who came out of the fire of Pure Consciousness." [1]

– From the *Lalita Sahasranama*, the 1,000 Names of the Goddess Lalita

CROSSING LINES FOR GOD THE MOTHER

In the last chapter, I discussed how looking for repeating symbols can sometimes take us to places where we force the connections, or where we are ignoring concepts that might stick in our craw about what we want to accomplish in creating associations. I mentioned how my own symbols and tokens of Mother are colored by my birth, heritage, and lived experience. One of the issues that arises in this same vein is the issue of speaking of, or appropriating even, concepts we are interested in from a culture that is not our own.

---

[1] Swami Tapasyananda, tran., *Sri Lalita Sahasranama: Text, Transliteration and English Translation* (Chennai, India: Sri Ramakrishna Math Printing Press, 1988), 88.

The worries around cultural appropriation have been present in Craft, contemporary Paganism, and magical practices for a long time now. The debate has gotten rather heated, particularly around the large growth of white practitioners of African Diasporic Traditions such as Santeria, Quimbanda, Vodou, and Palo. I have seen this debate swell and change with my time in the community, and it still (for now) raises strong emotions on all sides.

This chapter isn't meant to serve as a side in this debate, or to argue for any particular philosophy or stance about cultural appropriation. With this debate in mind, however, I do think that worship of the Goddess will inevitably lead devotees to search for Mother in other cultures, cultures outside of their own. This feels unavoidable, since the majority of those interested in Goddess worship and reading this book most likely come from a patriarchal Abrahamic background and have little connection to living Goddess traditions. When you are surrounded by atheists and Presbyterians, but want to worship God the Mother, of course you're going to look outside of what you know.

We have predominately looked at Hellenistic examples so far in this book, and in the cultures touched by Hellenism cultural mingling and pulling from foreign traditions was common. The cults of the Great Mother often (as seen in the prayers quoted earlier in this book) mingled African, Mid-Eastern, Greek, and Italic deities. Isis was born in Egypt but Hellenized in Greece and the wider Roman empire. Syrian Goddesses and deities from the Levant were brought to Rome by traders, prisoners, enslaved persons, and others, and their worship was mingled with and taken up by native Roman citizens. Celtic deities merged with the Roman imagination, and Romano-Celtic divinities were beloved throughout the Empire—figures such as Epona, the horse Goddess. And of course, one of the most influential cults was that of Mithras, an originally Persian figure. This was a common practice. "Foreign" deities were sometimes approached with mistrust, but at other times were integrated into local practice, becoming as centrally important to daily life as more "native" gods.

And as for the initiation cults we have covered, birthplace and individual culture were not the standards for entry. Anyone could be initiated at Eleusis if they could speak Greek, so that they understood the prayers and passwords, even enslaved persons who were normally barred from other major religious acts and offices. This is true in the Cult of Isis as well, particularly in Rome. In fact, it was the entry of enslaved persons and other oppressed peoples into the cult that made conservative Romans weary of it.

Hindu women painting one another with sandalwood paste during Durga Puja, a festival to the Goddess. (Adobe Stock)

I believe that a major reason these initiatory mystery cults were open to all, with few exceptions, was that they truly saw the Goddess as cosmic and all-encompassing. This is a crucial point in discussions around religious identity. For some religious identities, your birth, ethnicity, language, tribe, bloodline, and more are all crucial to the identity. Judaism is the classic example of a religion that involves a concept of birthright, bloodline, and cultural, ethnic, and national identity. Yazidis,

Mandaeans, Druze, and many Zoroastrians also believe that one must be born to the faith to belong to the faith. There are still debates in Hindu communities about whether or not conversion into Sanatana Dharma (the internal name of the faith) is possible, or whether or not conversion is an outsider concept, brought in by the colonial mindsets of Christianity.

This is a major crux of this entire conversation (or debate, if you view it as such). Do you believe that your path is a tribe, a community, a bloodline, or do you believe that what you seek is cosmic, or transcendent, and stands outside of cultural identity and birth? Perhaps both are true for you. I cannot answer that question. It is too personal, and each devotee will have to wrestle with those ideas on their own.

It is also important to remember that many cultural and religious groups are closed because of oppression, being forced into secrecy by missionaries and imperialistic forces. And there are also tribal faiths, and faiths of community that do not make sense outside of their own contexts. All of this complexity is present when we approach Mother. For me, Mother is transcendent. But I leave to the seeker what that means for them in their own practice. Policing the entry points of religious systems outside of your own culture and experience is rarely a good idea.

For devotees of the Goddess, the most common place to find yourself in this multicultural searching will most likely be at the feet of Kali, or of Durga, in the tradition of Goddess worship that comes from the dharmic, Indic tradition commonly known as Shaktism: the Goddess-centered branch of Hinduism.

Some devotees of Mother may also find her in African Diasporic Traditions, drawn by the traditions of Mami Wata, Ezulie, Pomba Gira, Yemaya, or any of the other powerful female figures of these paths. I cannot speak to these paths as I have never been initiated into any of them, nor do I practice with Orishas, Lwa, or other spiritual beings from these paths. That is not to say that I do not love to explore them, to study and read and learn. I simply do not find them to be a place for my development. I count myself as incredibly lucky that I know many priestesses, priests, and devotees in these traditions that have shared with me (that which they can share, anyway) and taught me. But I do not have the knowledge to speak with any authority on African traditions. It just isn't my place to do so.[2]

With Shaktism, however, I do have a relationship. As someone who found God the Mother, Shaktism loomed as an unbelievable discovery: an entire tradition of millions of devotees, all devoted to Devi, a word literally meaning "Goddess." For those of us who see the face of God in Mother, this tradition is a treasure of the world's spiritual heritage—a living, thriving tradition of devotion to God as Mother. I have been reading and studying about Shaktism for most of my time as a devotee to Mother, and many of the works I recommend to those that ask about the Goddess are drawn from this tradition. Some of those works are sourced within this chapter.

Shaktism is one of the major branches of Hinduism, and its worshippers focus on the Supreme Godhead as a Goddess, as Devi.[3] Some forms of Devi are widely known to Westerners, such as Kali, Durga, and Lakshmi. Others, such as certain tantric deities or local cultic Goddesses such as Manasa, the serpent deity, are less well-known outside of insiders to the traditions. Regardless, the image of Kali's terrible, lolling, blood-soaked tongue, and Durga's golden arms, ready to strike down demons, are powerful, and many who love Mother find their way to these traditions.

---

[2] For those seeking further information on this subject, I recommend *Voodoo and African Traditional Religion* (Warlock Press, 2021) and *Orishas, Goddesses, and Voodoo Queens: The Divine Feminine in the African Religious Traditions* (Weiser Books, 2020), both by Lilith Dorsey.

[3] It is important to note that boundaries between "denominations" in Hinduism are often porous, or even entirely constructed by Western scholars of religion. Many Hindus participate in festivals, ceremonies, and practices that span across lineages and established traditions. Shaktism is not a native term to India, even if its root *shakti* is. It is very difficult to parse "Shaktism" from the traditions rooted in Siva ("Saivism"), but I have used the term as a useful way of discussing the Goddess-centric traditions, texts, and practices that come from the Indian subcontinent.

I want to use this chapter to examine how many similarities there are between these traditions and Goddess worship in the West, in contemporary Craft and beyond. I am not here to say that they are exactly the same; of course, they aren't. And I am not here to say that you can approach these traditions lightly without running the risk of misrepresenting and misunderstanding them. Shaktism is centuries old and contains libraries of scriptures, many of which have not been translated into non-Indic languages.

It also is not a unified belief system. There are multiple schools of Shakti worship, and the philosophies behind Shakti Hindu systems vary depending on place, time, and the believers in question. Painting with broad strokes can be dangerous, as it obliterates the unique distinctions of the various Goddess traditions of the Indian subcontinent. But there are overarching themes and ideas that run through most Shakti traditions, and these are beautiful philosophical and theological fountains to drink from if you are seeking Mother.

The exploration of Shaktism is also complicated by Tantra. Tantra is a word misunderstood by many seekers in the West as something akin to sexual practices. The truth is, Tantra is not about sex. Tantra refers to multiple theological systems that exist in Hinduism and Buddhism, based on scriptures known as *Tantras* that relate practices of meditation, worship, and philosophy that lead to *moksha*, the ultimate goal of most Hindu practice: release from the cycle of life, death, and rebirth.[4] In Buddhist Tantra, the goal is *nirvana*, a slightly different concept. The word *tantra* itself is from a root meaning to weave, or a concept that references the loom.

Tantra contains multiple schools and traditions, but most of them do focus heavily on the Goddess. The interplay between the male force of

---

[4] One of the most intricate and well-established tantric movements is Sri Vidya, a school that focuses on the Goddess Lalita Tripura Sundari, often embodied in the complex geometric form known as the Sri Yantra, or Sri Cakra. For an exploration of Sri Vidya that is open to beginners, see: *Glorious Alchemy: Living the Lalitā Sahasranāma* (New Sarum Press, 2019) by Kavitha Chinnaiyan.

creation (often Siva) with the Goddess (Devi) is a central theme in most tantric practices. Some tantric practices (although they are a minority) also focus on what is known as "left-hand path" practices (*vanamarga* or *vamachara* in Sanskrit). These practices include the breaking of religious taboos such as drinking alcohol, engaging in ritual sex, eating meat, or touching the remains of the dead. These practices have been sensationalized in the West, in film and popular media, but they do not represent the majority of tantric religiosity.[5]

With these nuances in mind, I firmly believe that I cannot write about the Goddess without addressing the largest Goddess-focused religious system on the planet. There are tens of millions of *Shaktas* in the world. And even beyond those traditions that could firmly be labelled Goddess traditions in the wide and complex umbrella of Hinduism, more god-focused traditions still honor the Goddess.

Devotees of Krishna honor his beloved and equal, Radha.[6] Saivite Hindus (who honor Lord Siva as the supreme Godhead) honor the incarnations of Parvati (Kali, Durga, and more). And many Hindus attend festivals and pujas for Devi, regardless of their particular religious heritage. Saivite systems, in particular, are intimately linked to Shaktism, and many Siva-centric traditions mix and flow with Goddess-focused traditions. The point here is that, regardless of denomination, the Goddess is alive in the Indic traditions, and millions devote their lives to her. They raise their arms, as we do, and chant her names, eagerly seeking union with her absolute beauty, her foundational-to-existence being, and her inexhaustible love.

---

[5] For a solid overview of Tantra, I recommend: *The Hindu Tantric World: An Overview* by André Padoux (University of Chicago Press, 2017).

[6] Within the Krishna-centric forms of religiosity, there is one lineage that worships Radha as the Supreme Divinity, and Krishna as her servant. That lineage is the Radha Vallabh Sampradaya, founded in the 16th century.

Fragment of a statue of the Goddess Chamunda, a ferocious form of Kali. (Met Museum)

THE GODDESS AS POWER ITSELF

The word *shakti* in Sanskrit means "energy." Other translations link it to ability, force, or change. In Shakti philosophy, this moving, dynamic, powerful energy of the cosmos is personified as a Goddess. The male force of Creation, usually the god Siva, is more akin to the grounding forces of existence, the stable and the unchanging. The eternal dance, union, and relationship between Siva and Shakti form the basis of reality itself. Creation participates and emanates within the Siva-Shakti union.

In the stories of Shakti literature, this concept of power is often illustrated by the gods facing an *asura* (a demon, or malevolent being) that they cannot defeat. Often these *asuras* have been given great boons to survive almost any attack. When the gods realize that they cannot defeat the threat, they channel their devotion and power into one being which manifests as the supreme Goddess that then vanquishes the *asura* and restores order.

Sometimes, the Goddess emanates from herself as another form, a more vicious-looking or warrior form. In the *Devi Mahatmya*, one of the central texts of the Shakti tradition, the Goddess emanates a ferocious Goddess from between her brows to defeat two *asuras* known as Chama and Munda. This emanated Goddess is Kali. When she slays the two *asuras*, she returns their severed heads to the Goddess that emanated her and is given the name of Chamunda, in reference to the two beings she destroys. This Goddess, Chamunda, is a ferocious form of Kali, depicted as emaciated, skeletal, and wild. The text reads:

> *From her scowling brow, Kali sprang forth, frightful of*
>
> *countenance and armed with sword and noose,*
>
> *bearing a strange skull-topped staff, adorned with a*
>
> *garland of skulls, and clad in a tiger's skin. Her emaciated*
>
> *flesh appalling,*
>
> *her mouth gaping, her lolling tongue horrifying, her*
>
> *sunken eyes glowing red, she filled the four quarters of the*
>
> *sky with her roars.*"[7]

---

[7] Devadatta Kali, *In Praise of the Goddess: The Devimahatmya and Its Meaning* (Berwick, ME: Nicolas-Hays, Inc., 2003), 125.

For anyone who has looked at Kali, or Chamunda, it can be a truly shocking image for a divine figure. If we are used to Christian iconography, or romanticized images of past pagan gods, the blood-soaked Goddess is a terrifying deity. Her wider iconography paints her as wild, with untamed hair, skulls, severed limbs, decapitated heads, and a tongue dripping with blood. Sometimes she is shown with fangs, or a terrible maw of teeth. She brandishes weapons, many dripping in the blood of recently slain enemies. In the above incarnation she bears a noose. She is shown dancing on corpses, or haunting cremation grounds or other places of the dead or the dying.

These images are interpreted, by many Shakti philosophers and commentators, as powerful tools to jolt believers into realizations and awakening. What she is truly destroying is ego, delusion, malice, or fear. The severed heads are the deluded egos we leave behind when we take up the work of seeking enlightenment and release. The weapons are the tools of meditation and religious practice. In other commentaries, her ferocious nature is seen as protective. The demons she slays, she slays for her devotees, destroying that which would destroy us.

Icon of the Goddess Durga, shot during the Durga Puja festival in Kolkata. Durga is the slayer of the buffalo demon. (Adobe Stock)

Texts in this tradition also often include a sort of revelation from the Goddess to the gods or to gathered sages, explaining her nature as the supreme being, one with the *Brahman*, or ultimate reality. Just as Vaishnavism sees the *Brahman* as Vishnu or his incarnations such as Krishna, and Saivism sees the *Brahman* as Siva, the Shakti traditions see the *Brahman* as Goddess, as Devi.

In these revelations, there are often truths shared of Mother obliterating all distinctions and dualities, attempting to shatter our misconceptions and lead us into enlightenment. Many Shakti traditions are nondual, drawing from the teachings of *Advaita Vedanta*.[8] Her fearsome attributes are there to teach us and to shatter our dual thinking to reveal the oneness of our *atman*, the soul within, to the *Brahman*—the ultimate, the World Soul, the cosmic reality. The *Devi Gita*, part of a larger Goddess-centered text in Shakti tradition, contains the following revelation from the Goddess:

> *In me this whole world is woven in all directions, O Mountain. I am the Lord and the Cosmic Soul; I am myself the Cosmic Body. I am Brahma, Vishnu, and Rudra, as well as Gauri, Brahmi, and Vaishnavi.*
>
> *I am the sun and the stars and I am the Lord of the stars. I am the various species of beasts and birds; I am also the outcaste and thief.*
>
> *I am the evildoer and the wicked deed; I am the righteous person and the virtuous deed. I am certainly female and male, and asexual as well.*

---

8 Advaita Vedanta is a school of Hindu philosophy based in nondualism. In this system, the individual soul (atman) is considered one with the World Soul (Brahman) and the goal of spiritual practice is to realize and live within that unity.

> *And whatever thing, anywhere, you see or hear, that entire thing I pervade, ever abiding inside it and outside.*
>
> *There is nothing at all moving or unmoving that is devoid of me. For if it was, it would be a nonentity, like the son of a barren woman.*
>
> *Just as a single rope may appear variously as a serpent or wreath, so also I may appear in the form of the Lord and the like; there is no doubt in this matter.*
>
> *The world cannot appear without an underlying basis. Accordingly, the world comes by only through my own being and in no other way."* [9]

The Supreme Devi, here, obliterates all distinctions, associating herself with the highest gods, beyond male and female, beyond good and evil, the complete underlying reality of the cosmos. Nothing is said to exist outside of her presence. Her supreme nature even creates delusion. Devi is referred to in texts such as the Devi Gita as *Maya*, a term meaning delusion or misunderstanding. Even our misunderstandings are her doing, part of her endless dance of creation, destruction, and enlightenment. Every soul is Devi. The World Soul is Devi. Everything is Devi. Compare this with the revelation of Isis in *The Golden Ass* and see the comparisons. Mother is all.

---

[9] C. Mackenzie Brown, *The Devī Gītā: The Song of the Goddess, A Translation, Annotation, and Commentary* (Albany, NY: State University of New York Press, 1998), 118.

BHAKTI: THE PATH OF DEVOTION

Across all Hindu traditions, there are multiple paths that are seen as possible routes to enlightenment. In contemporary Hinduism, one of the most common paths of spiritual development is known as bhakti, which is the yoga[10] of devotion. Bhakti is a path where one falls in love with the divine, usually through ritual worship, chanting, prayer, and good living. The bhakti path has inspired many saints, sages, and poets, and devotional works from bhakti movements are still a central part of Hindu literature, music, drama, and theology. The concept is more well-known in the West now due to the efforts of ISKCON, the International Society for Krishna Consciousness, also known as the Hare Krishna movement.[11]

In both non-tantric and tantric traditions of Shaktism, bhakti is a common path. Devotees of the Goddess chant her names, repeat her mantras, offer worship and prayer in rituals known as puja and make offerings at her temples, shrines, and images (known as *Murti* in Sanskrit). In Bengal, there is a particular devotion to the Goddess Kali.[12] In Sri Vidya, a tantric school, devotion to Lalita Tripura Sundari—She

---

[10] Yoga is a complex term often mispresented by well-meaning seekers. Yoga, as a philosophical and religious term, has little to do with the proliferation of the body system of *asanas* (postures) in contemporary yoga-as-exercise. The word means "harness" or "yoke" in Sanskrit, and refers to mental, spiritual, and sometimes physical processes meant to explore consciousness or philosophical and/or religious truths. There are many paths of yoga in the Indian tradition, one of which is *bhakti*. The term also refers to one of the six orthodox (*astika*) schools of Hindu philosophy. For more information on Yoga as a spiritual and philosophical school, see: *Yoga Sutras of Patanjali: A New Edition, Translation, and Commentary* by Edwin F. Bryant (North Point Press, 2009).

[11] Many people mistakenly believe the Hare Krishna movement to be a modern, New Age institution. It actually is a lineage within Gaudiya Vaisnavism, a tradition that stretches back to the 15th century. For more information on Gaudiya Vaisnavism, and devotional *bhakti* from that perspective, see: *Bhakti Yoga: Tales and Teaching from the Bhagavata Purana, An Exploration of the Philosophy and Practices of Krishna Devotion* (North Point Press, 2017) by Edwin F. Bryant.

[12] For an incredible and deep look into Bengali worship of the Goddess, see: *Offering Flowers, Feeding Skulls: Popular Goddess Worship in West Bengal* (Oxford University Press, 2004) and *The Madness of the Saints: Ecstatic Religion in Bengal* (University of Chicago Press, 1989) both by June McDaniel.

Who is Beautiful in Three Realms—dominates religious practice. In many parts of India, particularly in Bengal and Tamil Nadu, the Goddess Durga is beloved, worshipped in the enormously popular Durga Puja festival.[13]

These emanations of the Goddess are not seen as entirely distinct, as each believer approaches the face of the ultimate Godhead through the worship of an *Ishta Deva*, which literally translates to "preferred, or personal deity." These "beloved deities" (another possible translation) are not separate gods, necessarily, but individual revelations, faces of the Goddess that we can approach the ultimate truth through and with.

Across all of these various bhakti paths, devotion is seen as transformative. Just as we've discussed in previous chapters, devotion is not just about honoring a figure that you fear or need to help you. Devotion is what leads to enlightenment in this system. There are many commonalities, for me at least, between Goddess worship in India and Goddess-centered theurgy in the Hellenistic world. Devotion to God the Mother teaches us, changes us, and promises good rebirth and eventual union with the ultimate.

The power of devotion in Goddess worship can be seen in the works and lives of two central Shakti practitioners, both fairly well-known in Western culture. The first is Ramakrishna, a 19th c. Bengali Hindu mystic with a strong devotion to Kali. The second is Ramprasad Sen, an 18th c. mystical poet and saint devoted to Kali as well.

Ramakrishna is known to the Western world through the proliferation of his teachings by his disciple, Swami Vivekananda, and the foundation and monastic order that bear his name. His writings and concepts have been popularized in the West for many years now. He was a devotee of Kali, writing and praying to her in a form of bhakti (devotion) that is almost childlike, viewing Kali as Mother and him-

---

[13] For an in-depth look at the Durga Puja, see: *Ritual Worship of the Great Goddess: The Liturgy of the Durga Puja with Interpretations* by Hillary Peter Rodrigues (State University of New York Press, 2003).

self as the devoted child or son of the Great Mother. In stories of his worship, Ramakrishna fed Ma Kali with morsels of food, like a child, and slept next to her statues, praying to her as if he were a young boy talking to his mother.[14]

Dakshineswar Temple in Kolkata, India. Ramakrishna served as a priest at the temple, which is dedicated to the worship of Kali. (Adobe Stock)

Ramakrishna saw Kali as his personal revelation of the Godhead, and his writings speak of periods of enlightenment and bliss, all spurred by the worship of her in the fearsome visage of Kali Ma. He says, "I wept before the Mother and prayed. 'O Mother, please tell me, please reveal to me what the yogis have realized through yoga and the jnanis through discrimination.' And the Mother has revealed everything to me. She reveals everything if the devotee cries to Her with a yearning heart. She has shown me everything that is in the Vedas, the Vedanta, the Puranas, and the Tantra."[15]

It is interesting to note that this fierce devotion to Kali is sometimes

---

[14] Elizabeth U. Harding, *Kali: The Black Goddess of Dakshineswar* (Berwick, ME: Nicolas-Hays, Inc., 1993), pp. 256-257.

[15] Swami Nikhilananda, trans., *The Gospel of Sri Ramakrishna* (New York, NY: Ramakrishna-Vivekananda Center, 1942), 225.

downplayed by those that have carried Ramakrishna's teachings and the stories of his life to the West. Many of those inspired by Ramakrishna focus more on the Vedantic teachings of Ramakrishna and the underlying monistic and elevated philosophy found in certain schools of Hindu philosophy and touched upon by Ramakrishna.

I firmly believe, however, that it is impossible to understand Ramakrishna and his equally adored and studied mate, Sarada Devi, without looking into the fierce devotional love (*bhakti*) displayed toward Kali Ma. When we repackage the practices of a saint like Ramakrishna to make them more palatable to Western, largely Christian-born, audiences, we really are losing something. Trying to "clean up" the image of a devotee by stripping away what post-Enlightenment readers could see as "superstitious" is, at least for me, to rob that devotee of their true power as a teacher and an example.

Ramprasad Sen, living centuries before Ramakrishna, was similar in his absolute devotion to Kali. Both of these figures, Sen in particular, often wrote about how challenging her worship was. They spoke to God their Mother in terms that shock and confuse many Westerners. We are used to prayers that speak to God as gentle, or powerful, or commanding. God the Father is a king, a just figure, a fountain of mercy. Kali is not always portrayed as such, even by her most devoted followers. Ramprasad Sen describes her in one of his poems as wearing a garland of infants and having a beauty "only deepened by blood."[16]

Even with the fear and anger that make up part of his worship, the poet still praises Kali as the ultimate revelation of Truth. Her terrible visage and fearsome attributes are handled as no more than beautiful adornments that teach concepts that must be understood by any devotee. Even when we are angry, terrified, or despairing, we find refuge in the terrifying Mother. The poet writes:

---

[16] Ramprasad Sen, "Mother, Incomparably Arrayed," in *The Norton Anthology of World Religions: Hinduism* eds. Wendy Doniger and Jack Miles (New York, NY: W.W. Norton & Company, 2015), 526.

> *How many times, Mother, are you going*
>
> *To trundle me on this wheel like a blind-*
>
> *Folded ox grinding out oil? You've got me*
>
> *Tied to this old trunk of a world, flogging me*
>
> *On and on. What have I done to be forced to serve*
>
> *These Six Oily Dealers, the Passions?*
>
> *All these births—eighty times 100,000—*
>
> *As beast and bird and still the door*
>
> *Of the womb is not shut on me*
>
> *And I come out hurting once more!*
>
> *When a child cries out, calling the precious name*
>
> *Of mother, then a mother takes it in her arms.*
>
> *Everywhere I look I see that's the rule,*
>
> *Except for me. All some sinners need to do*
>
> *Is should "Durga" and—pouf!—they're saved.*
>
> *Take this blindfold off so I can see*
>
> *The feet that give comfort. There are many*
>
> *Bad children, but who ever heard*
>
> *Of a bad mother?*
>
> *There's only one hope*
>
>> *For Ramprasad, Mother—that in the end*
>>
>> *He will be safe at Your feet.* [17]

---

[17] Ibid, pp. 523-24.

Both Ramakrishna and Ramprasad Sen are part of a much larger tradition of Hindu, particularly Bengali, devotionalism to the Goddess. Devotees make pilgrimages to the Shakti Peethas, temples with special significance in Shakti belief, and participate in large festivals in the Goddess' honor. All of this, as I've tried to show so far, is about the *power* behind devotion. These practices are not quid pro quo. These practices are meant to develop and change you at the deepest parts of your psyche. Whether it is rebirth in Elysium, for the Greeks, or *moksha* for the Hindus, devotion to the Goddess is an all-encompassing path of liberation and enlightenment, not a mere transaction of intelligences.

DRAWING FROM THE WELL

I want to stress again that Shaktism is a living tradition with tens of millions of devotees. In Bengal, devotional songs play in shops and in popular media, many dedicated to Kali Ma. Films retell the stories of Devi destroying demons and emanating from the worship of the gathered gods. We must be careful not to consider this path something that exists in books, or only in our imagination. India is a very real place, and the traditions that have arisen in the dharmic, Hindu traditions are the living cultural and religious traditions for many, many humans.

What that means is that we cannot approach the worship of Devi the same way we approach the worship of pre-Christian, European deities. A lot of what is written on Kali, for example, by non-Indian and non-Hindu Pagans approaches her as just another pagan deity. On Monday we worship Venus, and on Tuesday we worship Kali. I'm not sure this is the healthiest approach to the rich tradition of Shakti worship and devotionalism.[18]

---

[18] For an exploration of how the worship of Kali has impacted culture both within India and outside, and in contexts removed from traditional Hindu communities, see: *Encountering Kali: In the Margins, at the Center, in the West* edited by Rachel Fell McDermott and Jeffrey J. Kripal (University of California Press and Motilal Banarsidass Publishers, 2005).

There are also writings and classes given on Kali that really deviate entirely from the living Shakti tradition. I have seen classes and blogs hail Kali as a sexually liberated Goddess of rage and anarchy. I've seen Western artists render Kali in ways that would scandalize and offend many Hindus. There is an approach to Kali as something that very much is not a Goddess, but instead a representation of an agenda. As much as I appreciate the passion behind some of these approaches, they really are alien to the tradition as it is practiced by living devotees. All this is to drive home: be fastidious in your research and look for solid, primary sources and the voices of Indian worshippers and writers whenever you can.

None of that is to say that I do not believe we can draw from the Shakti tradition. I do, and the deeper I have gone into the study of Shakti texts and worship the more I discover. But I say that as someone who has only barely scratched the surface of what is available from this tradition, and that after years of study.

There is a steep learning curve when you approach Hindu scriptures and philosophical works if you don't have a base knowledge in the history, philosophies,[19] and religious traditions of South Asia. Concepts like karma, chakras, and Tantra, have all trickled to the West with growing numbers of adherents and seekers, but that has only complicated things. Sometimes, wading through the morass of texts available is disheartening. So much written on Tantra in particular is guilty of the worst kind of cultural theft and outright misrepresentation.

With all those worries, I still believe that the development of Shakti worship and devotional practice is one of the greatest flourishing founts of the Goddess the world has ever produced. Beyond textual study, I really encourage anyone interested in the worship of Devi to look at the visual art and music that has come from Shaktism. Bengali devotion-

---

[19] If you want to investigate the foundational ideas and philosophies of Indian thought, see: *Classical Indian Philosophy* (Oxford University Press, 2020), by Peter Adamson and Jonardon Ganeri.

alism in particular has produced incredibly moving devotional songs and painting traditions, used to depict loving renditions of Kali and other faces of Devi. Listen to the songs and examine the images, really looking at the complex web of symbols and the use of terrifying and shocking motifs to drive home points about the nature of the Goddess and the nature of our own souls.

CHAPTER 6
HERA
A CASE STUDY

> Rosy Eros with the golden wings held the reins and guided the chariot; 'twas he, who presided over the union of Zeus and the fortunate Hera." [1]
>
> -Aristophanes, *Birds*

A JILTED GODDESS

So far, we've touched upon the transformative practice of devotion to Mother, and how we may draw ourselves into her worship, but I want to take a step away from that, to investigate one deity in particular. It may seem that this chapter feels out of place, but my hope is that by the end you will see why we are going to do a deep dive into a face of the Mother that might seem a surprising choice.

The Goddess Hera, Queen of Olympus and wife of Zeus, is a name familiar to anyone with a cursory knowledge of pre-Christian Greek religion. She is a central figure in some of the major works of Greek writings that we have from the Classical era, and her Roman counterpart Juno figures just as prominently in the writings of poets, historians, and religionists from the Roman people, both republican and imperial. If

---

[1] Aristophanes, "Birds", trans. Eugene O'Neill, Jr., *The Complete Greek Drama*, vol. 2 (New York, NY: Random House, 1938), accessed April 23, 2023, https://www.perseus.tufts.edu/hopper/text?doc=Perseus%3Atext%3A1999.01.0026%3Acard%3D1737.

you ever studied mythology in your schooling, or read Greek classics or studied Latin, then you are more than familiar with her and her legends.

Roman copy of a Greek statue of Hera wearing veil and crown. (Wikimedia Commons)

Beyond the Classical era, Hera has been portrayed (and Juno as well) in paintings, literature, and poems, particularly in the works of Romantic and Classicist artists. She is frequently, in films, television shows, and novels, a character brought out to highlight vindictiveness and vitriol—the perfect incarnation of the stereotypical shrewish wife.

Hera, in the myths most known to us, is portrayed as a jealous, murderous deity whose chief role is to confound her husband, punish her adulterous partner's conquests, and to exist in a state of perpetual spite. In the *Iliad*, Homer's treatment of Hera is so extreme that it feels like he is writing about some demonic deity despised by his people, not one of the most worshipped figures in all the Greek-speaking world, and one that actually sided with the Greeks in the Trojan War that he is writing about.

The lovers of Zeus quake in fear, hide or disavow their children, or flee to the dark and hidden places of the earth to escape her. And Zeus is ready in many of these myths to punish or mock his wife for this behavior. At one point, after a particular entreaty from his wife in Homer's *Iliad*, Zeus answers Hera with the following:

> *Dear lady, I never escape you, you are always full of suspicion. Yet thus you can accomplish nothing surely, but be more distant from my heart than ever, and it will be the worse for you. If what you say is true, then that is the way I wish it. But go then, sit down in silence, and do as I tell you, for fear all the gods, as many as are on Olympus, can do nothing if I come close and lay my unconquerable hands upon you."* [2]

In Homer's epic, Zeus describes his wife as "shrill" and "hateful." He screams at her, abusive and unrelenting with more disdain than conjugal love. Scholar Walter Burkett has written that Homer almost turns Hera

---

[2] Homer, *The Iliad*, trans. Richmond Lattimore (Chicago, IL: Chicago University Press, 2011), 90.

into a "comic figure."[3] She is, to be blunt, a joke. And when she does try to move Zeus, she does it by borrowing a girdle from Aphrodite to make her more sexually appealing, using seduction to get what she wants. This only feeds into the image of Hera as jilted or conniving.

And other myths that surround Hera are no less ugly. Aside from the countless stories of Hera punishing her husband's lovers, lovers that did not always consent to being taken by Zeus, she is also portrayed as vindictive in other ways. She hurls Hephaestus off a mountain for being ugly or lame and is punished by him later by being locked into a chair in the Underworld. She punishes and persecutes Hercules (Herakles in Greek, ironically meaning "Glory of Hera"). She tries to lead a rebellion against her husband and is punished by being hanged by her feet from chains for all to see and jeer at, a show of Zeus' incredible, inviolable power.

There are, of course, gentler mythologies around Hera. She is the supporter and divine matron of Jason in his quest for the golden fleece, and even in Homer's *Iliad*, she is occasionally shown as caring for the fate of mortals. And many of the terrible myths about Hera are contradicted by other versions of the same story, depending on the writer and the time. The myth of the hurling of Hephaestus from Olympus, for example, does not appear in all accounts of the forge god's birth. These examples aside, in the majority of cases and most assuredly in the popular imagination, she's just a jealous wife. Nothing more.

I doubt most readers have an image of Hera different from the ugly sketch above. There really doesn't seem to be much else to grasp at, does there? The problem in this is that the *Iliad*, *Odyssey*, *Aeneid*, and other epic works are not indicative of the lived experience of worshippers in the Greek or Roman worlds. These works were read and studied by elites, often written solely from the point of view of a narrow segment of the population and their portrayal of the divine should no more be

---

[3] Walter Burkett, *Greek Religion* (Cambridge, MA: Harvard University Press, 1985), 132.

taken as canonical or perfect as we would accept *1001 Nights* as indicative of Islamic theology or Medieval European folklore as dogmatic for Christians. Many of these works have decidedly political aims behind them.[4] They are not pure theological treatises that we can approach as guidebooks to understanding how Greek or Roman peoples thought of their religious lives.

These classical works are epic literary creations, meant to inspire awe and to explain history in cosmic frameworks. They are not necessarily useful for understanding how the average Greek or Roman prayed, lived, and worshipped with the gods. Drawing theology from the *Iliad*, or any classical epic, can lead to a skewed view of the religious practices of the Greek and Roman world. These skewed views, however, have incredible staying power as they form the basis of so much art and literature that succeed them.

Sometimes we try to embrace the poor portrayal to make a larger point. There have been arguments made by some commentators that Hera is an example of a "conquered Goddess." Believers in the pre-patriarchy matriarchal theory have argued that Hera is an example of a Goddess beaten into submission and tarnished by the rise of patriarchy, taken from her lofty pedestal as Queen of Heaven and painted as a bitter wife. That argument doesn't hold a lot of historical water, really, since we have little evidence of what Hera may have been to pre-Classical Greeks. A lot of speculation is required to make the leaps necessary to talk of her as the supreme pre-patriarchal Mother that was then transmogrified by later voices.[5]

The reason I think there are better ways to approach the story of

---

[4] *The Aeneid* is dedicated to the emperor explicitly, for example.

[5] Note that while some scholars have disputed the existence of prehistorical matriarchal societies, there are works worth investigating around the ideas of matrilineal cultures, Goddess worship, and the emergence of patriarchy. Marija Gimbutas' books, including *The Living Goddesses*, *The Civilization of the Goddess*, and *The Goddesses and Gods of Old Europe*, as well as Riane Eisler's *The Chalice & the Blade*, are recommended starting points for further exploration. I am not suggesting these in regard to Hera, specifically, but instead as resources for those interested in the concept of prehistorical matriarchy and Goddess worship.

Hera than the prehistorical matriarchal focus is that Hera was not "conquered" in the eyes of Greek worshippers. The *Iliad* does not represent, in totality, how Hera existed in Greece, nor how her worship continued and developed in the later Hellenistic world. To admit that Hera was "conquered" due to a few elite texts misses the entirety of her story and the complexities of her worship.

The first great temples built by the Greeks were dedicated to Hera. In Argos, a city where Hera was a central figure in religious life, her high priestess held political import and power. In Argos, Hera was involved in protective rituals that blessed the entire city state and were crucial for the military success of the Argive people.[6] She was equally adored in Samos and Olympia. Her festivals were city-wide events in Greek-speaking city states, lauding her as the Queen of Heaven, the *basileia*, who even Zeus had to answer to. There are statues and shrines to Zeus that refer to him as Zeus Heraios: Hera's Zeus.[7]

In *The Golden Ass*, which we touched on before, there is another prayer that I want to highlight here. In this prayer, a pregnant girl in dire need prays to the Goddess Juno for aid. Juno was equated by the Romans to Hera. Although there are major differences in the development of Juno's cult in Rome and traditional cults of Hera in Greece, the two were conflated by Hellenistic times. With the following, heartfelt words, the devotee prays:

> *O sister and wife of the mighty Jupiter! whether thou dost possess the ancient temples of Samos, which glories in thy querulous infancy, and in thy nurture or whether thou dost frequent the blessed seats of the happy Carthage, which adores thee as a virgin, riding through the heavens in a lion-yoked car; or dost preside over the illustrious walls of the Argives, near the banks*

---

[6] Sue Blundell and Margaret Williamson, eds., *The Sacred and the Feminine in Ancient Greece* (London: Routledge, 1998), 14.

[7] Ibid, 17.

> *of Inachus, which celebrates thee now married to the Thunderer, and Queen of the Gods! O! thou whom all the east venerates under the name of Zygia, and all the west denominates Lucina! be thou, Juno, the saviour [Juno Sospita] in this my extreme misfortune, and deliver me, weary with the toils of such long-continued labours, from the fear of my present impending danger; for I know that thou art accustomed voluntarily to relieve the distresses of the pregnant."* [8]

We immediately see the connections to a Greek Hera within this prayer to Juno. The prayer mentions the temple of Samos, a temple to Hera, and uses a Greek (here: *eastern*) title, *Zygia*, to refer to the Goddess. This word means "yoked" and refers to the Goddess' role as the spouse of Jupiter, or Zeus. The title *Sospita* here means "savioress." This prayer is a glimpse at what Hera truly was: a supremely potent Goddess, the Queen of Heaven, the savior of women, and of all peoples. She was the one who governed marriage, childbirth, and is here linked with the lion-chariot, the vehicle of the Carthaginian Goddess. The Goddess nurtures her glory and accepts supplications and the love of devotees. She is our advocate.

This image may seem so far from the shrewish wife as to seem like I am inventing her history, but the archaeological and written record does not lie. Hera was not simply some bitter queen, but instead could be the life-sustaining force of maternal love, hardly a figure that should only be remembered for hurling her child from a mountain because he wasn't beautiful or murdering the unwilling conquests of an unfaithful spouse.

And in more mystery-based systems and Neoplatonic theurgic systems, Hera was far more than the spiteful spouse of Zeus. In the Orphic Hymn to Hera, she is said to be "the mother of rains" and is "part of

---

[8] Apuleius, *The Metamorphosis or Golden Ass of Apuleius*, trans. Thomas Taylor (London, UK: Universal Press, 1822), 89-90.

everything mixed in with the holy air."[9] Apart from her there is no life to be found.[10] And in the complex philosophy of Proclus, Hera and Zeus are in a perpetual state of creation, a dance of making, dissolution, and recombination.

This water jar from the 5th century BCE was awarded as a prize during games sacred to Hera and bears an inscription to "Argive Hera"—meaning Hera as she was worshipped at Argos. (Met Museum)

---

9   Barry B. Powerll, *Greek Hymns to the Gods: Hymns from Homer to Proclus* (Oakland, CA: University of California Press, 2021), 31.

10 Ibid.

Proclus takes the myths of strife between Hera and Zeus as a complex allegory of how souls come into being, with Zeus being the creative force and Hera the first principles of creative differentiation. The ugly myths of their interpersonal marital battles serve as rich theological stories that teach us about how mortal souls come into being and are related to the higher divine planes. In other Neoplatonist stories, Hera is associated with the *aether*, with air, and with the first breaths and waters of life itself.[11]

From everyday devotionalism (a *bhakti* of Hera if you will), to the dizzying philosophies of Neoplatonist theurgists, the Queen of Olympus is a supreme figure, a face of Mother that shines with power, authority, adamantine will, and even, yes—Love. We can sing to her as the Homeric Hymn does, saying: "I sing of Hera of the golden throne, whom Rhea bore, queen of the deathless ones, of exceptional beauty, the sister and wife of loud-thundering Zeus—glorious! whom all the blessed ones in tall Olympos revere and honor, like Zeus who delights in the thunder."[12] Think of that. *All the blessed ones.*

WHY HERA?

When I chose to write a case study of Hera, I had a few major reasons in mind that I hope I've clarified. The first is to show that what we think we know about mythology is often pulled from a handful of elite sources or from popular imagination more than from the actual lives of religious believers in the respective cultures of mythologies. The second is that devotion and worship of Mother was found even in the service

---

[11] To explore Proclus' theurgic understanding of the gods, see: *Proclus: An Introduction* (Cambridge University Press, 2016) by Radek Chlup as well as the multi-volume *Proclus: Commentary on Plato's Timaeus* by the same publisher (each volume has its own editor, translator, or other contributors).

[12] Barry B. Powerll, *Greek Hymns to the Gods: Hymns from Homer to Proclus* (Oakland, CA: University of California Press, 2021), 31.

of deities that we do not normally associate with a Mother Goddess. Hera is hardly portrayed as a blessed, loving divine Mother in most of the sources we have access to as students of history or consumers of pop culture.

And yet, Hera is all of these things. She is the protector and advocate of the troubled soul that calls out to her. She is also, yes, spiteful, dark, and terrifying. And that is why I have placed her after the discussion of Shaktism. Just as Kali and Durga and Chamunda teach through images and moments that terrify, awe, or intimidate, so can we find that in Hera. And she is also named our savior, Juno *Sospita*, the protectress of childbirth and giver of succor to all who honor and revere her. Her complete nature is the only nature worthy of reflecting the totality of God. That is Mother. Mother is always the All.

COMPARTMENTALIZATION

The other reason I have chosen Hera, apart from a personal devotion to her, is that I want to address something that I think can really be a pitfall for devotees of the Mother, and that is compartmentalization.

Among magical practitioners, compartmentalization is everywhere. Because of the influence of simplistic spell-writing advice and the long tradition of correspondences, mentioned earlier in this work, that comes from the occult traditions of European magic, we tend to compartmentalize absolutely everything. Magical books and workshops often hinge on long lists of herbal, geological, and angelic correspondence charts. We use these charts to create magical rituals or spells, using a simple, clean logic of one-to-one correspondence. Are you working a love spell? Well, gather rose quartz, rose petals, symbols of Venus, and dove feathers. Are you working a spell for money? Gather cloves, coins, paper currency, and images of Jupiter or the Sun. This line of thinking is very common.

I'm not saying this is an incorrect methodology for ritual creation.

Not at all. What I am saying, though, is that it presents a lot of thorns for devotional practice and for approaching the more ecstatic, transformational aspects of theurgic worship of Mother.

What happens, is that this same one-to-one logic is applied to the divine, and no mythology is more heavily treated with this correspondence-based thinking than the Greco-Roman gods. Poseidon is the god of the sea, so his altar should be absolutely covered in seashells, tridents, bottles of ocean water, or sand. He is good for spells about travel across the ocean. Aphrodite is the Goddess of love, so call on her for love spells and adorn her altars with flowers and jewels and sweet-smelling fragrances.

The problem with this is that the gods were not necessarily so compartmentalized, really, in Greco-Roman religion. Hera, as Goddess of marriage, may be seen as only "useful" for a marriage spell, but frankly that is just an odd way of approaching the Goddess. In Argos, Hera was a supremely potent deity, a Queen, worshipped alongside Zeus and petitioned for *anything*. You didn't just go to Hera for marriage, you went to Hera because she was the matron of the city, and her temple was the central hub of civic religious life. She wasn't just "a Goddess of marriage" she was simply a Goddess, powerful and divine and capable of handing out boons and curses equally, regardless of what section of life was assigned to her by certain myths.

And this is true beyond Hera. In Athens, Athena Parthenos was the dominant religious figure; in Sparta it was Orthia and Ares. To go back to the example of Poseidon, maybe you did worship Poseidon because you were dependent on fishing for your livelihood, or you worked by the water. But maybe you worshipped Poseidon because he was the chief deity of your city, or his temple was the one you had access to, or your family had always worshipped at his altar. And in that case, I highly doubt a worshipper thought, "Well, I can't ask Poseidon to help me with my crops because he's only the god of the sea. Darn. Guess I'll starve or start fishing so he can help me." No. He was a god, and in that moment before the altar, or in the ecstasy and union of prayer, he was *the* god. The one you saw and had access to.

Worship of the Mother is the same. What you find and have access to is enough. You do not need to seek out a "patron" or "matron" to have connection to Mother. How you see her is enough. How she comes to you is enough. And we don't need to wring our hands over whether a particular incarnation held dominion over an area of life that is troubling us. Hera may have been worshipped as protectress of family life and marriage but at Argos her temple also held festivals to honor and bless the military and protect the state. She was more than a box on a checked list.

The Goddess as a totality has been a concept that I've tried to hammer home throughout the first chapters of this book, and here is no different. Approaching the Goddess, even as a named deity from a very particular pantheon, does not require a simplistic concept of correspondence. Within the Goddess we name and specify is the Goddess beyond all names, beyond all specifications. The names are doors to teachings and experience, not cages. Hera had many epithets throughout the Greek world that can teach us.

She is *hyperkheiria*, which means "She whose hand is above" and she is *Akraia* meaning "of the high places." She rules, from above, her hand outstretched for the worshipper and the supplicant, mistress of the skies, mother of storms and rain, giver of those celestial things necessary for life on earth.

She is *Antheia*, "of the flowers", surrounded by the Horae, the seasons, and the Charities, or Graces. Her attendances are the flowing of time itself, the wheel of the year, the gifts of beauty, grace, and regal posture. Her throne is limitless, decorated for the supreme authority of Heaven and Earth, wife of thunder, *Basileia*, Queen.

And as Juno she is *Sospita*, a savioress, called upon to save us in the moments before tragedy. She is called *Lucina* and *Mater* and governs our very birth into this life. As *Moneta* she announces war and peril, and rules from high mountains and the glory of citadels. She is protectress of our community, defender with the spear, and supreme counselor. And she is lady of Carthage, glory of Dido, defender of the port and the temple. She is the Mother of the city.

The Temple of Juno in the Valley of the Temples at Agrigento, Sicily (Adobe Stock)

Do not allow your devotion to Mother to be hampered by some attempt to correspond particular incarnations or deities to worldly matters. Allow the face of Mother to come through your practices, your magic, and take the forms she takes. No one should be shoehorned into the worship of a deity because of a profession, or a childhood experience, or a momentary worry. I do not think the worship of Hera should be relegated to newlyweds, wedding planners, or caterers. Everyone can find the face of Mother in her. The Goddess is not a fractally shattered collection of patron saints. She is everything.

And I say all of this because letting go of these correspondence-based ways of thinking can break down barriers and open up our devotional life. Sometimes, I find that seekers are put off from the Hellenistic pantheon, or even the pantheons of other systems, because of this almost sitcom-like quality of bawdy myths and one-to-one rulerships. When you're seeking a deep, transformative religious experience, it can be jarring to approach incarnations of Mother in myths that read like soap operas. Hopefully, what I've given here can help ease that a little and allow those that *do* find Mother in Hera, Athena, Nephthys, Isis, or Venus to see her as a complex totality and a fountain of meaning.

THE PRIMEVAL

I mentioned earlier the idea that Hera was a matriarchal Goddess changed through later patriarchal myths, and I did cast doubt on that opinion. I do want, however, to point to a few major touchstones with Hera that do seem to link her to a deeper, earthier version of the divine than we may have of her. Despite her traditional image of matronly queenship and regal nature, Hera was not as far removed from the mud of earth as we might think.

At her cult in Argos, there are records of older images of her, aniconic images that do not represent human figurines.[13] In one myth, the horrifying figure of Typhon, a demonic force of destruction and chaos, was born from Hera, not Mother Earth as most myths state. And Hera was also gifted the golden apples from Mother Earth, on her wedding day, the same golden apples that are guarded by the Hesperides in the far West, a mythic land of evening and dream-like nature.

She is also referred to, by Homer, as *bo-opis*, a term often translated as "cow-eyed" but could equally mean "cow-faced." It may be that this is meant to paint her eyes as large, lashed, and beautiful. But it also seems to hint at deeper agricultural practices, reminiscent of cattle Goddesses such as Hathor. Hera was associated in many texts with cattle, and being

---

[13] Walter Burkett, "Hera," in *Greek Religion* (Cambridge, MA: Harvard University Press, 1985).

a Goddess that watched over cattle, or those that tended livestock.[14] The Spartans called Hera *Aigophagos*, which means "Eater of Goats."

All of this is to show how what we might know about a Goddess on the surface level is rarely the entire story of her worship. Devotees approached the Goddess in differing ways, often in ways that challenge our assumptions and our desire to fit the Mother into a predetermined box. Goddesses are often reflections of complex social and historical realities. Even today, devotees will approach Goddesses as incarnation of idealized femininity: either submissive virginal protectors or "holy whores." These archetypes do contain power, but we must be careful of approaching the divine as no more than a reflection of stereotypes or fantasies, particularly patriarchal fantasies.

To be fully transparent, I have a personal devotion to Hera and writing this chapter is, in a way, a service to an incarnation of Mother that speaks to my own religious life. In my own private devotion to Hera, seeking out other contemporary devotees, I have seen other worshippers write poetry and prayers to Hera referring to her as the "bitch Goddess" and "using" her for spells against unfaithful lovers. I'm not attacking this practice, necessarily, but I do hope that what I've shown in this chapter inspires people to look to Hera as more than a scorned wife.

Hera is sculpted in gold and ivory, and veiled as the wife of the Olympian King, but she is also everything else I've briefly sketched above. Hera, like many other Goddesses, moves in the hearts of believers and storytellers in various ways, meandering through biases and cultural prejudices and flowering into unique spiritual realities. Whenever we come to the Mother, we see a polished gem, a multifaceted reflection that refracts and bends the lights of devotion in countless ways, and based on many factors. We should always question our approach to this gem, looking at how our own beliefs and hopes are refracted, bent, or reflected back at us.

---

14 Ibid.

CHAPTER 7
QUEEN OF THE WITCHES

 ...the witches were usurping authority and the keys of the Church when they held their nocturnal meetings because by the light of waxen candles they would hurl the sentence of excommunication even at their own husbands, calling out, one by one, the names of each and every part of their body from the soles of their feet to the top of their head, and then at the end the witches would blow out the candles and say: 'fi: fi: fi: amen.'" [1]

– From the trial of Dame Alice Kyteler, 14th c.

FORMS DIVINE

In this and the following two chapters I want to dive into three visions of Mother that incorporate the potency of her worship. In each of these, we will approach her in a guise, a mask, a network of symbols and connected references that haunt the periphery of her worship. We will take these three "incarnations" as wells to draw from in our devotion.

These three incarnations are not meant to be Jungian archetypes alone, since I do not believe Mother is a simple archetype. They are meant, instead, to be like doorways to her living being. Each of the three doors leads to a different face, and with that face a different voice.

---

[1] Brian P. Levack, ed., *The Witchcraft Sourcebook* (New York, NY: Routledge, 2015), 44.

These are teachings, lived in the worship of Mother in both past and contemporary devotees. The first is one very dear to me, as an initiate of Craft, and that is Mother as the Queen of Witches.

The Witches, woodcut by Hans Baldung, Germany, 1510. Woodcuts depicting sabbats usually employ grotesque imagery and animals or objects associated with the Devil (here: goats) and often an all-female cast of characters. (Met Museum)

DEVIL OR WOMAN?

In popular imagery of the Witches' sabbat, from Early Modern woodcuts to contemporary film, the sabbat belongs, truly, to one figure: the Devil. The Man in Black, often as the Great Goat, dominates the devotion of the gathered Witches, followers who are frequently lurid and naked in their orgiastic dancing and feasting, worshipping the fallen angel and signing pacts that give them access to familiar spirits trapped in the bodies of animals such as toads, cats, and vermin. And they gain magical powers from their unholy pacts, often the ability to fly or to send out their spirit or "fetch" to haunt and torment their enemies.

The fascination with Devil-worship that haunts the period of the witch trials in Europe (and to a lesser extent, the Americas) is a complex historical phenomenon. There is an obvious over-sexualization of women at play, a fantastical almost pornographic obsession with sexual rites, nudity, and the kissing of the Devil's backside to invert the sign of peace given with a kiss in Christian worship.[2] The nominally celibate clerics of the Roman church write passages that read like nocturnal fantasies, masturbatory in their excruciating detail.

There is also a mistrust of any who stand outside of the established social order. Dominant women, midwives, folk healers, the lonely, the mentally ill, most likely many of those that did not fit into the dominant social paradigms of Christian European society were fair game for overzealous witch-hunters and murderous clerics.

And yet, this central figure of the Devil is not the only figure at play in the mythology, writings, and unfortunate loss of life that explodes out from the European witch hunts. What is not always addressed in popular retellings or imagery of the trials is that at the core of the witch trial records is not just the goat-foot Devil, but…a woman. There is a divine figure, a face of Mother, even in the trials of the Witches that

---

[2] The infamous *osculum infame* or "kiss of shame."

were linked to diabolism. In the 20th century, occultist and novelist Dion Fortune put a realization into the mouth of one of her characters, a realization that when Witches went to kiss the backside of the Devil, there they found instead the face of the Goddess.[3]

WITCH-GODDESS

In the *Canon Episcopi*, dating from the 10th century and parroting the views of Augustine of Hippo, we see the belief that Witchcraft is a delusion, particularly common with women, and that belief in Witchcraft is a heretical fantasy. Regardless of whether it was pure fantasy or reality (which later clerics most certainly believed, believed strongly enough to put fire to flesh and murder innocent people) the *Canon Episcopi* has a startling and interesting accusation at its core.

> *It is also not to be omitted that some unconstrained women, perverted by the Devil, seduced by illusions and phantasms of demons, believe and profess themselves, in the hours of night, to ride upon certain beasts with Diana, the Goddess of the pagans, and an innumerable multitude of women, and in the silence of the dead of the night to traverse great spaces of earth, and to obey her commands as if her mistress, and to be summoned to her service on certain nights. But I wish it were they alone who perished in their faithlessness and did not draw many with them into the destruction of infidelity. For an innumerable multitude, deceived by this false opinion, believe this to be true, and so believing, wander from the right faith and are involved in the error of the pagans when they think that there is anything of divinity or power except the one God."* [4]

---

3   Dion Fortune, *The Winged Bull* (York Beach, ME: Weiser, 1999), 145.

4   Brian P. Levack, ed., *The Witchcraft Sourcebook* (New York, NY: Routledge, 2015), 36

It is not the Devil at play here, in the minds of those seduced into a fantasy of Witchcraft, but a Goddess—it is Diana. The writer clearly believes Satan to be the power behind the throne, so to speak, in this delusion, but the "deluded" in question are professing faith in Diana, not the Son of Perdition. It is a flight with the Goddess that animates the mythology and power of the Witches' sabbath in the minds of those the so-called saints accuse of delusion.

And the *Canon Episcopi* is not the only Diana-centric document we have regarding the witch trials. In various documents, throughout the witch trial period, Diana or a figure resembling her or bearing a name derived from hers is worshipped and adored by gathered Witches.[5] Diana is also referred to as the "Goddess of the Pagans" in the *Canon* and elsewhere, which seems to suggest that in the popular imagination, even if not in reality, Diana had survived under the rule of Christendom as a symbol for pagan worship. More than any other pagan deity, Diana appears continually in our records.

Diana, usually associated with the hunt and the wilds, does have a deeper connection to Witchcraft, to death even, and to the darker aspects of a life lived at night. Throughout the Hellenistic world a strong association was developed between Diana (or Artemis) and Hekate. These two were often conflated with Selene as well, the moon, known in Rome as Luna. Diana is Diana Trivia, the three-formed Diana, lady of the crossroads, just as Hekate is *Hekate Triformis*, the thrice-formed Goddess associated with chthonic ritual and nighttime spell work.

An entire mythology developed about the continuation of Diana's worship in Christian Europe, an actual "society" that maintained belief in pagan customs and continued her worship underneath the nose of the Church.[6] This may have partially gathered steam due to the fact that Diana is the only named Goddess in the Latin translation of the

---

[5] Carlo Ginzburg, "Following the Goddess," in *Ecstasies: Deciphering the Witches' Sabbath* (Chicago, IL: University of Chicago Press, 2004).

[6] Ibid.

New Testament.[7] Paul refers to the temple of Artemis at Ephesus, but to most Christians in the Middle Ages and the Early Modern Age, that would have been read in Latin as "Diana of Ephesus."

Roman statue of Hekate in her three-formed guise. Hekate was associated with Witchcraft, as well as with the Goddesses Diana and Luna—the moon. (Met Museum)

---

[7] Acts 19:28 contains "Artemis" in Greek, but Latin translations render her name with the Roman Diana.

And there is a conflation in trial records with other figures in the Bible, particularly Herodias, the wife of Herod who demands the head of John the Baptist and is the mother of Salome. Her name appears in records of witch trials, and there she is something like a heathen Goddess that leads others into Witchcraft and blasphemy. She is a Goddess in her own right, the leader of the Witches, conflated with Diana and with other names of Goddesses found in Witchcraft writings, names such as Herodiana, Abundia, Habondea, Holda, and others.[8]

This Diana/Herodias mythology would end up being centrally important in the 19th century work of folklorist Charles Leland. His *Gospel of the Witches* claims to be the records of a surviving cult of Witches that worshipped Diana and her daughter Aradia in blasphemous rituals in defiance of the Catholic Church in Italy. The text is given by "Madalenna" and Leland purported that the text was a legitimate example of the survival of Goddess worship. In one section, we see the power of Diana (and her daughter) in their teaching of Witchcraft. In an invocation at the Witches' sabbat, to the daughter of Diana, the text states:

> *I implore Thee by the love which she did bear for thee!*
>
> *And by the love which I too feel for thee!*
>
> *I pray thee grant the grace which I require!*
>
> *And if this grace be granted, may there be*
>
> *One of three signs distinctly clear to me:*
>
> > *The hiss of a serpent,*
> >
> > *The light of a firefly,*

---

[8] Carlo Ginzburg, "Following the Goddess," in *Ecstasies: Deciphering the Witches' Sabbath* (Chicago, IL: University of Chicago Press, 2004).

The sound of a frog!" [9]

It is interesting to see the development of this concept of a "daughter of Diana" considering that almost all Greco-Roman sources view Diana as a virgin Goddess. There is obviously something going beyond literal myth-retelling here. The Witches' Goddess is not a virgin Goddess. She bears fruit, desires love, and couples with a consort. The text of Leland's *Gospel*, as well as trial records from the witch hunts, often include more open approaches to sexuality than might be expected from a "virgin" Goddess. This too is the power of change and adaptation in the faces of Mother. Literal retelling was never the point. It should not be for us, either.

When we approach the lore of the trials, we don't need to be fanatically literal in our readings. We can draw from the symbolism and experience of the spirituality we might find there, while still admitting that it is the reflection of its time. The trials contain a lot of human cruelty, for example, and needless death. That is a part of the story as well, and we cannot forget that. Human lives were snuffed out over religious fear. We can mourn that, of course, but I will always believe there is a certain power in lifting up the lore of the Witches into something more transformative, refusing to resign it solely to cruelty. Retelling is perhaps an odd work for healing, but healing it can be.

BEYOND DIANA

It is not just Diana reigning as a central female figure in the witch trials, or her associations with Herodias. Two Italian Witches, accused and persecuted during the trials, confessed to worshipping a figure known as *Madonna Oriente* that blessed her worshippers and acted in ways

---

9   Charles Godfrey Leland, *Aradia: Gospel of the Witches* (Custer, WA: Phoenix Publishing, 1996). 17.

similar to Diana.[10] The title, meaning "Lady from the East" is shockingly similar to incarnations of the Mother from antiquity, and hints at a figure far removed from strictly Christian sources.

Salome with the Head of Saint John the Baptist, painting by Andrea Solario, Italy, ca. 1507-1509. Witches were accused of worshipping certain diabolical or "wicked" figures from the Bible, including Herodias, the mother of Salome who convinces her daughter to dance for the head of John the Baptist. (Met Museum)

---

[10] Carlo Ginzburg, *Ecstasies: Deciphering the Witches' Sabbath* (Chicago, IL: Chicago University Press, 2004), 92.

Carlo Ginzburg is one of the few scholars that approaches the religiosity of the witch trials. Many schools of thought that investigate and draw conclusions from the European witch trials conclude that it was a case of mass hysteria. There are also those that see the trials as a period of misogynistic persecution, where the Church dominated largely female victims through fanaticism and the purging of undesirables from the community. Ginzburg, and he is not alone, argues that within the trials there are hints at folkloric, perhaps shamanic practices that survived into the era of Christian dominance. In his work of microhistory, *The Night Battles*, he investigates a unique cult-like group within Italy, the *Benandatti*, who engaged in astral battles with dark forces in trance-like states.[11]

Regardless of the complex debates surrounding the witch trials, I agree with Ginzburg's conclusions that there are spiritual practices and folk beliefs woven into the trials we have from the period of persecution and execution. Scholar Emma Wilby, in *Cunning Folk and Familiar Spirits*, investigates the incredible records of work with familiar spirits in the (specifically British) witch trials, connecting them with shamanistic spiritual practices throughout European cultures.[12]

Wilby's second book, a deep dive into the fascinating case of Isobel Gowdie, a young girl accused of Witchcraft in 17th century Scotland, argues (successfully I believe) that Gowdie may have practiced a form of trance.[13] The young girl's trial records are some of the most fascinating documents we have from the witch trials, including chants that she confessed to using to change her form and leave her body in the shape of a

---

[11] Carlo Ginzburg, *The Night Battles: Witchcraft and Agrarian Cults in the Sixteenth and Seventeenth Centuries* (Baltimore, MD: The Johns Hopkins University Press, 1983).

[12] Emma Wilby, *Cunning-Folk and Familiar Spirits: Shamanistic Visionary Traditions in Early Modern British Witchcraft and Magic* (Chicago, IL: Sussex Academic Press, 2005).

[13] Emma Wilby, *The Visions of Isobel Gowdie: Magic, Witchcraft and Dark Shamanism in Seventeenth-Century Scotland* (Chicago, IL: Sussex Academic Press, 2010).

hare.[14] Wilby and Ginzburg are looking into the spiritual dimensions of the legacy of the trials, realizing that a purely secular reading misses some key components that I believe speak to us, even today.

But beyond Diana, and the possibly shamanic practices of the trials, there are other faces of Mother at play in the lore. In the British Isles there is the figure of the Queen of the Fae, or the Queen of Elphame. She has been woven into so much of the folklore and legendary history of Britain.

In the British Isles, faerie lore mingled with Witchcraft lore to create unique mythologies that differ from continental witch trials. The fae were seen as intimately linked to Witchcraft and to magic, ruled over by various figures, including a Queen that appeared to supplicants and taught magic. She was frequently said to be wedded to the Devil, a husband figure given unique names such as *Christsonday*, a blasphemous rendering of Christ's Sunday.

In the famous ballad of Tam Lin, the title character relates to a lover that he was kidnapped by the Faerie Queen and became integrated into the life of the elfin lot. Every seven years, the fae are required to pay a tithe to Hell, which is one of their own handed over to the Devil. Tam Lin is fearful that he will be the one given, a rite that happens on Halloween. Eventually, the title character defeats the Queen and escapes this horrid fate.

The Faerie Queen would go on to inspire poetry, opera, and literature. Drawing from Celtic mythology, popularized by Romantic artists and popular folklore, her figure rose in prominence in the British imagination and continues to inspire popular writers and filmmakers today that draw from fae folklore and paint dealings with these figures as dangerous, complex, and often leading to disastrous consequences for those that do not follow taboos, rules, or good sense.

All of this mythology, from witch trials to the fae, would go on to

---

14   Folk musician Fay Hield has put Gowdie's confessed chant to music in the song *Hare Spell*.

inspire the foundational figures of the Witchcraft revival. Contemporary religious Witchcraft does in fact worship a Goddess of the moon, a Witches' Goddess that is worshipped in secret, oath-bound rites, and watches over the Witches with her consort who bears horns.

This is the central religious paradigm of Gardnerian and Alexandrian Craft and has gone on to inspire those outside of these traditions who still claim the title Witch or Wiccan or Pagan. Much of the early Witchcraft revival was rooted in the work of Margaret Murray. Regardless of how Murray's works are received in the current academic world, it is important for any devotee of these traditions to read her works, I believe, and understand how the founders and leaders of the contemporary revival of Witchcraft connected their practices to the lore, imagery, and spiritual egregore of the European witch trials.[15] This includes Diana, of course, but also the other faces of Mother we have discussed here. Mother is part and parcel of the legacy of Witchcraft.

WORSHIPPING THE WITCH

As a devotee of Mother, you approach the Queen of Witches in trepidation and temptation. There is no reason to fight against the fear laced throughout the mythology of the naked Diana in flight to orgiastic rites of abandon and freedom. Give in to it. Worship her in wild spaces, at night, hidden from others. Streak your offerings in sweet honey and good wine. Defy your shackles and give yourself over to freedom.

For that is the heart of the Queen of Witches. She is freedom, freedom from the constraints of patriarchal churches, and the fantasy-turned-murder of witch-hunters and violent clerics. In his 1970's work *Mastering Witchcraft*, Paul Huson recommends that would-be Witches struggling with their Christian upbringing go into the woods at midnight

---

[15] See: Margaret Murray, *The Witch-Cult in Western Europe: A Study in Anthropology* (Oxford: Oxford University Press, 1921) as well as *The God of the Witches* (London, UK: Sampson Low, Marston & Co. Ltd., 1931).

to recite the Lord's Prayer backwards in defiance of the Church.[16]

This may be nothing more than rebellious, anticlerical pique at first glance, but there is deeper magic at play here. To worship Mother as Witch is to worship her as breaking through social taboos and expectations. This is similar to the left-hand path practices of Tantra mentioned in a previous chapter. To break a taboo purposely, consciously, is to strip it of its power. And the Queen of Witches breaks many taboos. She is sexually active and free. She seeks magic and teaches it. She desires to feast and dance, even during Lent or times of mourning, even when we are told not to feast, not to dance.

That is Mother as Witch. And if you wish to worship her then you must be willing to face fear and doubt. Push your limits in your devotions to the Queen of Witches. Challenge those things that bring you fear: the darkness, nighttime, the woods, heights, the sea, nudity, unashamed dance and movement.

Prayer and devotional practices to the Queen of Witches can take the form of outdoor worship, under the moon's light, naked (as possible) and full of ululations, chanting, and dancing. Offer sumptuous food and dip your bread in sweet wine. Feed others. Touch others. Dance with others. Scare yourself.

The lesson of the Queen of Witches is this: the biological is theological. We are blessed to be incarnated in bodies, a union of consciousness with feeling, evolving, limited flesh. And our conscious mind experiences the cosmos because of these bodies, because of our nerves, and fingertips, and tongues, and lips, ears and eyes.

God the Mother is alive in the body, pressing up against our synapses, pumping within the walls of our veins and arteries. She is in our sweat and saliva, our scent, and the warmth of our breath. In the vein of Neoplatonic philosophy, Proclus—who we've met before—assigned Artemis (Diana) to the rulership of birth and the "completeness of mat-

---

[16] Paul Huson, *Mastering Witchcraft: A Practical Guide for Witches, Warlocks, and Covens* (Lincoln, NE: iUniverse, 2006) pp. 20-21.

ter."[17] She is a fleshy Mother, alive in the biological and evolutionary bodies we inhabit.

And if you feel terror, good. Let it be holy terror. Artemis and Diana were conflated with Hekate, with darker chthonic forces, and Artemis was no kind and gentle Goddess in every incarnation. She demands a human sacrifice in the *Iliad* for being slighted. She destroys those that peek at her Mystery against her will and knowledge. She refuses to be tamed, ever wild and alive within the forest, the Huntress, arrows ready to pierce the stag and the human being alike.

GODDESS OF MAGIC

And the Witch Goddess is the Mother of Magic. She is Hekate, worshipped in secret rituals at crossroads in the dead of night, and she is Isis, stealing the name of Ra with trickery to work her wonders. She is the Queen of the Fae, making pacts with mortal supplicants, trapping the unwary and the unworthy in prisons of time and confusion. She is the sorceress of Celtic lore, appearing at the edge of fog-cloaked forests, flying above the boughs of the sacred trees on ragwort. She *is* magic.

The hallmark of contemporary religious Witchcraft is the practice of magic, and that magic is linked and knit with the worship of the Goddess. With her consort she guides the practice of Craft and promises secret knowledge and initiation into the Mysteries. The same emotive current that drove initiates in the cults of Isis, Demeter, and Cybele drive us today.

Magic, as a practice, is frequently associated with the worship of the Goddess. Apart from the Witchcraft mythology explored in this chapter, we can look to the opinion of many conservative Hindus towards Tantra, which is often viewed as a form of black magic by outsiders. Some left-hand path *tantrikas* break all taboos and engage in practices that

---

[17] Spyridon Rangos, "Proclus and Artemis: On the Relevance of Neoplatonism to the Modern Study of Ancient Religion," *Kernos* 13 (2000): 62.

separate them from mainstream society. Accusations of black magic have haunted Tantra for centuries.

With the union I am painting between the Goddess and the practice of magic, I feel like I do have to speak a little on the practice of magic itself, and not just its connection to specific instances in history, or to particular traditions such as my own. In lieu of listing out spells, I want to convey what I feel might be the nature of magic when it is worked within the framework of devotion to Mother.

I say *might* because I have to tread very carefully here. Most works on magic are about the operational systems of magic. You are told which stones to gather, which sigil to etch into candle wax, or which herbs to grind and spread across your working altar. All of this is lovely, but it very rarely addresses the *why* or the *how* behind magic. When practitioners do start talking about how magic works, or what magic really is, the conversation can turn rancid quickly. People are very passionate about their practice.

For some, magic is a science. This is not a new concept. Throughout the history of magical practice, and I'm coming from a largely Eurocentric framework here, magic was something mechanical and operational. It was based in a complex interplay of correspondence and technical application of skill. This is the magic of grimoires. If you follow the steps, you will command spirits due to laws of the universe that are at your command and that these spirits must obey, just as falling objects "obey" the law of gravity. The names, sigils, and complex rituals are triggers to command spirits—almost always angels or demons—to follow your will and accomplish a desired goal.

Much of this is also tied to the concept of sympathetic magic. With a Platonic view of the cosmos, the magician is led to understand the reflection of higher worlds even in small things. Gold is not just a metal, it is a reflection of the sun, of God, of the angels. Knowing where the sympathies of the world lie is like knowing how to read a complex map. Once you understand the right systems, knowing all the turns of the road, you can drive the vehicle towards your destination more efficiently.

This mechanistic approach to magic was taken up by more modern seekers, from Aleister Crowley to the parapsychical researchers of the late 19th and early 20th centuries. For these systems, magic is simply a collection of abilities that traditional science does not yet understand. It is the application of psychic will, forcing change in physical reality through mental application. This is the root of why so much talk around magic centers around the word "intent." In these systems, it is the Witch or magician's will, projecting into the world, that causes change. These methods have been expanded in New Age magical systems through meditation techniques, intentional speaking, and even techniques labelled as "mind control."

Other practitioners, in an attempt to slough off the constricting world of Medieval and Early Modern philosophy and religion, have looked to Jungian concepts, like the collective unconscious, to explain and provide a framework for their magic. Other, more postmodern magicians do away with the entire frameworks that are constructed to explain and provide a foundation for magic. They prefer to experience magic as chaotic, experiential, and working solely because of belief, or the right timing, or sheer luck.

In more religious systems of magic, spells are more like contracts with spirits, beings that must be served, cajoled, or perhaps coerced. Grimoires do this, occasionally, but this approach is more common within traditions that worship certain powers that are believed to grant boons or power if you serve at their altars. It isn't about a particular series of laws that trigger a response (the right stone, at the right time, for example) but instead a foreign intelligence you are contacting. Working with spirits of the dead is similar to this as well, with historical examples of curse tablets often asking spirits of the vengeful dead to act on behalf of the petitioner. Working with the dead is very often a contractual form of spiritual magic.

As a Goddess devotee, I do think what I do falls under the category of "religious magic." But for me, the closest I have found as a satisfactory *why* or *how* behind my practice is (no surprise here) theurgy. I believe that magic is woven into faith and religious practice so tightly that forcing them into separate categories is unhelpful, at least for me.

I believe that magic is a divine act, a participatory act, where we align ourselves with divinity and channel the experience of that union to influence the world around us. Trance, ecstasy, and the power raised through worship and visionary experience can be used to give us altered states where we see the world through a new and startling lens. Through that lens we can focus our efforts and influence the ebb and flow of the energy we raise through practice. Channeling and controlling that flow, for me, is magic.

And that magic has risen, in my life, through Mother. Worshipping her in the circle, with her consort, has given me an entirely new perspective. In that moment, the world falls away and I feel just outside of reality, edged to the very periphery of vision, pushed slightly askance on my axis, and in that instability, I feel that I see differently, I act differently, I speak differently.

The world shifts, moving from rigid and mechanistic to something interconnected and far more malleable. That malleability allows me to touch on aspects of my life I wish to change, like a potter at the wheel. It is delicate work, and it does not always land the way I want it to, but it is the only experience that has ever made the word "magic" feel real to me, and not like fantasy or roleplay.

When I push my devotion and worship to the heights necessary for magic, I feel more capable of noticing the interconnections of life. It is like rising up to see a larger picture so that your strategy and knowledge contains more information, information that is crucial for success. I feel less narrow in magical practice, less constrained or fearful. It is the Mother that makes this possible for me.

To end, I want to give a prayer to the Goddess that embodies all we have covered here, the true glory and power behind the Witchmother.

This prayer is found in the Greek Magical Papyri and draws from harrowing imagery to portray an awesome mien of the Great Goddess. It is long, yes, and uses odd and seemingly incorrect grammar, but that is part of why I chose it. The Queen of Witches is a Goddess that inspires both liberation and dread. She is hard to pin down, and incapable of being confined. She is the dark moon and the black lake in the woods. She is the thing crying in the night. We can choose to join those cries in the ecstasy of her worship.

> *Come to me, O Beloved Mistress, Three-faced*
>
> *Selene; kindly hear my sacred chants;*
>
> *Night's ornament, young, bringing light to mortals,*
>
> *O child of morn who ride upon the fierce bulls,*
>
> *O Queen who drive your car on equal course*
>
> *With Helios, who with the triple forms*
>
> *Of triple graces dance in revel with*
>
> *The stars. You're Justice and the Moira's threads:*
>
> *Klotho and Lachesis and Atropos*
>
> *Three-headed, you're Persephone, Megaira,*
>
> *Allekto, many-formed, who arm your hands*
>
> *With dreaded, murky lamps, who shake your locks*
>
> *Of fearful serpents on your brow, who sound*
>
> *The roar of bulls out from your mouths, whose womb*
>
> *Is decked out with the scales of creeping things,*
>
> *With pois'nous rows of serpents down the back,*
>
> *Bound down your backs with horrifying chains*

Night-Crier, bull-faced, loving solitude,

Bull-headed, you have eyes of bulls, the voice

Of dogs; you hide your forms in shanks of lions,

Your ankle is wolf-shaped, fierce dogs are dear

To you, wherefore they call you Hekate,

Many-named, Mene, cleaving air just like

Dart-shooter Artemis, Persephone,

Shooter of deer, night shining, triple-sounding,

Triple-headed, triple-voiced Selene

Triple-pointed, triple-faced, triple-necked,

And Goddess of the triple ways, who hold

Untiring flaming fire in triple baskets,

And you who oft frequent the triple way

And rule the triple decades, unto me

Who'm calling you be gracious and with kindness

Give heed, you who protect the spacious world

At night, before whom daimons quake in fear

And gods immortal tremble, Goddess who

Exalt men, you of many names, who bear

Fair offspring, bull-eyed, horned, mother of gods

And men, and nature, Mother of all things,

For you frequent Olympos, and the broad

And boundless chasm you traverse. Beginning

And end are you, and you alone rule all.

For all things are from you, and in you do
All things, Eternal one, come to their end.
As everlasting band around your temples
You wear great Kronos' Chains, unbreakable
And unremovable, and you hold in
Your hands a golden scepter. Letters 'round
Your scepter Kronos wrote himself and gave
To you to wear that all things stay steadfast:
Subduer and subdued, mankind's subduer,
And force-subduer; Chaos, too, you rule.
Hail, Goddess, and attend your epithets,
I burn for you this spice, O child of Zeus,
Dart-shooter, heav'nly one, Goddess of harbors,
Who roam the mountains, Goddess of crossroads,
O nether and nocturnal, and infernal,
Goddess of dark, quiet and frightful one,
O you who have your meal amid the graves,
Night, Darkness, broad Chaos: Necessity
Hard to escape are you; You're Moira and
Erinys, torment, Justice and Destroyer,
And you keep Kerberos in chains, with scales
Of serpents are you dark, O you with hair
Of serpents, serpent-girded, who drink blood,
Who bring death and destruction, and who feast

> On hearts, flesh eater, who devour those Dead
>
> Untimely, and you who make grief resound
>
> And spread madness, come to my sacrifices,
>
> And now for me do you fulfill this matter." [18]

Roman sarcophagus depicting the stories of the moon Goddess, 3rd c. CE. (Met Museum)

---

[18] Hans Dieter Betz, *The Greek Magical Papyri in Translation, Including the Demotic Spells*, Volume 1 (Chicago, IL: Chicago University Press, 1992), 91-92.

CHAPTER 8
QUEEN OF HELL

> *Go into the underworld,*
>
> *Enter the door like flies.*
>
> *Ereshkigal, the Queen of the Underworld, is moaning*
>
> *With the cries of a woman about to give birth.*
>
> *No linen is spread over her body.*
>
> *Her breasts are uncovered.*
>
> *Her hair swirls about her head like leeks.*
>
> *When she cries, 'Oh! Oh! My inside!'*
>
> *Cry also, 'Oh! Oh! My inside!'*
>
> *The queen will be pleased.*
>
> *She will offer you a gift.*
>
> *Ask her only for the corpse that hangs from the hook*
>   *on the wall.*
>
> *One of you will sprinkle the food of life on it.*
>
> *The other will sprinkle the water of life.*

Inanna will rise." [1]

– From the Descent of Inanna

INTO THE DARK

The second mask of Mother we're going to investigate is the Queen of Hell. By this, I mean the Goddess as a darker figure, not dark in the sense of terrifying or wild (such as Kali, or the Queen of Witches) but something more personal, more painful. The Goddess as Queen of Hell is intimate with suffering, tied to our human experiences of trials, tribulations, and testing. She is the darker aspects of our psyche, the harrowing and shifting medium wherein lie shame, fear, disgust, regret, depression, and guilt. She is the Mother of Loss, who weeps when love is destroyed or when the last breath ekes out of a body.

No religious system or devotional practice can survive if it does not face the Mother in this guise. In some corners of the magical community, New Thought and New Age ideologies of avoiding negativity, or "manifesting" good vibes are meant to banish the uglier parts of our lives and uplift us until we are "vibrating" on a higher frequency, able to step over challenges and failures as if they were little cracks or potholes on the path. In this world, it's all about you! If you dream it and envision it, you *will* achieve it! It is a delightfully narcissistic way to live.

It is also a poisonous ideology. Many of the evils of this planet have nothing to do with what "vibrational frequency" you're living in but instead are the products of sheer human cruelty and the capacity of mortals to weave their hatred into the world with force. Refugees, famine victims, and oppressed minorities do not suffer because they don't *manifest their own will*. They suffer from human evils. To suggest that their suffering is their own fault, a failure of the imagination, or a karmic debt, is a monstrously cruel thing to say. I am continually horrified at

---

[1] Diane Wolkstein and Samuel Noah Kramer, *Inanna Queen of Heaven and Earth: Her Stories and Hymns from Sumer* (New York, NY: Harper & Row, 1983), 64.

how idiotic, doe-eyed positivity movements diminish the suffering of the oppressed.

The Queen of Hell stands as a stark reminder of the dangers in much of the approaches I've parodied here. Neglecting our fears, our failures, or the things that drag us into despondency is a recipe for self-destruction and egotistical delusion. Denial is not a healing technique. If we are going to see Mother as the totality of life, the font of consciousness, the All, then she must embody every aspect of our reality, even those that we wish were different or those we want to hide away, and even the things we are ashamed of or horrified by. In the chapter on the worship of Devi, we saw the Goddess declare that she was not just the wondrous things of life, or sages, but also thieves and evil-doers.

And it is not just the smiling prophets of the New Age who demand that we deny the dark. Modern secular consumerist culture despises a "downer." You are told to be continually upbeat, lest you bore your friends and alienate your partners. If you care too much about an injustice, then you are "obsessed" or "preachy." You must smile, and laugh, and be nonchalant even when you are anxious, fearful, or sad. If not, you might do something unthinkable such as put your mental health ahead of your career or offend someone by being a killjoy. We wouldn't want you anxious or sad at work because that will probably decrease your productivity. *Heaven forbid.*

I am not suggesting, to be clear, that to worship at her shrine demands that we live in perpetual darkness, or that we endlessly ruminate over the worst aspects of our lives or the world writ large. This is just as unhealthy as toxic positivity. Pushing up against saccharine New Age ideals, there has also been a rise of the darker-than-thou crowd. Constant, unending "shadow work" (a nebulous and ill-defined concept, in most of its contemporary uses) is not helpful in the least. Persephone eventually returns from the Underworld and so must we.

With that caveat, I do think that sitting with the Queen of Hell, sharing meager meals at her plain table, is a necessary part of Goddess devotion. But it is not just a necessity, it is a gift from Mother. The darkness is not only about pain, or misery. It is about respite. H. Byron Ballard, in her 2018 book *Earthworks: Ceremonies in Tower Time*, highlights the healing power of what she calls "going to ground."[2] This is a powerful lens through which to worship Mother.

She is the darkness as healing chamber of rest, as the muddy, gnarled roots beneath the tree of life. The blinding lights of modernity are demanding, and our sense of privacy and personal freedoms are eroding at a rapid pace. Our technology tracks us, recommends what to buy, shelters us in echo chambers, and constantly advertises. This is no wild-flung conspiracy, it is just a facet of the information age and its effects on human life.

The Queen of Hell is rest from the unending light of screens, scrutiny, and self-examination. She is that moment when you feel unwatched, untended, not constantly prodded and put upon to be better, brighter, happier, more perfect. Her home is under the earth, in the cairn, in the hollow mountain, the swamp shack, the mound of earth, the cool and damp cave in a dry and sunbaked desert.

She is the mourning Mother, tending over the rites of the dead, and guarding the shadowed passages between worlds, inhabiting a liminal space taken up by the monstrous entities that are grief and regret. She is the *momento mori* that we must all deal with as that which we love grows old, sickens, or dies. We cannot deny death, as the constant removal of death as a reality has led, in my mind, to an incredibly unhealthy relationship with loss in our modern situation.

She is also the lessons of our own moral failings and ethical mistakes. She is Medea who murders her children and Hera seeking vengeance for jilted love. She is Cerridwen, seeking to devour and consume someone for simply making a mistake that thwarted her desire. She is Tiamat, the great and terrible dragon, her belly opened up by a would-be savior.

---

[2] H. Byron Ballard, *Earth Works: Ceremonies in Tower Time* (Asheville, NC: Smith Bridge Press, 2018).

She is the Witch and the hag and the sorceress. She is all of this.

THE UNWILLING QUEEN OF HELL

Persephone, in her dual role as daughter of the fecund Demeter and wife of Hades, was at the core of the Mysteries of Eleusis. Her myth is still well-known and continues to inspire artists and writers today, regardless of their personal religious beliefs. Recently there has been an attempt to rewrite her story as a love affair between her and Hades. I applaud the attempts to remove the barbaric sexual assault at the core of her myth, but that assault *was* at the core. Death *takes* her. It takes her against her will and drags her down to a gloomy abode of asphodel and shades.

And there, she eats the seeds and seals her fate. There is a terrible ugliness in this story, and it isn't just the ugliness of the violation of her body and her freedom. Although the horror of that is remarkable. The ugliness is also about the utter fatalistic unfairness of it all. They're just seeds. It's just a pomegranate. The breaking of religious taboos, once a major part of cultures in the West,[3] is less stressed in modern culture. We look back at stories like this with more than a bit of disgust. Why should she be trapped in the abode of Death because she ate a few seeds? Why can't the mighty gods just change her situation? Zeus can't help her? Nobody?

The horror of her descent is that she is punished for no reason. It is human to long for a *meaning* behind tragedy. There has to be a reason for such indiscriminate suffering. On the one hand, there is a reason: someone took her. Someone forced himself on her. That is the agency

---

[3] We still find echoes of the power of taboos in fairy tales, and in much folklore from Celtic cultures, for example. There is the concept in Celtic lore of the *geis* which is a taboo, often random and oddly specific, that when broken creates chaos and punishment. Fairy tales and folklore are littered with examples of seemingly innocuous acts wreaking havoc. She ate the grapes when she shouldn't have. He picked a blossom from the wrong rose bush and lost the love of his life. The randomness, to me, is the point.

behind the descent. And that is the reminder that we all must fight for a better world, against those that would harm and destroy. Actively fighting for what we believe in is often the answer when we are faced with injustice and the callous and inhuman cruelty that makes up much of our world.

Woodcut of the abduction of Persephone by engraver Giuseppe Scolari, 1590-1607, Italy. Persephone's abduction by the God who ruled over the Underworld was a quintessential part of the Eleusinian Mysteries. (Met Museum)

But there are other moments where the answer is not a fight. Loss comes at us at random, seemingly unconnected to our actions, our beliefs, or our hopes. Someone is snatched out of our life, or a diagnosis hits us like a bullet train, screeching and horrible. In those moments, we think of the fates, spinning their threads with no regard for our feelings, no regard for our hopes and dreams. So much can be taken from us in less time than it takes to draw breath.

The Queen of Hell is the space to breathe and find rest when these horrors descend. She is seated on her cold obsidian throne, offering a place at an ashy but welcoming hearth. You do not have to explain everything here. You do not have to put on a strong face for your friends or family. Here, you can grieve in peace and gather your thoughts. That is why the Queen of Hell is our advocate and beloved, even if we are terrified to be called into her domain. Without this rest, we cannot heal.

She is also our reminder that we have to let go of control, sometimes. We have all eaten metaphorical pomegranate seeds at one point or another, engaging in a seemingly innocuous act that had ramifications we were not prepared for. This is a terribly human experience, to realize that we are stuck somewhere against our will, or that we have landed in a situation we cannot control, despite our magic, despite our will, despite it all. We are tied, for a period, to the experience of suffering. The Queen of Hell is the opportunity to survive that experience, to long for justice, or healing, and to move through the darkness with conviction that the path will be illuminated eventually.

SAINTS AND PSYCHOANALYSIS: UNDER THE GAZE OF MOTHER

Much has been written in contemporary Witchcraft and pagan literature about the concept of the "Dark Goddess."[4] This figure is often linked to the healing of deep trauma, and the facing of the more painful and

---

4 Two examples of this in contemporary pagan and Witchcraft writing would be *Mysteries of the Dark Moon: The Healing Power of the Dark Goddess* (HarperCollins, 1992) by Demetra George, and *Encountering the Dark Goddess: A Journey into the Shadow Realms* (Moon Books, 2021) by Frances Billinghurst.

difficult aspects of caring for our mental and physical well-being. Meditations, prayers, and rituals are designed with this Dark Goddess to force us to face our unhealed wounds, and to work out our own darker desires and hang-ups, working them out in fear and trembling, if need be. And the Queen of Hell is there through it all.

In Christian theology, this concept finds expression in the "dark night of the soul" which stems from the work of 16th century Catholic mystic John of the Cross, who wrote a poem describing his finding of God as a lover during a dark night. He would go on to write a book-length commentary on this work and the concept has continued to grow in Christian theology as a time of deep suffering, darkness, or a feeling of the absence of God. In those times, so the theology teaches, we must seek and trust God even more, even when we feel that a once flowing spring has become an endless, black desert of hopelessness.

With time, this concept has found expression in secular and psychological schools of thought as well. In psychoanalysis, two concepts arose to express the darker places within human consciousness. Within the work of Freud, there is the concept of *Id*. Freud describes the Id, writing, "It is the dark, inaccessible part of our personality, what little we know of it we have learned from our study of the dreamwork, and, of course, the construction of neurotic symptoms and most of that is of a negative character, and can be described only as a contrast to the ego. We approach the id with analogies: we call it a chaos, a cauldron full of seething excitation…"[5]

The student of Freud, Carl Jung, worked more with a concept of the "shadow." Although the term does not entirely originate with Jung, his exposition of the "shadow" has been taken up by many who desire a more spiritual approach to psychological healing. Jung describes the shadow as "a tight passage, a narrow door, whose painful constriction

---

[5] Sigmund Freud, "New Introductory Lectures on Psychoanalysis," in *The Standard Edition of the Complete Psychological Works of Sigmund Freud*, ed. and trans. James Strachey, vol. 22 (London, UK: Hogarth Press, 1964), 82.

no one is spared who goes down to the deep well."[6] Integrating the shadow is part of what Jung called "individuation" which is psychological wholeness and healing. To deny our darkness, or continually push it down, robs us of the ability to feel complete. There is nothing that will plunge you into a loss of self quicker than pretending to be something you are not or refusing to own up to what you've done or what has shaped you into the person you are.

I want to say that I am not suggesting we take on the processes of psychoanalysis, whether Freudian or Jungian, to help us heal. Modern psychotherapy has moved entirely away from these methods and there is an enormous amount of sloppy science and terrible misogyny in the psychoanalytic fields, particularly in Freud. These systems, however, were deeply influential on many cultural commentators and they have worked their way even into the modern occult and magical communities, particularly Jungian concepts of archetypes, integrating the shadow, and the collective unconscious. In discussions of divination, magic, and spiritual healing, many practitioners are quoting from the works of Jung whether they are aware of it or not.[7]

Whether Christian or psychoanalytic, the entire point here is that there are deep parts of ourselves that we tend to avoid, negate, or wish away. These parts of ourselves are often frightening to us. We may struggle with neuroses that embarrass us, or fantasies that make us feel guilty or ashamed of our bodies and sexuality. We may harbor resentment, even hatred, for people we claim to love and care for deeply. We may have debilitating addictions that curtail our attempt to live a full and healthy life. All of this is part of the human experience.

And the Queen of Hell is mistress of them all. There is no "sin" that

---

[6] Carl Jung, "The Archetypes and the Collective Unconscious," in *The Collected Works of C. G. Jung*, ed. Herbert Read, Michael Fordham, and Gerhard Adler, trans. R. F. C. Hull, 2nd ed., vol. 9, pt. 1 (Princeton, NJ: Princeton University Press, 1968), par. 44.

[7] For more information on the specifically occult or esoteric in Jung, see: *Jung: On Synchronicity and the Paranormal* (Princeton University Press, 1997) edited by Roderick Main.

she does not understand, intimately. There is no desire or petty hatred that she does not know. At first, this is a horrifying concept. We prefer to keep our "shadows" locked away from public viewing, firmly planted in the back of our minds and denied, negated, or swept under the rug. Not from her, though. We cannot hide from her. She is the gorgon, hair a mass of hissing snakes, a monstrous creature staring at us, threatening with her gaze to turn us into stone. Her gaze lets us know one thing, one thing that is painful: *I know what you're thinking, creature.* Nothing will turn you to stone quicker than realizing someone knows who you really are.

In Alcoholics Anonymous there is a statement bandied a lot: "You're only as sick as your secrets." They also often say "secrets kill." The Queen of Hell is the realization that the darker aspects of us only fester when they are left unexplored. They grow enormous when untended, like an ugly garden gone to seed and ruin, all fruiting plants choked out by the weeds we cannot bring ourselves to uproot.

The Queen of Hell is the reminder that you must face up to what lies beneath the surface of propriety and expectation if you wish to grow and heal yourself, mind and body. Therapy is a good thing. 12 step programs save lives. Psychiatric treatment is not a shameful thing, to be avoided and spoken of in hushed whispers. We must make an effort to care for our mental health, regardless of our religious or magical practices.

The Queen of Hell is, for me, the guiding principle behind all of this. She is the Mother as reminder, demanding that we probe and address our thoughts and deeds, discover what drives us, what challenges us, and what happened to us. Because sometimes it is trauma at the root of what ills us, and that should be dealt with in solid therapeutic settings with qualified professionals who are as much servants of the Great Goddess as any priest or devotee.

To put it more bluntly, and plainly, there have been quite a few times when I am discussing something with a Witch, a magical practitioner, or a seeker, and the only thought I have is, "You should really go to therapy."

That is not a statement rooted in judgment, either. I have thought the same thing about myself as well, many times.

None of this is to say that you cannot use spiritual and religious practice as part of your mental healthcare. Most therapists are open to their clients using spirituality or religion to help them navigate their lives. I do not think, personally, that I would benefit from an entirely secular framework for dealing with my mental health. That is my personal experience, however, and yours may differ. For me, the worship of the Mother is part and parcel of how I heal. She is inseparable from my work.

THE HAG

One of the aspects of life that we feel the most uncomfortable with is aging, sickness, and death. Disease haunts us. I am currently writing at the tail end of a pandemic that shuttered businesses, ended a staggering number of lives, broke families apart, and changed the way we live our lives in ways that I am sure we will continue to uncover as we charge ahead.

Disease and aging have so haunted us that they have become stock tropes in horror films and novels. What is a zombie movie, really, if not an examination of how terrified we are of outbreaks, illness, and infection? Pandemic films and novels about creeping, wasting illnesses are common enough to be considered a subgenre of horror. The more grotesque, the better. Then we get into what is called "body horror" with all of its gory glory.

And the Queen of Hell is there, in illness and the fear of illness, just as she is in everything. Many mythologies from varying cultures have "plague gods" devoted to dispelling of disease and protection from outbreaks. Catholicism even has "plague saints" such as St. Roch, who guard against illness, reminders of the Black Death that decimated Europe.[8] Sometimes, plagues and illnesses themselves were personified as malefic deities and demons. This is common in Mesopotamian folklore, for example, which influenced later Jewish mythologies surrounding demons that carried disease and spread poxes.

Aging, just as much as disease, has been maligned and set up as a horror. Our culture grows ever more youth obsessed. It is a canned, cliché joke at this point to include a female character in a sitcom who is terrified of aging and desperately attempts to hold off the signs of her changing body with expensive treatments, lying about her birthday, or changing the lighting. It is pretty unsurprising that, with few exceptions, these characters are never men. But men are not entirely spared. Many older men, particularly if they are divorced, are portrayed in media as bumbling oafs, sad and desperate. The message is clear, regardless of gender: aging makes you *less than*.

Although we have grown in our sensitivity, it is still not uncommon for uncouth strangers to remind a woman of a certain age that if she desires children she better "hurry up" and we still talk of ticking biological clocks and write films and television episodes addressing innate fears of not finding a partner or tying the knot by a certain age. Industries that promise to defy aging rake in billions playing off these fears.

In defiance of these cultural norms, many Goddess worshippers look to the Mother as Crone, or Hag. The concept of Mother, Maiden, and Crone (the Triple Goddess) has been attacked as ahistorical, which I address elsewhere in this book, but the archetype of the Crone, the reality of the Goddess as aging and reflecting the lived experience of all of us, because we all age, is part of the Mother. I see her as the Hag.

The Hag is the Mother as aging, growing in wisdom but dealing with a changing, failing flesh. As someone who has dealt with chronic

---

[8] Near where I currently live there is a cemetery and connected chapel devoted to Saint Roch. Within the chapel, petitioners have left casts of healed body parts that hang as beautifully macabre decorations and offerings.

pain since I was sixteen, I find much comfort in the Queen of Hell as the rheumy, wise Hag. She is the Cailleach here,[9] the gnarled Witch, the body that refuses to conform to expectations of beauty.

The Witch, woodcut by Albrecht Dürer, ca. 1500, Germany. Witches were often portrayed as aging women, disparagingly called "hags" or "crones." (Met Museum)

---

[9] For more information, see *Visions of the Cailleach: Exploring the Myths, Folklore and Legends of the Pre-eminent Celtic Hag Goddess* (Avalonia, 2009) by Sorita d'Este and David Rankine.

She is not here to be the object of your desire or fantasy. She is here to cook you alive and feed you to the rats or the crows. She is not here to care for your children while you gallivant and loaf. She will eat your children. She is not here to pat you on the back and feed your petty need to be uplifted or celebrated at all times and in all places. She is sharp-tongued, and her recommendations are the only thing that's going to wake you up and force you to change your ways before you get swallowed up in regret. Baba Yaga.[10] Cailleach. Fairy tale Witch. We know her.

What the Queen of Hell is, as Hag, is a complex dance between acceptance and defiance. We accept that we cannot fight death, or conquer aging, and sometimes we cannot heal illness. We defy expectations that demand we conform to someone else's view of what is desirable, or worthy of time or love. We walk the line between grace and rage. Mother is on that line.

STOPPING & STARTING

Mother, as Queen of Hell, is also the thrust to make change, even when that change is painful. The fearsome images of Devi, such as Kali and Durga, were used by Hindus in the fight against British colonial rule. And modern Goddess worshippers often call on fearsome or protective deities to inspire fights against injustice and human cruelty. This is a crucial aspect of the Queen of Hell.

When I wrote of respite earlier, it was not as a synonym for inaction. Sinking into despair with no hope for change is not a vision of the Mother that I am trying to reach into here. What I hope to be touching is the belief that Mother works within the darker periods to give succor. She is not a symbol of passive acceptance. We are not meant to take the dark aspects of her as tokens of defeat. Mother presses us to carry the memories of pain and inequality, of cruelty and wanton destruction,

---

[10] For a contemporary and artistic take on Baba Yaga, see: *Ask Baba Yaga: Otherworldly Advice for Everyday Troubles* (Andrews McMeel Publishing, 2017) by poet Taisia Kitaiskaia.

and transform them to the best of our ability. With those memories we can build the new.

There is much work to be done, and the Mother stands at the ready, inspiring us to fits of passion and a thirst for change. Healing at her hearth, or in the darkness of her caves, is not a symbol for retreat. It is also not an excuse for self-indulgence. One of the most powerful forms of healing is to heal others, to work for something we are passionate about. The Mother as Queen of Hell is not telling us that we can sink into our own sealed worlds, foregoing the world around us because we are suffering. That kind of isolation is rarely healthy and often exacerbates our struggle.

Absolute isolation is also not a goal in devotion to Mother. Taking time to recuperate is necessary, but often when we take that time, we should ask ourselves: are we really recuperating? Are we working on ourselves in any way, or reaching out to the support systems we have? If we lack those systems, what can be we do to find them? There are times when we want to forfeit any sense of ability or responsibility for our lives. Even if we call it "shadow work" it can sometimes be anything *but* work. The hollows of the Queen of Hell are places for you to stop and rest on the journey, not places to take up residence permanently. Never forget that.

CHAPTER 9
QUEEN OF HEAVEN

> *The Tao is called the Great Mother:*
>
> *empty yet inexhaustible,*
>
> *it gives birth to infinite worlds."* [1]
>
> – Tao Te Ching

> *Enlil gave me the heavens and the earth. I am Inanna! He gave me lordship and he gave me queenship...He placed the heavens on my head as a crown. He put the earth at my feet as sandals. He wrapped the holy garment around my body. He put the holy sceptre in my hand. The gods are small birds, but I am the falcon...I am heroic!*
>
> *...Which god compares to me?"* [2]
>
> – From a Sumerian text praising Inanna

---

1 Stephen Mitchell, trans., *Tao Te Ching* (New York, NY: HarperCollins, 2006), chap. 6.

2 Electronic Text Corpus of Sumerian Literature, "A *balbale* to Inanna," accessed November 20, 2022, https://etcsl.orinst.ox.ac.uk/cgi-bin/etcsl.cgi?text=t.4.07.6#.

COSMIC PROPORTIONS

The final incarnation in this three-part investigation of Mother is the Queen of Heaven. Here, Mother is enthroned and celestial, the ruler of the planetary spheres and the aether between the worlds. She is cosmic in proportion and dynamic, a never-ending being that is beyond human cognition. In the Queen of Heaven, we find our aspirations, the highest image of ourselves. Here is the Higher Guardian Angel of ceremonial magic, the *Adam Kadmon* of Kabbalah, the *atman* that is one with the *Brahman* in Vedanta, and the promise of rebirth in the Mysteries.

The Queen of Heaven is mistress of the astrological calculations that determine birth and fate. She is the loom-tender of the warp and weft of cosmic time. Mother rules over the endless, expanding creation that is within her and of her. Time and space are knit together at her will. Here is the Goddess as ultimate vision, the full expansion of Creation visible to the onlooker, devasting in its entirety.

To the non-theistic practitioner, or one that views the Goddess as merely psychological archetype, this is the most challenging of the incarnations of Mother. This is the Goddess far removed from earthly magics, from individual will, from the ground beneath our feet. She is the most God-like of Mothers, the absolute, non-contingent ground of existence, the only ontological reality.

I believe that a lot of occultists and magicians are wary of this kind of language because the language, philosophy, and theology of "God talk" has not really been handed down to us in the best of ways. Most of our philosophies in occultism are filtered, handed down piecemeal and by proxy via the mouths of early 20th century occultists and theosophists. These writers pulled from Plato and Aristotle, Neoplatonism, Kabbalah, particularly "hermetic Qabalah", and other philosophical traditions as well, sprinkled with concepts from dharmic religion to talk about a "perennial philosophy."

This has led to a vision of "the God concept" as a static figure, a larger-than-life superhero-like figure more in common with certain Protestant visions of God than anything Plato or Aristotle had in mind, or the sages behind the Vedantic tradition for that matter. In the theologies of Neoplatonism, as well as other Greco-Roman philosophical traditions, the "ground of all being" is not static. It is dynamic, and fluid, and constantly combining and emanating to pulse out creation from the central oneness of divinity.

18th century painting of Mahadevi (literally: Great Goddess). For many Hindus, the Goddess is the absolute reality that undergirds all of existence. (Met Museum)

Mother is this pulse, this eternal core of being, the very *is-ness* of the universe. Mother is not one being among other beings, she is being itself, with no predicate. She is, in short, bliss. She is the ultimate finality of causes that itself never ceases to create and remake. Release belongs to her. Enlightenment is hers. Peace is hers. And yet, she never ceases.

MOTHER-MIND: MEDITATION AND THE GODDESS

In this aspect, the Mother is the teacher of meditation and mindfulness. She is the spring where all sages drink. Meditation is almost always one of the first recommendations for magical practitioners, or seekers. It is so commonplace that sometimes I think we gloss over this practice. Meditation is not easy. Recommending a ten-minute moment of silence each day is not a bad idea, but it doesn't entirely cover the concept of meditation. So many self-help books demand us to begin a meditation practice with very little discussion of what meditation even is, beyond some sense of a rather beige calmness that promises to fix all of our woes.

And for new devotees or seekers, meditation is not really a unified branch of practice. There are many schools of meditation, and they differ greatly in practice, aim, and philosophy. Vipassana meditation, for example, draws from largely Theravada Buddhist sources and is marketed as Insight Meditation in the West. It is a venerable and incredibly rich tradition of meditative practice, but its aims are deeply Buddhist in nature and might not be the most fruitful path to follow for someone identifying as a Goddess devotee, a Witch, or a Pagan.

In Tantra, and wider Hindu practice, there are also unique schools and systems of meditation. The raising of the *kundalini* and the use of *chakras* are commonly known in the West. The meditative worship and visualization of complex *yantras*, geometric images meant to embody teachings and trigger meditative experiences, are used by many schools. These systems, however, were often initiatory in their beginnings, and still are in most cases. A qualified guru is necessary for many of these practices.

There are also secular forms of meditation, largely focused on calming breathwork and bringing attention to singular points to calm anxiety and quiet an overactive mind. These are useful techniques, but their aim is more for mental well-being and balance than spiritual development in a religious sense.

None of this is to say that devotees cannot benefit from these techniques, because they very much can. I have explored Vipassana meditation as well as simple breathwork in my own path and they did bear fruit for me. They are not, however, forms of meditation I use to connect to the Goddess, to the Queen of Heaven, to the Cosmic Mother.

The form of meditation I use most often is commonly referred to as "pathworking" in magical circles. The term was originally used, most often, to reference a very particular kind of meditative exercise. The "paths" in question were the paths on the Tree of Life, usually understood in the writings and teachings lumped under the category of "hermetic Qabalah."[3] Over time, I have seen this term applied to any form of meditation that involves visualization, magical goals, or occult concepts. It is similar to visualization techniques used in other traditions. In this form of meditation, we are focusing our mind on a path, a vision, a specific goal or conceptual framework that we bring alive in the theater of mind. It is a form of imaginal meditation.

Over the years I have participated in many meditations in this vein, often drawing from mythology or literature. I have done meditations based on the story of Taliesin and Cerridwen, the search for the Holy Grail, the legend and imagery of the Witches' sabbath, and more. Each time, the focus is on immersing the mind in the story until the images, revelations, teachings, and personages of the story are real, experienced

---

[3] For a classic example of Hermetic Qabala-based pathworkings, see: *The Shining Paths: An Experiential Journey Through the Tree of Life* (Thoth Publications, 1997) by Dolores Ashcroft-Nowicki.

in mind to teach us.

And specific historical legends are not the only inspiration for these meditations. Often, the work is focused on an archetypal journey to Mother. Frequently, I like to begin in caves or with a descent into the earth if the goal is union with Mother as Earth Goddess, mountain, or the Queen of the Underworld. Sometimes the journey is one of specific, triggering symbols and icons or tokens of the mother: a chalice, a cauldron, a triangle, the moon.

This method is not easier than other forms of meditation. In my experience, it is actually quite a bit more difficult as it requires consistent practice and a slow but potent build-up of mental images, triggers, and states of awareness. We all used to be a lot more gifted at this imaginal form of thinking when we were children, but time and mundanity rob us of a lot of our abilities in the realms of visualization and imagination. With effort, we can regain it. We can immerse ourselves into meditation so profound that we can slip into trance. And there, where infinite possibility and directed thought coalesce, we can meet Mother.

CALM

Regardless of the goal of meditation, or the specific technique, there is a necessity across all systems to quiet the mind. What is often referred to as "monkey mind" by a lot of meditation teachers is a hurdle to a solid and rewarding meditative practice. It is difficult to find time to meditate, and our current world is hell bent on distracting us as much as possible. Schedules for most modern practitioners are nothing akin to the schedules of nuns, monks, or contemplatives in cloistered communities. When we read texts on meditation, it is important to remember that they were often for specific religious communities that had access to a life we simply do not have.

This is an important point to remember, as it helps assuage a lot of the guilt and nervousness around meditation. For many would-be meditators, finding the time and quiet to meditate is rather difficult. This is exacerbated by a false image of spiritual perfectionism that is sold to us. When we think of meditation, we often imagine a serene, perfectly still person, absorbed in peaceful contemplation in a room of minimalist, Zen-inspired décor. Perhaps there is one silk painting on the wall, or a bromeliad. How lovely.

10th century Indian image of the Buddhist Goddess Mahapratisara in deep meditation. (Met Museum)

The truth is this image is unhelpful. Meditation is for everyone, even if you cannot build a meditation chamber as an addition to your house where you ring a bell and sit in silence for hours, unbothered by the responsibilities of life. And remember, many traditions of meditation understood very well how difficult meditation is and how mastering it was often left to contemplatives who devoted their life to a monastery or an ashram.

To give an example of this, we can look to Buddhism, as it is the world religion most often associated with meditation practice, at least by Westerners. In much of the Buddhist world, and this shocks a lot of people when they learn it, meditation is not a common, daily practice amongst lay devotees. The rise of lay meditation is actually a rather modern phenomenon in Buddhism. Historically, meditation was a practice most often engaged by monks and nuns. Lay devotees focused on supporting monasteries, cultivating merit by good deeds, and living an ethical life according to Buddhist principles. In Theravada Buddhism, some teachers still believe that only monks can attain enlightenment in this life, because the life of a householder has too much anxiety and too many responsibilities.

In many Buddhist communities, chanting has taken the place of meditative practice. As I mentioned before in the discussion around prayer, Pure Land practice is one of the most common forms of Buddhist practice on the planet, and it has very little to do with meditation as it is commonly understood. Chanting is also central to the schools of Buddhism that focus on the *Lotus Sutra*, such as Nichiren Buddhism in Japan. These practices do involve a level of mindfulness, for sure, but they are not the insight meditation practices we most associate in the West with images and concepts of Buddhism.

All of this is to say to you that you should approach mediation with a heavy dose of realism. Most of us cannot afford to devote entire hours of every day to meditative practice, nor do we often live in communities where we have that much free time. If you set yourself up with an image of meditative practice that demands absolute perfectionism, you're setting yourself up to fail. It is not uncommon for someone to chuck out a lot of money for special cushions, meditation timers, and cycles of classes only to eventually give up when the practice is too demanding, the expensive cushion gathering dust and the last few classes unattended.

So, what *can* we do to calm the monkey mind and prepare ourselves for solid meditation practice? The first is to consider our environment. Despite my warnings about meditation rooms, it is important to find a space where you can meditate undisturbed. And I do believe that we can strive to make that space sacred for our practice. The use of ritual incense, the ringing of bells, and the conscious use of dim lighting all serve to trigger our mind into a different place. That is the key: differentiation and consciousness.

When burning incense, for example, choose a blend or create one that ties into the visions and meditation practice you are focusing on. If you are going on a visualization meditation deep into the forest, burn arboreal incenses heavy with pine and cedar. If you are visualizing the deep caves that lead to the Underworld, where Mother waits for you enthroned as Queen of Hell, then burn patchouli, oakmoss, and other earthy scents that tickle the nose with the odor of dirt and clay. If you plan to meet her in ancient temples, let myrrh and frankincense sizzle on the charcoals.

None of this is about superstitious connection, it is about triggering the mind. We are sensual beings, and Mother is the Queen of Witches and Queen of the Earth. She is not pure mind alone. She is expressed in our bodies, even when we are mind-focused during meditation. Mind is part of body. It is not separate. Cartesian dualism is not Mother's way.

And my recommendation is to build these practices with diligence. If we burn myrrh, say, because we believe it has some occult connection to something we desire, that is one thing. But, if we continually burn myrrh for a particular meditative visualization, then eventually our mind will be easily triggered into the right space for our work. The trigger is the key, not an esoteric correspondence. There is a particular scent that is used in many of my Craft rituals that when I smell now immediately pulls me into the headspace of a ritual. These triggers are built with time, and they have an incredible effect if repeatedly used with intent.

Posture and breathing are next in the search for calm, centered meditative practice. Specific meditative traditions can sometimes be very strict about correct posture and breath counting. If you are working within one of these traditions, then by all means keep at it. But for most people, the important thing to remember about posture is that it should leave you comfortable enough not to be distracted by pain or numbness, but alert enough not to sleep. This goal is going to be achieved in different ways, depending on the body. For me, the half-lotus position is the most comfortable for meditation. For others, a seated meditation in a hard-backed chair is best.

And as for breathing, focusing on the in and out-flow of breath is a classic technique to center your thoughts before a meditation. Counting the breath, following a repeated pattern, is most common but (borrowing here from insight meditation) it can be as simple as noticing the breath, mentally, and returning to it as a focal point whenever the mind strays.

These techniques should be mastered first, before moving into complex visualizations. Take the time to practice noticing or counting your breath, inhaling your incense, and focusing your mind. Allow thoughts to come and go but do not grasp them if they are distracting or worrisome. Start slowly and build your stamina, as with any practice.

Also, you can return to a repetitive prayer practice to center yourself, as discussed in the chapter on prayer. Building your "staying power" with a mantric repetition for Mother is a powerful system to grow in your ability to withstand long periods of meditative practice.

THE VISIONS OF MOTHER

After you have become comfortable in the centering practices of breath, posture, and setting sacred space, you can move into visualizations and pathworkings to Mother. To prepare to create or participate in these meditations, you can study images, stories, or legends that tie into a particular visualization. If you are going on a journey to the Cauldron of Cerridwen, then you should immerse yourself in the stories available from Welsh literature. If you are going to meet Venus by the sea, take a trip to the beach if possible. Breathe in the scent of ocean water. Read the legends of the Goddess Venus, her prayers and orations from the past. If you are going to focus on tokens and icons of Mother, then examine those tokens in depth, devote time to studying and memorizing forms and shapes, color and line.

Developing visualization practices takes time, as there is an element of storytelling and scene-setting that is necessary for meaningful practice. Those with backgrounds in writing, or theater, are often excellent at this practice and make great teachers for pathworking meditations. Lean on the writings of others, if you need, and examine strong narrative stories of the Goddess or her symbols. Recommendations of where to look could include:

- Greek and Roman mythology, particularly stories of mortals meeting Mother such as Jason and Hera, Odysseus and Athena, or lovers before Aphrodite.
- Stories that are built on the concept of the hero or heroine's journey, such as the quest for the Holy Grail, or the transformations of Taliesin and Cerridwen.
- Descents into the Underworld such as the Descent of Ishtar to her sister Ereshkigal, Orpheus and Eurydice, the drama of Isis, Osiris, Horus and Set, or the descent and crowning of Persephone.
- Unsettling and powerful imagery of otherworldly union such as the Witches' sabbath, initiatory temple settings such as at Eleusis, or meeting the Goddess in the desert or inside grottoes, mountain caves, or the edge of the ocean.

With time you will develop pathworkings that you can come back to, reexamine, or probe more deeply for revelation and union with Mother.

Sometimes, you will develop strong connections to visual tokens that arise in your meditations, and entire sessions can be spent on contemplation of Mother in these symbols. You may begin your meditation with a complex journey of descending into the Underworld, there to find Persephone on an iron throne, veiled, guarded by the three-headed dog, and holding the burst pomegranate that seals her fate. With time, perhaps the pomegranate alone will take up your entire visual space, and you will have revelations from Mother solely from the contemplation of the glistening, blood-like seeds inside the fruit.

Orpheus and Eurydice, by Marcantonio Raimondi, early 16th century, Italy. A journey to the Underworld (called a catabasis) is a common and powerful starting place from which to build a visualization meditation. Orpheus travels to the Underworld for his lover, Eurydice, and their fate is the inspiration for many works of art. (Met Museum)

That may seem extreme, that you can find revelations of Mother in a piece of fruit, but meditation leads to unique experience and with practice these situations do arise. Contemplation of the sacred things belonging to Mother leads to union with Mother. Whether it is a pomegranate, a cup, or a spindle twined with spun thread, the tokens *are* Mother. This ties to our chapter on symbols, our discussion of the *sunthemata*, or sacred tokens that bring with them reflections of Goddess.

EXAMPLE

To end this chapter on the meditative Queen of Heaven that we find within and without, I want to give an example of a pathworking to Mother. This meditation can be read and then repeated mentally, or you can record yourself reading it to use during your visualization. I recommend a dim space for this, with as little light as necessary, and preferably in complete darkness. Burn good, resin-based incense. For this particular meditation, I recommend copal or frankincense. When you are done, record your revelations. Compare them as you develop other pathworkings and meditations. Look for the symbols and words that Mother leaves for you. Fall in love with her, again and again.

PATHWORKING: THE ALTAR
You are in darkness. There is no light to pierce the endless night around you. Breathe it in. The dark is a living, breathing thing. Feel it against your skin, pressing up against you. It crawls across you, into the pores and hollows of your body, filling you up, covering you in complete emptiness. Nothing extends from your body except for the endless, starless night. No moon hangs, crescent or full, and no far-flung light pierces the veil. It is pure in its absolute, voided negation.

Now, in your mind, allow yourself to fall into the starless night. The floor, the seat, the body, all fall away and you collapse down, moving towards the bottom of nothing, the floor of infinity. Only the gentle change of air lets you know that you are moving, nauseatingly falling through the hole of creation, faster and faster. Increase your breath. Reach, if you want. There is nothing to grasp. There is nothing here to slow your descent. Faster. Breathe. Faster. Hold your body. Tighten your muscles. Squirm. Nothing. Nothing comes. You fall, free, untethered from the earth. Untethered from the body. Untethered from the senses. Fall. Fall. Endlessly.

Beneath you, or perhaps it is above you as space feels unmoored and dizzying, you see something flicker. It is like the face of a small, minutely small, mirror. It is silvery bright in the darkness, a growing circle. Watch it. Look for it. Strain to see the shining surface reflecting back at you, reflecting light from a source you cannot see. That circle is growing closer, expanding, silver, shining, perfectly round.

Realization comes to you. It is the surface of a lake, a deep underground reservoir of shining water, eerily illuminated from within. Its light casts long tendrils of shadow against walls that now become visible to you, stony, rocky outcroppings in black and earthen brown. You are falling towards the surface of a great, underground body of water, waiting for you to break its surface. You hurtle as a falling star towards the water.

And then, as you hold your breath, you break into the icy water, sinking far into the silvery depths. Water fills your nostrils, soaks your body, shocking in its cold and startling depth. You have sliced into the lake like the blade of a knife, pushing deep into the water. Too deep. Begin to rise. Fight against the water pressing into your body, threatening at your closed mouth. Feel that burn at the base of the lungs, the frantic quaking of your body, the bubbling, churning, frothy water washing around you in currents and cold pressure.

Just when the lungs demand from their burning that you swallow something, be it air or water, you break the surface. Take a few deep breaths. Float there. Adjust to the dim and otherworldly light. Look out across the enormous lake and see the gentle lapping at its shores, a gravelly, stony beach of dull gray and black sand.

Shivering from the water, drenched, you make your way to the shore. Your feet eventually find purchase in silty earth as you crawl up and out of the lake, onto the sandy, gravelly shore. You cannot make out much of the enormous cavern, save for the curving, rocky walls. The gentle lapping of the water behind you is the only sound apart from your breathing and the crunch of your feet on the gravel.

In the dim light, not far from the shore, you see a large stone slab, rising to about the height of your stomach, twice as long as your body is high. It is old, and hewn from the living rock of this place, gray and flecked with the sparkle of mineral deposits and trapped quartz. There is nothing on the altar, nor beside it.

Wait before it. Your nose smells the mineral tang of this place, and something else, something earthy and old, wet and musky. You go to your knees before the great stone slab, feeling the little gravels and bits of sand dig into your kneecaps. Place your hands on the cold stone. Feel the rough-hewn surface. Feel the hum underneath it. It is so cool, so solid.

As your hands rest on the stone, you realize you are not alone. Someone is with you here, staring down at you from behind the great stone altar. Your hands feel the thrumming beneath the stone grow stronger. You take a deep breath and fill your lungs. And then you look up.

She is standing behind the great stone altar, veiled in black. She stands taller than any mortal, the black veil cascading down, obscuring her face, covering her body. You slowly stand, facing her across the great stone table. You see that there are three objects, lined up between the two of you on the altar. What are they? Note them. Take your time to study each part of them, but do not touch or pick them up with your hands. Learn them. Remember them. Go from one to the next, slowly, focusing on every detail you are able to pick up from them. Commit this to your memory.

Finally, when you have seared the tokens from her into your mind, look into the veiled countenance across the great stone altar. Watch as her arms slowly rise, pulling at the veil as they come up from beneath the edge of the altar. Wait. Hold your breath. Time is slowed. Focus on the rhythmic beat of your heart, filling your ears, echoing in the hollow of your skull. Her arms keep coming up, the veil slipping, falling away. Until, yes, there: her face. You see her. You are looking into the face. And you know, beyond any doubt, who she is. You know her name.

Now, *scream Her name.*

Open your eyes.

Aztec water Goddess, 15th-16th c. CE. (Met Museum)

CHAPTER 10
MOTHER OF MANY MOTHERS
SAINTS, QUEENS, AND MONSTERS

> " The Goddess who exists in our lives today speaks in our languages and suggests courses of action suitable to our times. And, as the small voice told me years ago, she has suffered and had her history stolen from her. This has affected her, as it has affected all of us." [1]
>
> – Carol P. Christ

WHAT MAKES A GODDESS?

Exploring so far, we have seen Mother in the form of large, archetypal figures such as the Queen of Hell and we have examined more individual deities such as Hera and the Goddesses of the mystery cults. What I want to address here is the incarnations of the Mother that exist in the consciousness of Goddess worship but may not be, in the strictest sense, deities.

One of the most common places in contemporary practice where we see Mother in these forms is within figures from Celtic mythology. Celtic mythology is a quagmire for anyone who cares about "historical accuracy." Many of our texts and traditions come from one of three

---

[1] Carol P. Christ, *Rebirth of the Goddess: Finding Meaning in Feminist Spirituality* (New York, NY: Routledge, 1997), 44.

somewhat untrustworthy places. The first is the writings of conquerors, the Romans, who wrote propagandistic pieces about the Celtic peoples that were subdued by Roman forces. The second is from Christians, who wrote down local, regional folklore, but colored their writings through the lens of Christian theology. The third source is romantic reimagining and the works of poets, amateur historians, and nationalistic writers who desired to paint an image of the Celtic motherlands and their past glories to inspire contemporary revivals among Celtic peoples.

These sources are all somewhat problematic as they do not give us much insight into what Celtic peoples might have actually believed about their gods or their religious practices. Romans painted the Celts as murderous barbarians. Christians painted them as superstitious and mystical, almost like figures from fantasy. And romantic and nationalistic poets wanted to create an idyllic past of inspirational figures to inspire movements of Celtic independence and identity.

It is also difficult to speak of the Celts in any broad sense, considering how diverse the people were that are put under this umbrella. Many people who are interested in Celtic history or mythology are unaware of just how enormous a category it all really is. The Galatians, famous from the New Testament, were a Celtic people living in Greece. So, we have a community of peoples that span from settled invaders in Greece to the furthest reaches of the British Isles, in Wales, Scotland, and Ireland.

Despite all of this, many faces of the Mother popular today come from these sources and inspire current devotees. Cerridwen, Brigid, Morgana, and others are worshipped as Goddesses by many Pagans and Witches alive today. With some figures from Celtic mythology, I think we can definitively assert that a certain personality was indeed a Goddess, as that word is most commonly understood. Brigid is most assuredly a Goddess, for example. Figures like Cerridwen, or Queen Medb, are different. We are unsure of what these figures represent, historically, and most of what we know about them comes with heavy caveats.

Even when we are sure that a figure is a Goddess, we cannot avoid the build-up, so to speak, of romanticism and poetic license. Brigid, for example, is frequently listed as a "fire Goddess" even though there is little evidence to support this conclusion, and it is largely a fabrication from rather recent sources.[2] And much of her imagery comes from sources that are penned solely by Christian writers.

Ceridwen, by Welsh artist Christopher Williams. (Wikimedia Commons)

But, and this may be uncomfortable for some, I don't think it matters. The fact is that the worship of ancestors, great queens, important personages, and other figures developed constantly in pre-Christian

---

2   Mark Williams, *The Celtic Myths that Shape the Way We Think* (London, UK: Thames & Hudson, 2021), pp. 12-13.

religion. In Egypt, Imhotep was a deified architect worshipped as a god. Cleopatra was, for many, a living deity, drawing from the long tradition of pharaonic divinity. Her children and partners were portrayed as gods, and after her death she continued to inspire the spread of the cult of Isis throughout the Roman Empire.[3] The imperial cults of Rome deified mortals and built lavish altars and temples where sacrifices and offerings were made to the souls of dead emperors, their wives, and even Hadrian's male lover (Antinous), all apotheosized post-mortem and made into gods. There is a humorous legend that the emperor Vespasian, nearing death, uttered, "O dear, I think I'm becoming a god!"[4]

And it isn't just Celtic mythology or Roman practice that provide incarnations of the Mother that find devotees in contemporary worship. Circe, the sorceress from *The Odyssey* has her followers. As does the priestess Medea, and the gorgon Medusa. Saints from folkloric Catholicism and incarnations of the Virgin Mary are worshipped as Goddesses by many of the faithful. Our Ladies of Lourdes, Fatima, and Guadeloupe are every inch Goddesses, despite the tedious theology used to try and explain away their worship as something other than what is due to God.

And perhaps one of the largest current trends in this vein is the rehabilitation of Lilith and the recasting of her as a Goddess. Originally a demoness or malefic figure from Jewish mythology, drawn from earlier Mesopotamian mythologies (where she was still a harrowing, terrifying figure) Lilith now has worshippers and devotees across traditions and her image is used as a symbol of sexual freedom, personal power, and liberation. She is a frequent guest in pop culture, as well, usually as a champion of sexual liberty, or a *femme fatale*. Is this defying her "history" or is something else going on?

Well, as for the importance of "history," I tend to think of Guan Yin

---

[3] Kara Cooney, *When Women Ruled the World: Six Queen of Egypt* (Washington, D.C.: National Geographic Partners, 2018), 309.

[4] Reported in Suetonius' *Lives of the Twelve Caesars*.

as a fascinating example of how religious belief develops on its own trajectory, regardless of "historical accuracy." Guan Yin is the Chinese name for the bodhisattva Avalokitesvara. In all historical texts in Mahayana Buddhism, Avalokitesvara is a male devotee of Buddhism who vowed to stay in samsara until all sentient beings could reach enlightenment. Through time, this figure became a female in East Asia. Now, Guan Yin has millions of devotees who pray, chant to her, and seek her out as a Goddess regardless of what the historical roots have to say about the matter. She is one of the most worshipped female images in the world today.

But let us return to figures like Medusa and Lilith. Part of why some of these figures have risen, I believe, is the conscious effort of devotees to give their energy and faith to those beings maligned in history by patriarchal sources. Reimagining or reconnecting with the story of a figure such as Medusa has a certain power to it. Medusa, punished for being violated by a rapacious god and then murdered by a young male hero, can be taken as a launching pad for a refusal to accept unhealthy paradigms.

Another reason for the deification of these beings is that many of the legends of these figures have an incredible human pathos to them. Since these figures come from epic stories, tortured legends, and sometimes very real, historical cultures, we can sink our teeth into them in a way that is more difficult with larger, ethereal conceptions of the Mother. It is the narrative power of these beings that gives them such ability to evolve and inspire.

THE POPULAR AND THE SCHOLARLY

Going back to Guan Yin, we can address an important issue in contemporary Goddess worship, a point that revolves around the worries of "bad scholarship" and inaccurate history. We start with a question: is Guan Yin a Goddess?

CHAPTER 10 – MOTHER OF MANY MOTHERS: SAINTS, QUEENS, AND MONSTERS | 171

Statue of Guan Yin. Here, she is portrayed as having 1,000 hands. This relates to Guan Yin as "She Who Hears the Cries of the World" as she is associated with reaching out across the cycle of life, death, and rebirth to help devotees. (Adobe Stock)

In the strictest reading of Buddhism, no, she is not. She is a bodhisattva (again, a male one at that). A bodhisattva is not a god or a Goddess. A bodhisattva is a person who takes vows to accept being reborn in the cycle of births called samsara to help other practitioners who are working toward enlightenment. They have not attained nirvana yet, as they wish to continue to serve. They are beings of loving-kindness (*metta*). They represent a deep commitment to easing human suffering. They are not gods, which do exist in Buddhism (called *devas*) as a separate category of entity.

That is the bare-bones Mahayana Buddhist take, but whether that trickles down to popular religious practices is up for debate. Many worshippers of Guan Yin in East Asia are not Buddhists, necessarily. Guan Yin is worshipped by Daoists, folk religionists, Confucians, and members of unique traditions called "Salvationist" religions. Many of these identities are fluid, anyway, with religious identity in East Asia much more complex than it is in predominately Christian or Muslim countries, where a singular religious identity is more common. A worshipper of Guan Yin in Taiwan, for example, may be a Buddhist with Confucian ethics who consults Daoist oracles for advice.

All of this is to say, does it matter if the texts or the authorities call her a Goddess if millions of living, breathing human beings are praying to her as one? How can you control a Goddess? The fact is you can't. Devotion and religious practice grow through popular practice, not by academic or theological decree. One look at folk Catholicism is enough to see how many of the faithful feel about "official dogma." No matter how much Mexican bishops scream and vent against the worship of Santa Muerte, her cult still continues to grow. And many Catholics still wear St. Christopher medals, even though the Church's official position is that there is no historical basis for his cult, and he is not on the roster of saints feted in the Church calendar. The Archangel Uriel has also been banished from Catholic worship, despite his survival in other traditions. There are many more examples such as these. Religion evolves and lives within the practitioners, and their faith can sometimes resemble very little of official doctrine.

But intellectual elitism is very common in those who approach religions that are not dominant in their own cultures. Converts to "Eastern" religions in the West, and even those just casually interested in them, often have very skewed images of the traditions they are fascinated by. Many people, for example, associate Daoism solely with the *Dao De Jing*, and believe it to be a pure, nature-based philosophy with no "superstition" (a judgment-heavy word). This is sharply contrasted to the Daoist schools alive and well in East Asia, which have enormous corpuses of sacred texts, practice divination, mediumship, internal alchemy, and have unbelievably rich devotional practices towards huge families of deities and spirits.

And that is why so many Westerners might consider Buddhism a solely atheistic philosophy of meditation, whereas millions outside of the West see worshipping Guan Yin as a Goddess, or praying for rebirth in the Pure Land, as completely and authentically Buddhist. I bring all of this up to reiterate: scholarly and dogmatic decrees rarely communicate the whole of a tradition. And traditions morph and change over time. This is no different with the Goddess. Mother is expressed in so many ways and trying to "purify" our practice to something spotlessly historical is often a dead-end road.

GODDESSES OF CONTEMPORARY CRAFT AND PAGANISM

With all this in mind, I think it's important to state that religious Witchcraft and Paganism are held to a level of scrutiny that is alien to most people in religious studies. If modern Goddess worshippers and Witches offer their prayers to Cerridwen as a Goddess of transformation, does it matter if she happens to just be a figure from folklore, or perhaps an earthly queen, or whatever else she might have been? It shouldn't. If you were to go up to worshippers of Guan Yin in China and tell them "You know she isn't *actually* a Goddess. She's just a bodhisattva, which means…" well you probably wouldn't start any healthy conversations.

This attitude of "gotcha!" moments in contemporary Goddess worship is unhelpful. Unless you are a strict reconstructionist (and I most certainly am not), then religion is allowed to develop and evolve with time. And even the strict reconstructionists have a lot to answer for if pure historical accuracy is the measure of faith. I don't know many devotees of the Norse gods dying in battle to attain Valhalla. I don't know many Hellenistic polytheistic reconstructionists slitting the throats of heifers on altars in Greece, following manuals of ritual slaughter from the Greek world to the letter, manuals that are written in a Greek that is no longer spoken as a living language.

None of this is to say that wanting to practice a pagan religion as it might have been practiced in pre-Christian epochs is *wrong* necessarily.

I don't think that. What I do think though is that Goddess worship, both within and outside of religious Witchcraft, is often lambasted for "re-writing" history or worshipping figures that "weren't even gods" with not too little vitriol, whereas other paths are given so much wiggle room if they are deemed *serious*—a seriousness determined by some bizarre rubric that I have never understood. I'm fairly certain the rubric is mostly about aesthetic and personal judgments that certain people in occult communities have surrounding the Goddess movements and the Witchcraft revival of Gerald Gardner, the Sanders, et al.

Many people who come to Goddess worship are faced with a lot of judgment and misunderstanding. I might sound like I am hammering a point home a little too harshly, but I want to give those that come to the Mother some ammunition, or at least some support, when they are questioned and prodded by the anti-Goddess crowd which, unfortunately, is quite *en vogue* at the time of this writing.

Much of this scrutiny comes, I truly feel, from the belief that Goddess worship is not *real* religion. I believe one of the reasons people would feel much more comfortable telling a Pagan worshipper of Cerridwen that she was never a Goddess than they would be telling a Chinese worshipper of Guan Yin that she was never a Goddess is simple. It's because they do not view devotion to the Goddess by Witches and Pagans as worthy, or valid. Buddhism is a "real religion" or a "serious religion" whereas Goddess worship, including Witchcraft, is labelled as silly, hokey, or a phase.

"Serious religion" is the religion that leads to ecstasy and transformation. If that happens in the drum circles and rituals of Goddess worshippers, then who is anyone to look down on that? Never forget, it is time and money that give religions their veneer of respectability. Christianity was once viewed as a fringe cult of lunatics and was accused of sexual immorality and godlessness, even drunkenness and debauchery, by Roman sources. It is only time and conquest that have made certain religious traditions respectable. Buddhism may have been integrated into East Asian culture, but it was once reviled by Confucian scholars who were horrified of the idea of leaving your family to join a monastic community.

Time also has a way of blurring our memory. That blurring has happened in the community of those that are interested in what we label as the "occult" in remarkable ways. I am grateful for the trend in the occult community of producing beautiful, annotated grimoires in leatherbound editions, often painstakingly crafted to be real works of literary art. These are frequently printed by serious scholars, who devote a lot of ink and time to expounding on the rites and magical rituals of the grimoires.

But never forget, the grimoires were viewed by many scholars and elites as ridiculous, garbled handbooks of cheap black magic. They contain spells for getting women to like you [5] and turning invisible and finding buried treasure. Somehow, though, they are held in high esteem by *serious practitioners*. Be suspicious of this. What we talk about now as a glorious, scholarly work of angelic magic, just might've been seen at one point as poorly written hokey nonsense. [6]

Debates aside, the fact is that worship and devotion of the Great Mother has always rankled. Good. Let it rankle. Conservative Roman senators thought the cultists of the Mother were charlatans and lunatics. They particularly brought up the lurid use of makeup, theatrics, effeminacy, and music in this faith. The Cult of Isis was persecuted for being secretive, foreign, and politically dangerous. Tantra is reviled by many conservative Hindus. Contemporary Witches have been fired from their jobs, mocked, and jeered at for practicing magic and devoting

---

[5] Many of the most beloved grimoires contain spells that frankly seem to be written for what contemporary internet culture would call an "incel."

[6] To be clear, I do love grimoire magic. In my previous book, *The Art Cosmic*, I draw heavily from the grimoire tradition. I also collect them myself, so don't think I'm being too much of a naysayer here, just trying to provide a little added context.

their worship to the Mother.[7]

Do not let this damper your devotion to Mother. Many live outside of the Mysteries. Let them. It is not our burden to recreate any particular cult from time immemorial. The Goddess is alive, evolving, dynamic and real in the lives of her worshippers. If you feel her call, you can find her face in the queens and spirits of mythology and legend with wild abandon, as far as I am concerned. In that spirit, I offer a prayer for you:

Sister Medusa, hear my prayer. Come, slithering and stony-eyed. Work upon the Earth again, beloved one, beautiful one, shining one. Face of glory, I adore you. Serpent-haired, I adore you. You I put before me, sister to the Gray Ones, winged and lustrous Gorgo. Slayer of fools, I adore you. Mystery of the blood, I adore you. Spring from the sea's belly, again, again, ever again!

Terracotta face of Medusa from the 6th century BCE. The face of the Gorgon was used in antiquity to ward off evil. (Met Museum)

---

[7] Co-founder of my own tradition, Maxine Sanders, details some of the persecution she faced as a public Witch in her autobiography *Firechild* (Mandrake, 2007).

THE FOUNTAINS OF THE MOTHER

Another concept that I want to address here is that the Mother has her prophets and saints as much as any religious tradition. In many religious traditions, gurus, monks, nuns, heroes, and teachers are elevated to a semi-divine nature. There is danger in this, of course, as guru-worship has produced much misery in the world and led to systematic abuse and disenfranchisement. But there is also the power of a connective line of belief that unites us in community and shared vision.

In my tradition, I have a lineage of initiators. I view them as voices of the Mother, priestesses and priests of the Goddess that I value and honor. They are not holier than I am, or more important, but they are honored humans in my mind that made the life I live possible by their teaching, their sacrifice, and their devotion to the Craft. The elders of Witchcraft made the enriching path I walk possible. I go beyond my own Alexandrian tradition to honor the elders of Gardnerian Craft, the progenitors of Witchcraft like Gerald Gardner, Patricia Crowther, Lois Bourne, and Doreen Valiente, who regardless of her shifting allegiances was responsible for much of my liturgical practice.

That lineage, though, is an initiatory lineage and most readers of this will not take initiation into Craft. So, I want to address a larger concept of what Christians might refer to as the "cloud of witnesses." The Mother has her own cloud of witnesses. And many of the figures addressed in this chapter, along with others I have missed, could count, on a deep psychological level, as those witnesses. Debating *what* they are, or *who* they are is not necessary for honoring the mouthpieces, incarnations, prophets, voices, and faces of Mother.

Of course, living traditions such as Shaktism have their own complex lineages and initiatory practices. As do other Goddess-focused communities. Those, I will leave to their respective devotees out of respect. Here, I want to give voice to the figures of legend that live, eternally, as prophetic visions of Mother. What do they say to us, even now, from the depths of their stories? Let us pray.

To Cerridwen, we pray for trials and tests that improve our life. Honor her, the sorceress and cauldron-tender, as the transforming Witch that brews the liquid of inspiration. She chases you, wild in vengeance, brutal in desire, single-minded, all-consuming. She comes to swallow you up and make you worthy. A great black hen, a slithering otter in the river, and so much more she comes. She comes even now, pushing you, asking you what you have done, demanding that you make an accounting of your life. She is not gentle. She will never be gentle. She will test you and bend you and push you ever forward. She is the face of Mother.

To Marie Laveau, we pray for wisdom, and cunning, and strength in the face of adversity. She is a mind sharp as polished glass, a bridge between a so-called New World and cultures demolished through cruelty and empire. She builds and transforms for her family, for her future. She is faithful, and willing to help. She demands a price. She calls for you to create and claim what is rightfully yours. No one comes to steal from you, now. She is the face of Mother.

To Tiamat, we pray for justice. Work to make the Mother's will manifest upon the earth. Refuse to worship unworthy heroes and murderous fools. Deny your prayers to rapacious gods. Scream and bellow for the fall of tyrants. Raise the seas, if need be, to wash away the cruel and merciless sons of destruction. They will call you chaos. They will call you evil. They will smear you with lies. Devour them. She is the face of Mother.

To Medea, we pray for understanding. Regardless of how much I sing the praises of Mother, I will fail. I will lash out in anger. I will slip into habits I wish to eradicate. Perhaps, even, I will commit some great crime, and alienate my supporters. Perhaps I will be abandoned. Give me strength to forgive myself and give me the authority and privilege to write my own history. She comes, now, a priestess and a Witch. She is the face of Mother.

To all the faces and witnesses of Mother we offer praise. We remember burned Witches, victims that may have loved Christ even and only been smeared with lie and scandal. We can remember forgotten heroines, overshadowed by neglect and disdain. We sing of teachers, and lovers, and partners, and fellow devotees, all of them a great cloud of memory, a host of believers and magic-workers, eager and hungry for transformation and release. All of this is Mother. Her names are legion.

HISTORY

To end, I do want to say that I am not "anti-history" in any way. I think historically accurate information about the myths and legends we inherit is crucial. And I do agree with a lot of critics that the Goddess movement, religious Witchcraft, and contemporary Paganism have all put forward ideas, books, and concepts that play very fast and loose with history, archaeology, and literature. I may be guilty of it here. But I am not writing as a historian. If I were, this chapter would look very different. A history of Cerridwen is not going to be the same as a theological work about Cerridwen, for example. If I were writing her history, I would go into the complex debates about the Welsh literary canon and Celtic studies that form the ground of discussions around her. But at some point, spiritual practice is simply a separate world from historical recordkeeping.

In Christianity, there is a strong movement to seek out what is called "the historical Jesus." Scholars such as Marcus Borg and others have poured forth a mountain of scholarship and ideology to ground Jesus of Nazareth in a historical framework. Many of the members of this movement are self-identified Christians, as well. They have attempted to marry faith with a scrupulous attention to historical fact.

To be frank, it has not born a lot of fruit among churches. The movement does have a loyal following, but it has not had a massive impact on the religious lives of most Christians. Why? Shouldn't Christians *want* to know about the "real" Jesus? Maybe. Or maybe, the lived religious faith of Christianity is aiming for, touching on, and living within something very different than the historians desire to understand. Neither side is wrong, but their goals and experiences are too different to marry together seamlessly.

I believe that if we approach religious Witchcraft, Goddess worship, or Paganism with the lens of history or archaeology alone, we are tacitly admitting, in some way, that the gods are dead. If discussion of our spirituality can only be had with artifacts and textual examination, then we are worshipping a butterfly collection. It may be beautiful and diverse, but it is pinned under glass, breathless and inert. The butterflies are fascinating, but they're still dead.

This is a central issue in those that seek Mother in Witchcraft, or traditions inspired by the revival of religious Witchcraft. It is an issue for contemporary Pagans who draw from pre-Christian pantheons and practices. The rise of Christianity as the solely accepted social religious framework means that we often do not always have access to the unbroken lineages and continually lived practices of other traditions such as Shakti Hinduism, including Tantra, or African Diasporic Traditions. This "gap" creates angst.

The only solution I have found is to find the Mother even in the "gap." I believe that Mother transcends culture and space. This is not to denigrate or disregard the importance of unique cultural flowerings around the Goddess, or lineage traditions. I belong to a lineage tradition, so I am definitely not saying that tradition itself is something bad. What I am hopefully putting out there to any seekers is that the practice of connecting to the Goddess through worship and the hunger for her ecstasy is not the same thing as unknitting the past and repeating systems from it. We draw from the past so that we may practice in our present lives.

And it is important always to remember that worship is not the same as recreation. When I study a particular Goddess from history, or a cultural idea that I believe could inform my practice or my devotion, I do care about sources. I care deeply about good scholarship, and comparative studies. But, when I step into the worship of Mother, I care about connection. I care about the transformation of myself at the deepest levels of my being. And that experience is going to overflow the containers of history, time, and scholarship. Mother is simply too expansive to be contained.

History as a Goddess: 16th century print of the Muse Clio. (Met Museum)

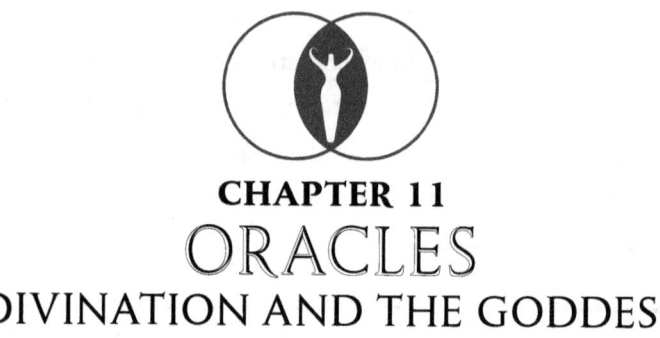

CHAPTER 11
ORACLES
DIVINATION AND THE GODDESS

> *Suddenly the priestess of Phoebus is silent. Her cheeks are pale, and her whole body shakes. Her fillets stiffen; her soft hair stands on end; her inner being hisses frantically with a choking sound. Her glance wanders unsteadily in different directions; her eyes seem to twist and turn inward and then again just to stare motionless. Now she lifts her head up into the air, higher than usual, and walks erect. Now she is getting ready to unseal her vocal chords against their will; now she tries to close her lips but cannot keep her words inside. Here is a priestess in ecstasy who fights against her god!"* [1]
>
> – From Seneca's *Agamemnon*

READING FORTUNES

For something around fifteen years, I've been a reader. By reader, I mean psychic reader, but I'm not entirely sold on that term, for reasons that will probably be clear by the end of this chapter. Even when I was a practicing Catholic, I read tarot and studied traditional astrology. Catholicism has an odd relationship to many magical and divinatory practices. Officially, a grave sin. In reality? Well, let's just say most of

---

[1] Georg Luck, *Arcana Mundi: Magic and the Occult in the Greek and Roman Worlds*, (Baltimore, MD: Johns Hopkins University Press, 2006), 337.

my clients were pretty devout when I was younger, and they were no strangers to a Mass. I feel like most Catholics don't remember what happens to fortune tellers in Hell, according to Dante. They're forced to live with their heads facing backwards, for having claimed the sight of seeing too far forward. Regardless of Catholic guilt, divination is a core practice for many practitioners and seekers, and just as I touched on magic, I feel like I have to touch on divination as a practice in worship of the Mother.

"La Papessa" (female pope) card of the Tarot deck playing at the inversion of male religious authority. She is more frequently called the High Priestess in more modern decks. (Wikimedia Commons)

Divination has a long history of being associated with women, at least in a Western context. The oracles, or sibyls, of ancient Greece were women. Two of the most famous were at Delphi and Dodona, the first a temple to Apollo and the latter sacred to Zeus. There were other major sites that contained oracles, or sibyls, and they are pretty much uniformly women. This is an interesting reality of oracular practice in the past: male gods had female oracles.

And in contemporary practice, the majority of readers and clients are women as well, with women being more likely to hold beliefs that others label as "New Age."[2] Spiritualism, perhaps the largest divinatory-based spiritual system of the modern era, maybe in history, was intimately associated with suffragettes and first-wave feminism.[3] So many of the leaders were women that propaganda against the Spiritualist movement frequently tarred the organization as a haven for suffragettes and disaffected women.

All of this I bring up to tie the practice of oracular seeing and psychism to the Mother. These practices go through phases of trend, rise and fall, and they are currently going through a bit of a renaissance. I can now purchase tarot cards at chain stores, and I have precious few friends on social media who do not share about their horoscope or memes containing astrological facts based around sun signs. Despite the protestations of more secular, scientific voices, divination does not seem to be going anywhere as a cultural practice.

And divination has not always, nor does it now, rest solely in the realms of hobby or mere interest. For certain religious systems, divination is a sacred practice, not relegated to the fringes of the faith. The reading of shells is an initiatory, deeply spiritual system in certain African Diasporic Traditions. In Daoism, the consulting of diviners and the use of the *I Ching (or Yi Jing:* 易經) is more than simple lot casting for fun. It guides major life decisions. In India, the practice of Jyotisha, often

---

[2] "New Age beliefs common among both religious and nonreligious Americans," Pew Research Center, Fact Tank, October 1, 2018, https://www.pewresearch.org/fact-tank/2018/10/01/new-age-beliefs-common-among-both-religious-and-nonreligious-americans/.

[3] For more information, see *Radical Spirits: Spiritualism and Women's Rights in Nineteenth-Century America* (Indiana University Press, 1989).

referred to in the West as Vedic or Hindu astrology, is a major aspect of life and universities even offer degrees in Jyotisha. This has led to heated debates in India between practitioners and those that relegate astrology to the category of superstition.[4]

The Fortune Teller by Georges de La Tour, 17th century. Fortune tellers, in European art, were frequently shown as hags, cutthroats, or thieves. (Met Museum)

And traditions of the Goddess as well have been tied to these practices. Many of the progenitors of the modern Goddess movement and the revival of religious Witchcraft engaged in divinatory practices, from tarot cards and astrology to scrying mirrors and mediumship. Raymond Buckland, who helped introduce initiatory Witchcraft into America, was raised in Spiritualism and continued the practice throughout his life. Alex and Maxine Sanders, Gerald Gardner, Patricia Crowther, and

---

4   "Supreme Court Questions 'Jyotir Vigyan,'" *The Times of India*, September 3, 2001.

others have written on, or alluded to, divinatory practices. Crowther in particular developed a series of rites tied to the zodiac.[5] I once had the privilege of listening to Maxine Sanders describe how her coven members in the Temple of the Mother, in London, created black mirrors for scrying. Wherever Mother is, we see the practice of divination.

But divination is a complex practice, with detractors and devoutly faithful locked in argument over the worth of seeking out oracles or picking at the threads of fate. Nothing makes my secular friends more apoplectic than my love of traditional astrology, and nothing can send a devout believer of cards into a rage quicker than a snarky denier. My hope is to provide a different perspective here and introduce divination into your practice within the realm of service to the Mother.

SIBYLS: MOUTHPIECES OF GOD

The oracle at Delphi stood as one of the most important religious centers in the Greek-speaking world.[6] I've had the good fortune to visit Delphi, and it still thrums with a certain power, overlooking groves of olive orchards and still bearing the ruins of what were once great structures built to honor the god Apollo. I have a very fond memory of fellow initiates almost being chased away from the site by guards for reading tarot cards at the site. It seems the Greek Orthodox guards did not appreciate a coven of Witches using the site for divination. Ironic.

The oracle herself, a priestess of Apollo, gave arcane pronouncements at Delphi in religious rites and was frequented by queens, emperors, and potentates. We say the "oracle at Delphi" because the living oracles were rarely known by name. Instead, they were referred to by the deity they served—by the deity that was over their temple or shrine (hence

---

[5] *The Zodiac Experience: Initiation Through the Twelve Signs* (Fenix Flames Publishing, 2020).

[6] For a very readable and solid overview of Delphi's history, see: *Delphi: A History of the Center of the Ancient World* (Princeton University Press, 2014) by Michael Scott.

the Temple of Apollo at Delphi gives us the Oracle of Delphi). The list of visitors to this oracle, and how seriously her pronouncements were taken, is rather impressive. Countless emperors, and even Alexander the Great, visited the oracle, taking her wisdom as Gospel on how to engage with war, diplomacy, and affairs of state. Detractors did exist, but frankly they appear to be few. Oracles were serious business.

Ruins of religious structures at Delphi, Greece. The Oracle at Delphi was a priestess of Apollo. (Adobe Stock)

Their methodology was unique, compared to how we discuss "psychism" today. These oracles were not pulling from inward sources of ability—what modern readers often refer to as "a gift." They were instead seen as mouthpieces for God. It is not the power innate within the human that speaks from the oracle; it is the god, working through the oracle. This ties into the very concept of religious ecstasy that I believe the worship of Mother opens us up to. She works through us, particularly when our minds are loosed from our bearings in trance.

This "working through" is very similar to the modern Spiritualist concept of a "medium." The very word connotes a half-way substance, a conduit, something that is tapped into or embodied by a spirit, a deity, a power beyond the mortal coil to speak truth or provide revelation. Many of the greatest Spiritualist leaders from the movement were never really claiming to speak of their own power, but instead of having connections to spirits or guides that could speak through them. We can also see this concept of mediumship with other entities in the rise of "channeled material" such as the Seth material, or the *Urantia Book*.

This is the oracular power of worship. What happened at the oracles may be lost to time, reconstructed from the bits we have left to study, but what we do know is that it was a deeply religious practice. It was not all about internal gifts, or vague "energies" discussed through whatever science was available at the time. Instead, it was ecstasy. And in that ecstasy, the oracle spoke as though divine herself.

Before we leave the oracle of Delphi, I want to make an important detour. The high priestess (and thus, the oracle) of Delphi was called the *Pythia*. This title comes from the story of Apollo slaying a vicious female beast named Python at the location of the future temple at Delphi. In the Homeric Hymn to Apollo, Hera births a demonic force of evil named Typhon to spite her husband and it is given to the creature Python to be reared.[7]

The Python does much evil on the earth until Apollo slays it and thus the title of the priestess, *Pythia*, is explained. It literally means "to rot" as it was believed the rotting carcass of the Python gave up fumes at Delphi.[8] I think there is a lot going on in this story of a male deity slaying a female monster and then a young woman being made the sole mouthpiece. As Apollo-centric as Delphi is, there is something else going on—a vilified face of Mother peering up from beneath the rubble of the past. The great serpent, the dragoness, the wicked figure...I see Mother here, reminding of us a deeper power, deeper than the golden-faced

---

[7] Barry B. Powell, *Greek Poems to the Gods: Hymns from Homer to Proclus* (Oakland, CA: University of California Press, 2021), 132-133.

[8] Ibid.

male Apollo and his quiver of arrows.

Beyond the oracle of Delphi, there are other examples of divination in the Hellenistic world that are deep wells to explore. In Neoplatonism, the consultation of oracles and the practice of divination were seen as a worthwhile, religious practice, particularly by later philosophers such as Iamblichus and Proclus. In these philosophers' minds, the oracles were conduits of divine intelligence, speaking for the gods and offering valid readings that could be taken as holy pronouncements. I find it particularly interesting that many of these late-stage Neoplatonist philosophers were heavily interested in the Chaldean Oracles.

These Oracles are an arcane collection of unique philosophical and religious ideas that were seen almost like a revealed scripture by believers. And in the Oracles, the World-Soul is embodied as Hekate Soteira (Hekate the Savioress).[9] It was a Goddess that mediated between the higher divine emanation and the lower world—a Goddess that bore associations with Witchcraft and magic. It is not that the Hekate of the Oracles is the same as every other incarnation of Hekate in the Hellenistic world; that's far from true.[10] The Neoplatonic scheme has its own unique understandings surrounding the gods. But, still, the Goddess stands as a central figure in the system, and as the mediator between the higher planes and the world we inhabit.

All of this is to say, oracles were a major part of the lived religious life of mystics, theurgists, and seekers of the Mother. And they were not drawing solely from some paranormal ability, or ESP. They were speaking for the gods in significant religious rituals, rituals that read and feel very much like the ecstatic trance states experienced in other traditions, and available to devotees today.

---

[9] Ruth Majercik, *The Chaldean Oracles: Text, Translation, and Commentary* (Wiltshire, UK: The Promethean Trust, 2013), 7.

[10] For more information, see: *Hekate Soteira: A Study of Hekate's Roles in the Chaldean Oracles and Related Literature* (The American Philological Association, 1990) by Sarah Iles Johnston.

Priestess of Delphi by John Collier (1891). A reimagining of the Oracle, prophesying for the gods. (Wikimedia Commons)

THE WORTH OF A READING

Regardless of the practices of long-gone cultures, divination still remains part of our lives, particularly in communities of Witches, Pagans, and seekers. Predominately, we use mediumship, tarot or other forms of cartomancy, astrology, palmistry, scrying, or clairvoyance induced by touch. Less common forms of divination are growing in popularity, as are divinatory traditions from specific traditions such as Runes, from Germanic Pagans.

At the core of the experience of divination is an uncomfortable question that believers and practitioners tend to get very passionate about. What really is happening in a reading? The answer to that will depend a lot on your worldview, your experience, traditions you may belong to, and what your beliefs are regarding death, science, and much more.

I will be honest here. For me, trying to unknit divination with a scientific lens is unhelpful. Most scientific attempts to prove certain divinatory or extra-sensory abilities have ended in failure.[11] The rise of paranormal and parapsychical research has yet to provide concrete proof, or even strong examples, that are accepted by any large portion of academia or the scientific community.

For me, and I tread carefully here, a solid experience of divination is about connection. It is about the connection between the reader and the seeker, and connection with a larger matrix of symbol, divinity, aspiration, memory, and culture. It doesn't really inspire me, frankly, to think of readers as superhuman agents with powers beyond mortal understanding—some gift from birth that sets them apart from the world. For me, it is much more potent to think of a reading as a connection between two spiritual beings, attempting to peer into the loom of fate

---

[11] I know many readers will have personal experiences they believe contradict this, or certain examples from parapsychical research that they do believe are valid. I am not attacking this, only pointing out that none of these examples (as of yet) has been accepted by anything resembling a large segment of the scientific community.

and discern the threads a bit more clearly. Divination is, after all, from the same root as *divine*.

Some of the most powerful readings I've ever had, or given for that matter, have felt more therapeutic than scientific. Divination is like staring into a mirror. You are looking at yourself intensely or asking someone else to look at you and repeat back what they see. That practice, when done in a good setting with the right people, can provide incredibly healing results. Long before psychoanalysts dissected the dreams of patients strewn across fainting couches in the salons of central Europe, oracles and soothsayers dissected the fates of clients in backrooms, temples, and homes.

Don't think I am saying that all readers are angels, there to heal us from past traumas or talk us through difficult decisions with pure objectivity. No. Of course there are abuses in the system, and charlatans, and those that induce fear in clients and sow paranoia to reap money and gifts. We have all heard these stories. And serious health concerns and mental health concerns should be treated by qualified professionals, not just by self-proclaimed spiritual leaders.

But that's just the thing, for me: sometimes the oracle is the right professional. I know this is controversial, but it has simply been something true for me for so long that I cannot deny it as a reality in my life. Of course, a serious mental health issue should be discussed with your therapist. And of course, a serious medical issue should be discussed with your doctor. But, often, why we seek out a reading is because we are stuck at a crossroads, unable to decide on a path regarding important choices in our lives.

These are the moments where divination can work wonders. We sit down with another seeker, another spiritual creature, and pour our hearts out. We give it all over to fate and chance and let the cards fall where they may, or the stars align how they must. It allows us to let go of a lot of our choice anxiety and settle into our decisions with more clarity and peace.

Fate is an unpopular concept in our current world, and most people turn their nose up at the idea of some destiny being worked out in the universe. We prefer choice. We prefer personal power. That's all well and good until we have too many choices, or until we are torn so equally between two decisions that our mind freezes up, our body unable to turn right or left at the fork in the road. Fate is that thing that softens the choice anxiety of the human condition. Sometimes, blaming the stars (or thanking them), or letting the decisions unfold as they will on a table of cards, is the only way we can break through and see our situation through a new lens, or appreciate another perspective.

Approaching divination in this way has made the practice something rewarding and fruitful for me, as opposed to something oppositional. I don't play games of "stump the psychic" and I don't expect readers to bend spoons or levitate tables. The worst excesses of what was called "physical mediumship" tarnished the Spiritualist movement in many eyes, and much of what we associate with fake mediums comes from the desperate attempt to have a spiritual practice validated by the scientific community. I simply do not see the value in chasing after approval from the priesthood of materialism.

In a good reading we are sacralizing the moment. We are setting ourselves apart, stepping out of our mundane world for a moment to feel a little magic. We are seeking the Mother, reaching out across the ether and hoping that we pull something from beyond her veil, from the emanations of her divinity. A very dear friend of mine, and a High Priestess of my Craft, begins her readings with a small prayer that includes, "the universe is infinite; it contains all knowledge." I believe we could say, just as meaningfully, that the Mother is infinite, and she contains all knowledge.

MOTHER-KNOWLEDGE

The Goddess stands as a different kind of approach to knowing. Patriarchal agents are obsessed with two kinds of knowledge, and little else. The first is authority-based knowledge. Something is true because it is revealed in the text or pronounced as true *ex cathedra* by an authority that bears a mantle of teaching. This is particularly common in Abrahamic religion. Christian theologians frequently quote, as one of the principal authorities of the faith, a group known as the Church Fathers, an all-male cast of early Christian leaders and writers such as Justin Martyr, Ignatius of Antioch, and John Chrysostom. They were the leaders and defenders of what came to be considered orthodoxy in Christendom at its earliest stages.

I'm not sure I would want to take this group as a source of wisdom. Tertullian, one of the most important of the Church Fathers, once wrote to women, "And do you not know that you are an Eve? The sentence of God on this sex of yours lives in this age: the guilt must of necessity live too. You are the devil's gateway: you are the unsealer of that tree: you are the first deserter of the divine law: you are she who persuaded him whom the devil was not valiant enough to attack. You destroyed so easily God's image, man. On account of your desert—that is, death—even the Son of God had to die. And do you think about adorning yourself over and above your tunics of skins?"[12] So, there it is. No thank you.

But we cannot lay the blame solely on Christianity, or any traditional religion for that matter. Many of the philosophical works I've alluded to or sourced throughout this book come from Neoplatonism, which is a tradition that is very dear to my heart. Although there are powerful arguments and nuanced, beautiful discussions in these works, many

---

[12] Tertullian, "On the Apparel of Women," in *Ante-Nicene Church Fathers* vol. 4, edited by Alexander Roberts, James Donaldson, and A. Cleveland Coxe (Buffalo, NY: Christian Literature Publishing Co., 1885) revised for New Advent by Kevin Knight. https://www.newadvent.org/fathers/0402.htm.

of the great philosophers in this tradition appeal to authority as much as they do reason. They often will simply state that something is true because, well...Plato said it. So, it *must* be true! Even the most reasoned thinkers in antiquity were guilty of believing great knowledge was to be found in citing authority.

Hildegard of Bingen receiving a divine vision. Hildegard of Bingen was a polymath and mystic whose works touched upon art, music, theology, and science. (Wikimedia Commons)

The other form of knowledge that many love, particularly secular and academic authorities, is knowledge gained through the scientific method—the "cold hard facts" as we like to say. But there are other ways to approach "knowing" beyond just historical authority and scientific investigation. I know what the poems of certain authors mean to me in a fashion that I cannot use the language of religious dogma or scientific materialism to explain. And these feelings do not feel like mere opinions. They feel like a type of truth, a connection to something my soul knows as "The Real" even if it is about a numinous experience such as art, faith, or love.

This is an important realization in the practice of any spiritual work. When we relegate everything we believe to "just a hunch" then we are denigrating our experience. The knowledge that comes from emotional experience is not mere opinion. It is a different kind of knowledge entirely, one that is no less real or true, but exists in a separate framework from the laboratory or the church house. The classic example of this, used in a lot of these discussions is, "Do you love your partner? Do they love you?" Can we really explain the connection we have to a lover with the language of synapses and neurochemicals? Does that actually grasp the Truth?

You may be able to explain to someone the interaction of complex neurochemicals, using biology. You may also be able to explain the cultural trends and power structures that influence partnership and marriage choices. You may be able to summon up a mountain of fact to "explain" Love. Will you have done so? I firmly believe you will have missed the truth entirely.

Mother is the source of experiential knowledge, the knowledge contained in art, myth, metaphor, and ecstatic joy. Hildegard of Bingen, an extraordinary polymath, mystic, and contemplative, wrote of her ecstatic states, saying that she "...spoke and wrote these things not by the invention of my heart or that of any other person, but as by the secret mysteries of God I heard and received them in the heavenly places."[13]

Hildegard's knowledge was revealed knowledge, and she experienced it through ecstasy, what we might call trance in the modern context. Mother-knowledge is the knowledge of how to navigate this experience, and divination is a major tool to induce, control, understand, and dissect these experiences so that we can learn from them. It is not necessarily a "scientific process" as much as a moment of connection, revelation, and synthesis.

It may upset more traditional minds to associate someone like Hildegard of Bingen with "fortune-telling", but I think the link is crystal clear. If Hildegard were alive today, I highly doubt she'd be praised and adored. We'd think she was insane or lying, just like people think of readers today and those that consult oracles or visit mediums. Not every mystic from history was adored in their own time, and women in particular were often victims of religious violence when they stepped outside of accepted norms or claimed knowledge beyond what was acceptable.

For me, this is the power of divination as a devotee of Mother: I can use the complex web of symbols we have built up in tarot, or astrology, or any other method, and I can peer at the decisions that give me pause and the areas of my psyche that I feel perturbed by or confused with. She is there through it all, the matrix through which I'm looking, just like Hekate in the Chaldean Oracles, transmuting and diffusing higher information into material methods that I can see, touch, and understand more easily.

RITUALIZING

I want to end by giving something a bit more practical in terms of divination and the Goddess. This book is not really meant as an instruction manual for certain techniques, so if anything I've spoken to in this

---

[13] Hildegard von Bingen, *Scivias*, trans. Columba Hart, Jane Bishop, Barbara J. Newman, and Caroline Walker Bynum (New York, NY: Paulist Press, 1990), 65.

chapter ignites a passion in you for divination, I encourage you to seek out works on techniques that interest you and do your research. Tarot, astrology, runes, whatever it may be. You will find a treasure trove of information through good, solid research and practice.

What I want to give here is an idea for approaching divination specifically as a devotee of Mother and how you can incorporate devotion to the Goddess in acts of reading. Many artists and writers have created oracle decks and divinatory tools that focus on Goddess worship, and these are all worth a solid investigation. When the only images we have ever used to study or practice divination are marked by a lack of the Goddess, then new tools that include her can reorient our practice and speak to us with symbols and language that open up new experiences.

Beyond just tools, I also recommend trying to ground readings in devotional practice. By taking the time to make a reading a truly sacred moment, we can connect with the experience in ways that may shake loose old ways of thinking or open us up to new stories. The burning of incense before a sacred image, and prayers to figures of wisdom or oracular power can begin your sessions. Take the time to connect, through devotional service, before you shuffle the cards or map the planets.

Sources for the divine in divination include the oracles, or sibyls, I mentioned above as well as Hekate Soteira. Beyond these figures I would also recommend looking into the figures that control fate, chance, or destiny in many mythologies (often Goddesses, or divine female figures). These include personages such as the Fates (the *Moirae*), the Norns, or Fortuna. I would also look to figures that guard oaths, such as the Goddess of the river Styx, whose oaths even the gods must obey, as well as figures of revelatory wisdom such as Sophia.

And with time, we can begin to appreciate oracular or divinatory practice in ways that go outside traditional tools such as cards or palmistry. We can begin to use trance and the revelations we receive during our experiences of worship and connection as tools for reflection. Keeping track of repeating symbols, experiences, words, or images can open us up to seeing a truth we may be avoiding in our more conscious selves. The goal of ecstasy is knowledge. That is the goal of divination as well.

To end, I want to say that I am aware that divination and trance are often practices that can make people uncomfortable. Most of us live far removed from cultures that truly believed in the miraculous, the mystical, or the visionary. Attempts to wedge divination into science have not been much help to reorient us to the ecstatic and the beautiful, in my opinion. Instead, I believe we should try our best to let go of the hard dualism that pervades the modern, materialist worldview.

For the mystic in search of Mother: everything participates in her mind. Our divination is a conversation with the emanations of Mother. Perhaps, more than anything, it is an act of remembering. When we slip into the ecstasy of her knowledge, we become aware that we have always been with her. We come from the divine. We are destined to return. We have never left. All of this is true.

CHAPTER 12
CYCLES UPON CYCLES
THE DANCE OF THE GODDESS

> *At that time, she herself is the great destroyer. Existing from all eternity, she herself becomes the creation. She, the eternal one, sustains all beings."* [1]
>
> – From the *Devi Mahatmya*

THE CIRCLE AND THE LINE

The Goddess is worshipped, in my tradition, in a circle. The magic circle is not exclusive to religious Witchcraft. It exists in ceremonial magic as well, and in other practices that drink from the shared well of European esotericism. And in the wider Pagan community, gathering in circles for ritual, drumming, sharing, or feasting, is so common that gatherings are frequently referred to just as circles.

Beyond the world of Pagans and Witches, the circle is also featured in designs used in the worship of Devi in Shaktism, where lotuses, triangles, and other forms are transcribed within a circle, worked into the intricate geometric *yantras*.[2] I've already mentioned the full moon, or new moon, as a token of the Goddess. We could also look at the circle

---

[1] Devadatta Kali, *In Praise of the Goddess: The Devimahatmya and Its Meaning* (Berwick, ME: Nicolas-Hays, Inc., 2003), 173.

[2] For a look into how these geometric designs are understood in practice, see *Fractals of Reality: Living the Śrīcakra* (Sfaim Press, 2022) by Kavitha Chinnaiyan.

in Pythagorean, or Hermetic texts and the sacred geometry of arcane philosophy. It seems that everywhere we look in traditions of Mother and magic there are circles. Circles upon circles upon circles.

1922 reprint of a 15th century German woodcut of the Last Judgment. Religions with a "Judgment Day" inculcate into believers a purely linear view of both our history and our future. (Met Museum)

The reason for this, I believe, is the cyclical nature of the Goddess. The Mother's path is one of life, death, and rebirth—an endless cycle of creation, dissolution, destruction, and renewal. We see this, in many traditions, reflected in the "Wheel of the Year" or other major festivals that mark the changing seasons and keep time.

But it isn't just about the nature of the seasons; it's something much deeper. Goddess-mind is a recursive mind. It falls back on itself. It repeats itself. It meanders and wanders and recreates itself. It is more than a simple symbol; it is a way of thinking, a way of living. The circle is our reminder that life is endlessly coming up, experiencing itself, discovering new ways of being, shifting and changing in ways that are difficult to pin down and quantify.

The cycle is the method of thinking most likely to provide insight. We are, in falling into the cycles of Mother, looking at things from all sides, from above and below, delving into them in ways that traditional logic cannot accomplish. The modern Western world is decidedly *logocentric*, meaning that we believe that language can clearly define everything and that logic reigns supreme as the ultimate mode of knowing. Logic is a beautiful thing, but the cyclical and sometimes divergent methods of Mother open us to new revelations that more traditional discourse misses.

Linear thinking is not healthy for most areas that touch our psyche. In some endeavors it can indeed be incredibly helpful. If you're constructing a rocket, for example, or following a recipe. Step A comes before step B and cause X leads to effect Y. Great. But for most of the crucial areas of life, particularly the ones that relate to our mental, spiritual, or psychological wellbeing, strict linear thinking lands us in mental prisons and poisons our ability to heal and develop.

The modern world, unfortunately, adores linear thinking, particularly in cultures with European heritage or touched by Abrahamic religion. Life is not a circle within these worldviews; it is a line, starting from the point of your birth and ending, abruptly and finitely, at the grave. Naturally, this turns life into a race. You must hustle, constantly, or you'll risk missing out on something. You'll risk failing and being mocked. There are no second chances. The New Testament declared that humans are "fated to die once, and then face judgment."[3] There is nothing but the grind and the looming fear of judgmental destiny.

Go! Work! Make a choice! Do it now! There is no rest for the ambitious. Even if it eats you alive, you have to keep going, because your time is running out. Evangelical preachers are infamous for their use of finality to garner converts. Many Christian sermons, in Protestant churches at least, hammer home the idea that we are all one breath away from eternal damnation.

The anxiety of this thinking is bleak. We are hopelessly hurtling towards oblivion or judgment, and all things must end. There are no cycles of becoming and being, only a fired bullet, shot into the void and fizzling out at some predetermined point. Plenty of Western thinkers made the experience of this thinking the central focus of their philosophy. Continental philosophers in particular seem obsessed with the angst of being alive, the looming worry of death. Heidegger, perhaps one of the most controversial of well-known European philosophers,[4] invented a word in German to describe our condition. He called it *Geworfenheit*, which means "thrownness." We are *thrown* into existence. How horrible.

I do believe the influence of Christianity had a lot to do with this development and conceptual framework. Christianity has a concept of an *eschaton*, a word in Greek signifying "the end" or "the last." Eschatology is the branch of theology dealing with the end, with how things wrap up in the story of God and humanity.

Islam has a similar concept of final judgment, and belief in the "Last Day" is a central tenant for devout Muslims. In both traditions, the two largest religions on the planet, there is a definitive end to history, at least in its mortal form. The story will wrap up, at some point, and wherever

---

[3] Hebrews 9:27

[4] For good reason. He publicly supported the Nazi Party to maintain his university position.

the dice fall, they fall there for eternity. It is a suffocating concept.

The Mother is decidedly not this linear, bleak thinking. The Goddess is circular, because we cannot accept the rigid line of blind ambition on a hopeless trajectory. Nor can we accept the decree of a singular religious history that demands that all souls come to an accounting, consigned to flames or paradise as their deeds decree. We rebel, from the very core of our being, against this. Some part of us, some deep part that refuses to succumb to despair, revolts against this thinking.

There is the risk here, of course, of wishful thinking. Detractors to the Mother's way might say that we wish it were true that rebirth guarantees continuance, or that life is a circular, recreating, interconnected thing. This all sounds rather like touchy-feely hopeful nonsense to the nonbeliever. Many existentialist writers believed that facing up to the empty, meaningless slog of life was a decidedly brave and masculine[5] thing to do. It was just so courageous to admit there is nothing behind the clockwork of the cosmos.

Albert Camus, who embodies much of this existentialist thinking, thought religious belief of any kind was a colossal cop-out to facing up to our mortality, to give just one example of such thinkers. Camus, and other existentialists like Sartre, portrayed spiritual belief as infantile. Letting go of your beliefs is something good, strong, intelligent grown-up people do.

I don't necessarily think it's helpful to argue with the prophets of nihilism, but I would turn their accusations back on them. Isn't it just as facile and suspect to think that a linear movement from A to B is all there is? Isn't that a little, well, simplistic? Our experiences tell us otherwise. We have an inborn bent to infinity. Even Nietzsche, perhaps the most hostile-to-belief of the European philosophical tradition, toyed with an idea of "eternal recurrence," not in a literal reincarnation way mind you, but as a deeper concept of endless, cyclical repetition and

---

[5] It is interesting to note the male-centered language of these worldviews. "Man up" is a constant refrain from those who think they are helping us to face up to the difficulties of life.

finding peace within our actions inside of the cycle.[6]

I'm not convinced that the cyclical worldview of Mother is simply there as a comfort. There is something terrifying, something even Nietzsche recognized as unnerving, in the concept of recurrence. There is a swirling, miasma-like continual coming into being and crashing back into the void. The Mother is not just a beautiful, perfect circle. She is Charybdis, the monster of the whirlpool. Chaos is here, and fear.

Eternity is as deeply an unsettling concept as finitude, in many ways. It is not "infantile" comfort to approach the concepts of cyclical rebirth. I think a powerful example of this comes from the scriptures of Buddhism. Even though I am not a Buddhist, I do think there is a lot of pathos and power behind Buddhist scripture's reflection on what it means to cycle through lives:

> *Which is greater, the tears you have shed while transmigrating & wandering this long, long time — crying & weeping from being joined with what is displeasing, being separated from what is pleasing — or the water in the four great oceans?... This is the greater: the tears you have shed..."* [7]

Regardless of the angst-riddled work of theologians, existentialists and the like, or the terror of eternity, Mother's cycles can be a balm to so much of what slows our progress. Anyone who has spent time with a good therapist will tell you to avoid black and white thinking, or absolutes. The circle is the infinite symbol of that knowledge. There is no end, no beginning, only the circle. It can "begin" at any point and once begun, there is no ending. Fighting the flow of nature, going against

---

[6] Nietzsche first explores this in *Die fröhliche Wissenschaft*, usually translated as *The Gay Science*.

[7] "The Round of Rebirth: *samsara*", edited by Access to Insight. Access to Insight (BCBS Edition), 5 November 2013, http://www.accesstoinsight.org/ptf/dhamma/sacca/sacca1/samsara.html.

what Daoism calls *wu wei* (or action through inaction) is a recipe for disappointment. Sometimes we must work our magics in the flow of Mother, rising and falling in time with her tides.

LIFE AND DEATH

The primary cycle we all participate in, regardless of culture, religion, or climate, is the cycle of the lived human experience. We are born. We age. We die. Devotees would add *and are reborn*, but regardless of beliefs surrounding the afterlife, the cycle of the human life is a primary token of the Mother. Within it are contained all her mysteries. There is no stage of life that does not contain her, and yet she is greater than them all.

Childbirth is watched over by the Goddess. As Hera and Eileithyia her daughter, in Greece, or as Lucina in Rome. In Egypt the great monstrous figure of Taweret, part hippopotamus, part lion, part crocodile, watched over childbirth and was the special protectress of midwifery and children.[8] In Egypt we also find the frog-headed Goddess Heqet, who breathes life into children at the last moment of their birth, including being part of the story of Isis, the Goddess Heqet being she who breathes life into Horus. Among the Aztec, Coatlicue was the birther of the stars, the sun, and the moon, and in one of her aspects watched over those who died in childbirth.[9]

None of this is to say that we must associate Mother with physical childbirth, or that someone choosing not to have children, or choosing different methods to be a parent are outside this mystery. Not at all. Birth is also creation, art, and magic. It is the choice to create, to make a mark within the flow of time and space. Mother guards the mysteries of the workshop, the canvas, the flute and piano and horn, just as much

---

[8] Taweret was also depicted in amulets of protection and as a powerful figure across Egyptian magical practice. For more information on the magics of Egyptian deities, see: *Magic in Ancient Egypt* (British Museum Press, 1994) by Geraldine Pinch.

[9] Richard F. Townsend. *The Aztecs* (London: Thames & Hudson, 2009), 136.

as she guards the cradle. But regardless of our own choices, we are all the products of birth.

Outside of birth and creation, the care of the dying has also long been the domain of women, and of Mother. Although embalmers, undertakers, and funeral directors may be seen as predominately a male field, the actual care of those on the verge of death has largely been taken up by women. Most end of life care is the responsibility of women, and research shows that women experience more negative impacts on their wellbeing from the responsibilities of end of life care than men.[10] As women tend to outlive men, the population of the elderly grows more and more populated by women as age increases as well.[11] A dear person in my life, who worked as a hospice nurse for many years, once told me that in the last stages of dying, many patients had one thing in common: they asked for their mother.

Death deities run the gamut between god and Goddess, with many well-known deities associated with the lands of Death or personifications of death being male gods: Anubis, Hades, Thanatos, Osiris, and more. But there are many faces of Mother in the land of death. Ereshkigal, the sister of Ishtar, rules over the Underworld. Persephone is enthroned beside Hades. It is Nephthys and Isis who gather the remains of Osiris, and Isis who breathes new life into her husband, reanimating him with soul and mind. And Nephthys was a protective deity over the embalming process in Egypt and was a guide for the departed as they continued into the complex afterlife of Egyptian belief.

And there are other figures, faces of Mother, that act as harbingers, reminders of our mortality, or associates near the end of life. In Celtic myth, the Morrigan heralds the deaths of warriors and prophesizes the

---

[10] Karla T. Washington et al., "Gender Differences in Caregiving at End of Life: Implications for Hospice Teams," Journal of Palliative Medicine 18, no. 12 (2015): 1048-1053, doi:10.1089/jpm.2015.0214.

[11] Administration for Community Living, "A Profile of Older Americans: 2020," (2020), accessed April 25, 2023, https://acl.gov/sites/default/files/Aging%20and%20Disability%20in%20America/2020ProfileOlderAmericans.Final_.pdf.

fall of Cuchulainn. She is the great and terrible Carrion Crow. Banshees hurl and scream, developing through folklore as the sign of impending doom. Among the Norse, Freyja claims half the slain in battle and Hel rules over the cold and dreary abode of death that bears her name, not a personification of death itself, but landed there as a daughter of Loki; her body is half-corpse.

Image of the Goddess Taweret, ca. 330 BCE, Egypt. Protectress of childbirth. Her form may have been purposefully menacing to frighten away bad spirits or evil from the birthing process. (Met Museum)

Birth and death are both heralded by the Mother. She is present as the watcher, the initiator, the doula, the midwife, the hospice worker, and the dread lady. The messy things of life belong to her—circular, terrifying, and often hidden away. The birthing chamber and the deathbed are hers, equally. The very difficult work of bringing life into the world and sitting with it in the end are under the care of Mother. Even if we are terrified to look into these worlds, our sensibilities and fears triggered, hackles raised at the terror of life and death, Mother still is present.

For me, I take these as truths from Mother: we come from her, and we return to her. That is why she guards the cradle and the coffin. It is a reminder that we affirm the reality and immortality of the soul. We are born into matter, into the body (not a curse, as some would have it!) but it does age, sicken, and die. When that comes, as it will come for all of us, we can remember that her indestructible being makes up a part of our own being, just as much as our failing flesh. We participate in the dance of the Goddess, and that dance cannot die.

AND AFTER...

The devotee, as I said, would add rebirth into the great cycle. Initiates into the mystery cults believed that their devotion ensured a wondrous afterlife. In most records we have of the Underworld in Greek writing, the Underworld is a gloomy fate, full of asphodel fields and lost shades. Hades has no love for the dead, left to rule over a kingdom he did not want. Elysium, the land of the blessed, is reserved for great souls and for the souls of initiates. The rest of the fated dead face something rather, well, *unpleasant*. It seems that a lot of Greek writers did not have a positive outlook on the afterlife. Reading about Greeks and the Underworld makes me think of a quote in Dona Tartt's novel *The Secret History*, where one character says of another that he "had a pagan's gloomy view of death."[12]

Rebirth is a central tenet of my Craft. It is the only definitive thing we really state about death and the afterlife. We acknowledge rebirth as a primary doctrine. This is true in the writings of our progenitors such as Gardner, the Sanders, and others. But beyond that, we do not proclaim concrete dogmas regarding the afterlife. Reincarnation is the stated belief, but with little explanation of the mechanics of that system.

I prefer this, personally, as strict belief surrounding the afterlife can quickly become a carrot and stick control methodology. I also find it presumptuous when someone is sure of the exact specifications of the afterlife. Be very wary of someone who claims to know the path beyond the veil of death better than anyone else. We're all in the dark here.

But that concept of rebirth is something I find central to the worship of Mother. Her cyclical nature, her endless circle of being, is the token, for me, of our promised rebirth. Life as an endless cycle of consciousness incarnating is how I view it—the eternal marriage of flesh and spirit, unifying, separating, and coming back together.

But I think it is most likely far more complex than we think. Outside of material existence, there really is no concept of time, so it's not so much *one thing after another* as much as *everything happening at once*. What sense would it make to call something a "past life" if there is no "past"? I tend to see it instead as all happening in the infinite moment, the dance of Mother.

Regardless of the mechanics, rebirth is not my dogma; it is my hope. Worship of the Mother is hope. It is the succor to our anxiety about death and dying. Mother is the circle, the cycle, the endless beginning. At her shrine, the moment stretches infinite and indestructible. She is oneness with time and the acceptance of change, the glowing dynamism of life. I *hope* for rebirth.

Cicero, writing on the Mysteries of Eleusis, said that through the

---

12   Donna Tartt, *The Secret History* (New York, NY: Vintage Books, 1992), 440.

initiations of the mysteries we "gain, not only the art of living agreeably, but even that too of dying with a better hope."[13] I live within that hope, in the dance of Mother. I agree with Starhawk, who wrote that the Goddess is "the turning spiral that whirls us in and out of existence, whose winking eye is the pulse of being—birth, death, rebirth—whose laughter bubbles and courses through all things..."[14] Our rebirth may be a terrifying prospect, but behind it is that infinite spiral that echoes and reverberates with eternal creation. And yes, even laughter.

THE WIDE WEB OF EARTH

In religious Witchcraft, another cyclical form of worship for Mother is the cycle of the seasons, honored in Craft with the eight Sabbats that make up the Wheel of the Year. These holy days are based on a collection of historical festivals marking the equinoxes, solstices, and quarter days. Outside of initiatory Craft, contemporary Pagan traditions have also taken up this system of Sabbats and often organize their worship around the same framework.

The cycle of the year, regardless of climate or geography, is about understanding our present situation and what has built us to be where we stand and what we can expect or hope for in our futures. As we grow in our technological capacity, we separate ourselves more and more from the agricultural and the pastoral. We do not always know where our food comes from. Many of us exist in a hermetically sealed timeline where we eat fresh fruit in the winter, trucked from many miles away, and obliterate the heat of summer with air conditioning. There is little sense of change if we do not pay attention.

None of this is to suggest that we are supposed to give up the creature

---

[13] Cicero, *Treatises of M.T. Cicero*, trans. by C.D. Yonge (London, UK: Henry G. Bohne, 1853), 445.

[14] Starhawk, *The Spiral Dance: A Rebirth of the Ancient Religion of the Great Goddess* (San Francisco: HarperOne, 1999), 39.

comforts of our lives. I don't think becoming a Luddite is the answer. What I do believe is that Mother is the reminder of our dependency and connection in the biosphere. It is common to refer to "Mother Earth" or to Gaia, but Mother as Gaia is something I believe many devotees misunderstand. If we view Gaia as a foreign concept, something outside of ourselves, then we are missing the point entirely.

18th c. British depiction of dancers around a maypole. Celebrating the fertility of the changing seasons survived, even in Christian Europe. (Met Museum)

Our language uses phrases like *upon the face of the earth* or *on the surface of the earth*. This language leads us to separation. The fact is. We *are* the earth. We are a part of a living, interconnected biosphere. It isn't something "out there" that we can commune with, protect, take care of, or understand as a foreign entity. We participate within it. We are dependent on the web of life, the interplay of atmospheric condition, magnetic field, flora and fauna. Many environmentalists worry that we are destroying the earth, but it might be more accurate to say *we are destroying ourselves*. Cruelty to the planet is not damage done to someone or something else. It is an act of self-harm.

The earth in her entirety is frequently sacralized as a deity, or a divine figure. I've already mentioned Gaia, who was Terra in Rome, but there is also Bhumi in the Indian subcontinent, and Mau Dia in Vietnam, literally: Earth Mother. She is Pachamama among the Indigenous peoples of the Andes Mountain range, and held sacred in many other cultures. The earth as a living mind has even inspired Green-leaning scientists, commentators, and others to the idea of "Gaia Theory" where it is hinted that there is an interconnectedness between the material environment of earth and the evolution of biological creatures.[15] One influences the other.

All of this, in the ecstasy of service to Mother, is about connection. It forms the basis of an ethic, one of reciprocity and interdependence. Harm to the whole is harm to the self. The cycles of Mother are embedded into our world, repeating and refracting across the pattern of Creation. She is the pupa and the chrysalis, the evaporated water and the rain. She is the Golden Rule on a cosmic scale. Not only "do unto others" but "do unto the world" as you would like it done for you or to you.

This may seem a bit of a stretch, to begin this section talking about the Wheel of the Year and end with environmental and interpersonal ethics, but I don't think it is. I truly believe there is an intimate connection between the cycles of the earth we are part of and the ethical, spiritual, and psychological foundations of our being. For me, the knowledge of this connection is expanded, clarified, and experienced in the worship of Mother. Within her ecstasies, I don't just realize there is a web of connection, *I feel it.*

In ecstatic worship, many devotees describe a feeling of being absorbed into a cosmic whole, or what is called "ego death" in many systems. This is a crucial part of countless spiritual traditions. It is the absorption into *samadhi* in Buddhist meditation and the realization of the individual soul and the World Soul as one in the practices of Hindu traditions that

---

[15] The Gaia Theory, also known as the Gaia Hypothesis, was introduced in the 1970s by James Lovelock, Lynn Margulis, and other scientists. Lovelock's 1971 book *Gaia: A New Look at Life on Earth* laid out the main tenets of the theory. It is important to note that the theory has received criticism from some scientists, and that there is a range of opinions within the scientific community about the validity and applicability of Gaia Theory.

draw from nondualism. It is the ocean of love and bliss experienced by Sufi and Catholic saints. It is even the ego death achieved through the consumption of ritual hallucinogens.

This mystical oneness is reflected in our cycles of seasonal change. Each time we honor a turning of the wheel, we are honoring the whole. We are recognizing the evolving, changing nature of life. It is not just Halloween as a death festival that we enact, but Halloween as the reminder that all things must come to decay, and yet without decay there is no life. It is not just that May Day is a festival of fertility and life, but a reminder that life is diverse, clever, and constantly evolving. These festivals and celebrations are chances to worship Mother as the totality of *bios*, the totality of life. We are called, as devotees, to *biophilia*, the love of life and love of the biosphere, in all its terrifying and wondrous glory.

MAKING THE DIFFICULT HOLY

In this chapter, I hope that I've shown how the cyclical, emerging, and evolving nature of the Goddess is a medicine against absolutism and strict linear thought. I do want to highlight, though, how truly difficult it is to break free from these learned ways of thinking. One of the reasons I recommend ecstatic worship is precisely because it often takes something as drastic as transformative, abandoned religious experience to shake loose the learned behaviors that limit us.

One of the major hurdles in this process is the labelling of all "good" things as rational, clean, and upright. Rising with that is the labelling of all things difficult, terrifying, or dark as irrational, dirty, or "evil." Throughout this book I've used words like chaotic, dark, terrifying, and other so-called "negative" words to describe the Goddess. And with those words I have been describing a Goddess of Love, an absolutely transcendent figure in whose creation we participate and grow. There is no contradiction here.

Throughout the history of religion, across cultures, there has been an effort to equate the Goddess with darkness and evil. One of the major themes of patriarchal religion is the conquest of a chthonic, wicked, terrifying female form by a male hero. We see this is in the murder of Tiamat in Mesopotamian mythology, and the fact that Gaia is the mother of monsters and horrors to the Greeks. In many colonialist writings on Kali, or Shaktism in general, the face of Kali represents a base, evil religion that was nothing like the upright, clean, and "logical" Christian faith. There are many more examples of this, and to list them all would take up an entire book in and of itself.

In all of this is the fear of the Goddess and what she represents in her totality, as well as an enormous mountain of misogyny. We fear the Mother because we do not want to die. We fear the Mother because birth can be nerve-wracking and often soaked in blood and danger. We have frequently hoisted all our fears of the darkness and the unknown onto the shoulders of the Goddess (and thus onto the shoulders of women). This has continued into the fairy tales and legends of folklore, into the character of the Witch, the hag, the ogress, and the succubus. All of these are fantasies, foisting the worst of our patriarchal neuroses onto the Mother. We can try to rehabilitate these images, as many do, or we can just accept them.

By accept, I mean we can try to sacralize the difficult. We can make the hard things into holy things. The worship of Mother is the worship of *all* her incarnations and cycles, even those that destroy or horrify. Accepting change is painful and admitting limitations or finality even harder still. But in the cyclical nature of the Goddess, there is a freedom from limitation. We can be our entire selves in her worship, even the versions of ourselves that haunt us or shame us. We can worship her when times are full of laughter and ease, as well as at times where we feel very near the brink of complete destruction. The entirety of her being is the entirety of our devotion. The circle of the Goddess is the reminder of these truths, whether it is a circle for magic or the circle of the season.

CHAPTER 13

FINDING MOTHER IN HOSTILE LANDS
SOPHIA AND OTHER FACES

 The children gather wood, and the fathers kindle the fire, and the women knead their dough, to make cakes to the queen of heaven, and to pour out drink offerings unto other gods, that they may provoke me to anger."

– Jeremiah 7:18

WISDOM BEYOND THE VEIL

I have tried, throughout this book, to speak of the Mother as a lived reality, hopefully showing the continuation of her worship. I hope I have shown how even historical examples, ones we relegate firmly to the past, still live and breathe and thrum with power today, for us. With that hope, I do think it is important to address how difficult it can be to find Mother when the entire paradigm of our world, for many of us, is worked together in systems that deny her. Despite my faith in the Goddess, I realize how much of the world is dominated by religious frameworks that have no truck with the Mother of the Cosmos, or actively try to negate her.

And beyond that, I also want to think of those devotees who are seeking God the Mother, but do not connect necessarily to contemporary Paganism or religious Witchcraft. Not every person who feels the

CHAPTER 13 – FINDING MOTHER IN HOSTILE LANDS: SOPHIA AND OTHER FACES | 217

call of Mother is going to pray to the Queen of Witches, or to pagan Goddesses from pre-Christian pantheons. I have mentioned the living tradition of Shaktism, and there are many faces of Mother in African Diasporic Traditions, but these journeys come with cultural barriers that are difficult to cross for many.

What I hope to achieve here is to show that Mother shines in nearly every spiritual path. We do not have to abandon the frameworks and traditions that we know in order to approach her altar. Even in the most patriarchal faiths, Mother has shone forth, speaking in powerful and paradigm-shifting ways. Across Abrahamic faiths, within Buddhism, and elsewhere, the Mother is present. She is often veiled, or difficult to find, worked into mystical theologies that we must delve into if we wish to explore her mysteries. But she is still very much alive and guiding the faithful.

In this chapter we are going to investigate concepts of God that stand outside of popularly accepted orthodoxy, many of which include a face (or faces) of Mother. One of the most attested faces of Mother in these traditions is Sophia. The name means wisdom in Greek, and her incarnations span across several differing worlds. To Hellenistic philosophers, she was a Goddess-like personification of wisdom itself, at times a being, and at other times a literary turn of phrase. To the sects of early Christianity labelled "Gnostic", she was a central figure in the story of our creation in the material world, and more importantly our salvation from it. And even to Eastern Orthodox Christians, she is a living and breathing fount of spiritual wisdom.

She is a complex concept that is difficult to pin down. Gnostic perceptions of Sophia are radically different than concepts of Sophia by Eastern Orthodox Christians drawn forth in more modern times. Despite these challenges, she still stands as a voice of Mother, growing and breathing within a patriarchal religion that attempts to deny her. But before we look through the veil of Sophia, a few important areas must be covered.

MARY: AN INTERLUDE

> *Remember, O most gracious Virgin Mary, that never was it known that anyone who fled to your protection, implored your help or sought your intercession, was left unaided. Inspired with this confidence, I fly to you, O Virgin of virgins, my Mother; to you do I come, before you I stand, sinful and sorrowful. O Mother of the Word Incarnate, despise not my petitions, but in your mercy hear and answer me. Amen."*
>
> – The Memorare

It may be surprising to some that I chose Sophia and not the Virgin Mary to find the face of the Goddess in an Abrahamic path. The truth is, this is for more personal reasons than anything else. To be clear, the Virgin Mary is indeed, in my opinion, an incarnation of Mother. She is perhaps one of the most worshipped incarnations of Mother alive today. Devotion to Mary is incredibly potent in many communities of Roman Catholic, Orthodox, and Anglican Christians and this devotion inspires incredible works of art, intense pilgrimages, and visionary experiences. Images and incarnations of the Blessed Virgin are also used in many African Diasporic Traditions to represent certain divine figures and spirits. I happen to live in a city with a long tradition of Marian devotion, and prayers are offered to Our Lady of Prompt Succor regularly here.

Mary is also the bearer of so many of Mother's tokens. The moon and stars, the serpent beneath her feet, and the crown upon her head: these are all the symbols of Mother. There are Christian churches dedicated to Maria Maggiore (Great Mary), built in the same cities that once worshipped Magna Mater (Great Mother). And in many Christian communities, she is absolutely the supreme divine figure that touches the hearts of believers—far more than any member of the Trinity. I have been at shrines to the Blessed Virgin, and I have seen the emotional responses of believers as they pray to her. I still remember one of my favorite prayers to Mary from when I was a communicant Catholic, the *Salve Regina*, which begins with "Hail Holy Queen, Mother of Mercy, our life our sweetness and our hope…" What is this, truly, if not a prayer to Mother?

All of that being understood, I still have reservations about finding transformative, ecstatic revelation of Mother in the figure of the Virgin Mary. When I first began my journey to the Mother, I did use a lot of Marian devotion as part of my practice, particularly with art. There are still representations of her in my home, although I have added to them in certain ways to reflect the Goddess I worship. As time has gone on, to be honest, I simply do not feel that connection to the Blessed Virgin I once did. The servile nature of what has been done to her by the clerics of the Church is damaging. Praying for intercession from a figure of absolute submission to the Father (*Let it be done to me according to thy Word*) frankly sours my spirit.

There is also another aspect of Marian devotion that I want to address. Although we associate Mary with being one of the only images of Mother in a male-dominated tradition, she is not really the face of female power per se, but instead something that might be a bit more insidious. Within the long tradition of women mystics in Catholicism, devotion to Mary was not as common as devotion to Jesus. Many women mystics from Catholic history were far more moved by the idea of being a "child of God" or the "bride of Christ" than enamored with Mary, and devotion to Mary was truthfully more popular amongst male clerics and leaders of the Church.[1]

Even today, the most intense Marian devotion in the Catholic Church is frequently found in the most rigidly traditional and conservative branches of the faithful. Anyone who has been in the Latin-Mass-only crowd of the Church knows this. The strictest traditionalist bishops

---

[1] Gerda Lerner, *The Creation of Feminist Consciousness: From the Middle Ages to Eighteen-seventy* (New York, NY: Oxford University Press, 1993), 88-89.

and priests in the Church are frequently the most pointed in their love for Mary, even calling her a "co-redemptrix" with Christ. This trend of entrenched misogyny coexisting with fanatical devotion to Mary is truly remarkable.

Virgin and Child, Joos van Cleve, ca. 1525. The Virgin Mary became the most depicted woman in Christian art, frequently portrayed as an ideal mother. (Met Museum)

And there is a certain sense to this male adoration for Mary. Gerda Lerner argues that devotion to Mary is used to gentrify and sweeten the absolute male-only rule of the Catholic clergy, and I think there is a lot of truth in this.[2] For many priests, bishops, and popes, Mary is the perfect woman: submissive, and perpetually virginal.[3] In theological works, Mary is the inversion of Eve, or the "Second Eve." This is a central concept in much of Christian theology, and it comes with a lot of baggage.

Eve is the tempted, weak, and dishonest creature that is the fault of our fall from Edenic grace. Mary, on the other hand, obeys God entirely with no reservation and is thus the inversion of that original sin. This is pointedly expressed, among many other places, in Paul who says in 1 Timothy, "Let the woman learn in silence with all subjection. But I suffer not a woman to teach, nor to usurp authority over the man, but to be in silence. For Adam was first formed, then Eve. And Adam was not deceived, but the woman being deceived was in the transgression. Notwithstanding she shall be saved in childbearing..."

This theology is a strong barrier to me in approaching Marian devotion as Goddess devotion. If, however, you still feel the pull of Mother in the face of Mary, I would recommend looking into the history and devotion to the black Madonna,[4] or researching folk Catholicism, particularly around female devotees of Mary and other great saints in the Church. I also think it's important to look at growing movements of Catholic women, particularly in the Global South, who are using

---

[2] Ibid.

[3] There have been multiple clarifications of Mary's perpetual virginity in Christian history. Councils of Orthodox and Catholic authorities have consistently declared her perpetually virginal. Even early Protestant works, both Lutheran and Calvinist, mark Mary as eternally virginal. All of this is despite clear references in the New Testament to Jesus having brothers. The level of complex justifications for how the text can give Jesus brothers and yet Mary is perpetually virginal are almost stunning in their desperation to make sure Mary never had sex with Joseph, or anyone else for that matter. Many modern Protestants reject the doctrine entirely.

[4] For more, see: *The Black Madonna in Latin America and Europe: Tradition and Transformation* (University of New Mexico Press, 2007) by Malgorzata Oleszkiewicz-Peralba.

images of Mary in unique ways, mixing their devotion to the Mother of God with activism and a hunger for change. If the transformative and ecstatic Goddess shines within Mary, it definitely shines there.

In the vein of what I've said, I offer this prayer:

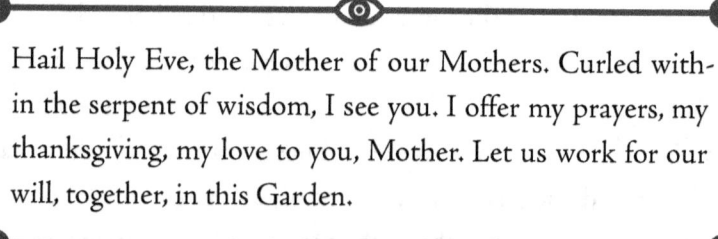

Hail Holy Eve, the Mother of our Mothers. Curled within the serpent of wisdom, I see you. I offer my prayers, my thanksgiving, my love to you, Mother. Let us work for our will, together, in this Garden.

EXTRA ECCLESIAM: OUTSIDE OF THE CHURCH

I also want to take one more detour before we dive behind the veil of Sophia. There are many other rich places of Mother's worship, devotion, and magic available in religious traditions that (on the surface) deny the Goddess. I am not doing a deep dive into them because I am not a member of these traditions. Christian belief I feel comfortable discussing, and with a few caveats Shaktism as well, but unknitting the Mother's presence in traditions that are not my own feels uncomfortable and runs the risk of oversimplification and misrepresentation.

With that worry, I still want to provide some touchpoints for seeking Mother in these worlds. They won't be deep dives, but hopefully I can provide some guidance to devotees. The first place, within Judaism, is the rich mystical tradition of Kabbalah. Despite its popularity as a New Age system, due to certain enterprising individuals, Kabbalah is largely a field plumbed to its depth in Orthodox Jewish communities. Most of the literature we have on Kabbalistic theology comes from quite Orthodox Jews, not from modern reformers. The Orthodox Jewish community is not often a place where we think we would find Mother, but that is not necessarily true.

Within Kabbalah, there is a mystical concept of the *Shekinah*. This word, meaning "dwelling", is the presence of God, and is often personified or visualized in a female form. Although the word appears in traditional rabbinic writing, it is taken to new heights in Kabbalistic thinking. There is also a concept of the "Bride of the Sabbath", at times unified with study of the *Shekinah* and sometimes separated from her. For those that are interested in these concepts, of the *Shekinah* and the *Bride*, diving into Kabbalistic sources provides a rich field of exploration for divine feminine forces within the complex workings of the Godhead in Jewish thought.[5]

Within Buddhism, it can be difficult for seekers to find Mother as well. Theravada Buddhism is still debating whether to continue or reinstate the ordination of nuns, and therefore is a largely male-dominated religious tradition. In the Pali Canon, the scriptures of Theravada Buddhists, women cannot become Buddhas.[6] Most Mahayana Buddhist traditions, on the contrary, do have female voices and leaders, but Buddhism can still be a tradition where finding Mother is difficult. Despite this, there are rich traditions that have developed Mother's voice within the path.

In Mahayana schools, devotion to Guan Yin (addressed elsewhere in this book) is widespread and she has taken on an almost cosmic Goddess-form for many believers. There are also the incarnations of

---

[5] For a more traditional, scholarly look into Kabbalistic thought, see: *Major Trends in Jewish Mysticism* (Schocken Books, 1961) and *On the Mystical Shape of the Godhead: Basic Concepts in the Kabbalah* (Schocken Books, 1991), both by Gershom Scholem. For a more modern and feminist exploration of the Shekinah, see: *On the Wings of Shekhinah: Rediscovering Judaism's Divine Feminine* (Quest Books, 2008) by Leah Novick.

[6] Bhikkhu Sujato, trans., "MN 115: Bahudhātukasutta," Sutta Central, accessed January 4, 2023, https://suttacentral.net/mn115/en/sujato?layout=plain&reference=none&notes=asterisk&highlight=false&script=latin.

Tara, particularly popular in Tibetan Buddhism.[7] Goddess figures, such as Tara, are often worked into complex systems of philosophy and practice in tantric Buddhism. Exploration of Mother in Buddhism will likely be most fruitful in the world of Mahayana Buddhism and tantric Buddhism.

14th century figure of Tara from Nepal. Tara, in Tibetan Buddhism, is a powerful figure who embodies active compassion. (Met Museum)

---

[7] For two accessible works, see: *Tara's Enlightened Activity: An Oral Commentary on the Twenty-One Praises to Tara* (Snow Lion, 2007) by Khenchen Palden Sherab and Khenpo Tsewang Dongyal, as well as *Tara: The Liberating Power of the Female Buddha* (Sounds True, 2020) by Rachael Wooten.

It is also important to note how Buddhism in East Asia is not always defined with rigid doctrinal systems. Many Buddhists in East Asia participate in religious rituals and hold beliefs that draw from folk religion (also called "popular religion"), Shinto, Daoism, Confucianism, and even new religious movements that are eclectic. In China, Salvationist Religions have adherents that number in the millions. Many of the sects and groups within these religions worship a supreme Goddess, a primordial mother of the cosmos. This Goddess is linked with Daoist and folk religion figures such as Doumu, the mother of the stars that make of the big dipper, or Xi Wang Mu, the Queen Mother of the West who holds the peaches of immortality. Mazu, the Goddess of the Sea, is also widely worshipped across Chinese communities.

And in Japan, Shinto has a long history of intertwining with Japanese schools of Buddhism. Many Shinto shrines are dedicated to female *kami* (divinities) such as Amaterasu and Inari.[8] Within Japan, Shinto beliefs and Buddhist dharma weave and integrate across the lives of many believers. Unique figures exist in Japanese religious practice such as Benzaiten, a Goddess associated with the arts and eloquence. She originated in the mention of certain Hindu deities in Buddhist scriptures, such as Saraswati, but developed into her own unique being within Japanese religious life. She is a perfect example of how fluid religion can be: an originally Hindu concept of the divine, brought to a largely Shinto, *kami*-worshipping culture, by Buddhist texts and missionaries.

Outside of these traditions, there are other places I recommend looking for Mother within more traditional spiritual communities. One is the tradition of female saints worshipped in unique communities of believers, such as Saint Sarah (or Saint Sara e Kali) among the Romany people, and the traditions of visionary saints such as Teresa of Avila, Hildegard of Bingen, and Catherine of Sienna. Female saint

---

[8] For a solid dive into Shinto, see: *Shinto: A History* (Oxford University Press, 2016) by Helen Hardacre. There are many powerful faces of Mother in Shinto practice, and it is an often-neglected tradition by Western seekers.

worship was often a place where devotees could find reprieve from an almost obsessively male paradigm. Hopefully these avenues provide rich resources for your journey, but now we dive behind the veil of Sophia.

SOPHIA AND THE GNOSTICS

 Then the mother began to move. She knew about the lack when the radiation of her light diminished. And she grew darker, for her consort had not come into harmony with her. [9]

—The Apocryphon of John

The Gnostics are not a unified group, and it is crucial to remember that they are the losing side in the history of Christianity. Much of what we know about them was written by their detractors, Christians who called themselves "orthodox" and denounced the Gnostics as heretics. The Gnostics did not see themselves as some foreign cult, separate from the teachings of Christ. Many of them just saw themselves as Christians, and they believed that their systems, ideas, and theologies were completely within the Christian faith.

It also is crucial to note that the term "Gnostic" is not referencing any particular unified theology. The word may be somewhat useless as an identifier, as unknitting what was "Gnostic" and what was just "extracanonical" can get very complicated, and the term has been used by modern theologians to paint any worldview or theology they hate (from secular worldviews to specific Christian denominations) as "Gnostic."[10] Despite this, there are collections of texts that seem to share common strains of belief and religious practice that we might put under this

---

[9] Bentley Layton, ed., *The Gnostic Scriptures: A New Translation with Annotations and Introductions, Second Edition* (New Haven, CT: Yale University Press, 2021), 44.

[10] For a solid overview, see: *The Gnostics: Myth, Ritual, and Diversity in Early Christianity* (Harvard University Press, 2012) by David Brakke.

shifting umbrella of "Gnostic thought."

Gnostic scriptures vary greatly, with each group's scriptures containing unique worldviews and complex explanations of the relationship between human beings, God, Jesus, Sophia, and salvation. There are some well-studied examples of Gnostic belief, such as Valentinians, but they do differ a lot in how they approach the faith. Despite this diversity, Sophia is a major being in the *dramatis personae* of much of the corpus of Gnostic texts.

Most Gnostic systems work from a concept called the *pleroma*. This word in Greek means "fullness" and it is the designation for the totality of the divine powers, including God, Christ, angels, and unique figures that only exist within Gnostic belief, such as the Aeons and an even wider array of cosmic characters with unique and semantically packed names. All of these beings participate, really, in one being: God. God is a wonderfully complex and full concept in Gnostic thought. Among this *pleroma*, or standing in relation to it, is Sophia.

How Sophia comes to be differs depending on the text, but most of the accounts center around the process of creation and the emanation of creation from a perfect, unknowable God that is beyond all designations such as gender or representation. This perfect mind or being emanates various entities, one of which is Wisdom, or Sophia. Many other emanations also bear the titles of "Mother" including spirits that are simultaneously Mother and Father. Chief amongst these Father-Mother figures is the Barbelo, the first emanation of God, which is an androgynous, nearly supreme being. But the last emanation, in many systems, is Sophia.

Sophia attempts to go forth and create without a mate, alone, in secret, or in some other fashion that does not fit into the cosmology correctly, and...disaster strikes. She unwittingly creates material reality, and in doing so, a figure known as the Demiurge emerges. This figure is often named Yaldabaoth.

Many Gnostic sources believe the God of the Hebrew Scriptures is this Demiurge, and that it is unworthy of our worship. In some systems, this Demiurge is simply ignorant, but in other systems is purposefully and willfully malevolent. Material reality is, in most Gnostic schools, a trap for spirit or the true light of divinity, and it is ruled over by a false tyrant. Our goal, as seekers, is to escape this false reality and participate in the real fullness of God from which we all originate.[11]

Sophia, realizing the mistake she made that led to her fall, hopes to save the souls that will be trapped in the material realm. With help from other beings of the divine worlds, she convinces the Demiurge to breathe into the first created humans. What is breathed out by the Demiurge is actually the divine spark that originates from Sophia (and ultimately, from the Supreme Godhead). The Demiurge had stolen it from Sophia, its Mother. In this act, Sophia creates a pathway back to the Divine for created human beings.

There are many issues with this story as a devotee of Mother, principally the issue of Gnostic disdain for the body, and for materiality. I have written elsewhere that I believe the Mother's worship requires a love for our bodies, an appreciation for our incarnation as a blessing from Mother and not a curse to escape. All that being said, I still believe there is power in the Gnostic Sophia for the seeker of Mother, particularly a seeker who still feels connection to the Christian story.

The power here is that the story of our journey to salvation (wholeness) is *incomplete* without Sophia. Reading the text, it may seem at first glance to be all about the redemption of Sophia, but remember it is Sophia that provides our route back to salvation and completion through her acts of redemption. Outside of Sophia, the story is incomplete. That is the power of Mother within this story. Despite my reservations about the anti-material and anti-body rhetoric, at the very core we are reminded that Mother is a necessary piece of our spiritual

---

[11] Christian theologian David Bentley Hart has written a novel based on the Gnostic *Hymn of the Pearl* that I recommend to anyone interested in Gnostic thought. *Kenogaia (A Gnostic Tale)* (Angelico Press, 2021).

fulfilment. The lone figure of a male god cannot bring us to salvation, to union with the divine. Sophia must be a part of the equation, or the cosmic mathematics do not balance. The entire Gnostic worldview, in many of its constituent schools, requires the emanations of God to be in sacred union. Mother is a necessity in this view.

One of my teachers once said to me that the patriarchy's image of God, alone and with no Goddess, is "diseased." I tend to agree. Sophia is the medicine of Mother, the eternal wisdom and the mediatrix of the World Soul. For those that find Mother, even in the Christian faith, Sophia stands as the heart of Mother, the opening of holy wisdom and the blessed union that conquers the chasm between us and the divine, collapsing it into the beatific vision. Exploring the rich Gnostic corpus of texts, and their dizzying but also, at times, deeply moving theology, is a rich field for devotees of Mother.

THE ORTHODOX SOPHIA

It surprises some Western Christians to discover that the Eastern Orthodox Church has a concept of Sophia. If we do know of Sophia in this context, it is usually in the name of the church in Istanbul, Hagia Sofia (holy wisdom), that was the jewel of Byzantine Christianity and was turned into a mosque by the Ottomans. But it is true that there is a spiritually significant concept of Sophia that survives in Eastern Orthodoxy, a version that is little known by Western Christians.

Part of the reason for the ignorance is that Eastern Orthodoxy is still seen as truly foreign to many Western Christians. Many believers are still unaware that it represents the second largest branch of Christianity in the world. Orthodox theology, never having lost its use of Greek, carried on many ideas and concepts of early Christianity and Greek philosophy that are not as pronounced in Western sources.

Latin Christianity, including the Roman Church and the Protestant churches that split from it, is far more inspired by the writings of

Augustine of Hippo and later theologians in a European context than Orthodoxy is. Orthodoxy still retains a very different theological approach to the Christian story, one that is somewhat less legalistic and more focused on the union of human beings with God. This process is called *theosis* in Eastern Orthodoxy, the act of becoming one with God.

Orthodox icon of Holy Wisdom (Sophia), portrayed as a winged female beneath Christ and surrounded by angels and other sacred figures. (Wikimedia Commons)

This has led to a certain mystical tradition still very much at the heart of Eastern Orthodoxy. They refer to the sacraments as "mysteries" and methods of contemplative prayer are very common across the Orthodox world. Monasticism still guides the churches of the East in ways that it simply does not in the West. Eastern Orthodox bishops, for example, are usually pulled from monastic communities and have spent time in communal, contemplative life.

This split between the churches, dating back to a schism between Rome and Constantinople, has led to a disconnect between the traditions that has only grown with time, particularly with the rise of Protestantism. Orthodoxy has developed unique theological traditions and ideologies that the rest of global Christendom are usually unaware of, and one of these is Sophia.

Historically, the Orthodox Sophia was the embodiment of God's wisdom, not the Gnostic being I described above. It is important not to conflate these two visions of Sophia. Orthodox churches and iconography represented Wisdom, or Sophia, in art and liturgy. As time developed, Sophia began to take on a mystical connotation, becoming a living representation of God's wisdom as it works through creation.

This vision of Sophia reached new heights in Russian Orthodox mystical writings in the late 19th and early 20th centuries. Writers and theologians began to speak of Sophia almost as a living being, consubstantial with the Trinity and perhaps even equal to it. The writings of Orthodox mystics created an entire field, Sophiology, for the study of Sophia, or Holy Wisdom, within the context of Christian life. This movement became so popular and its teachings so controversial that the leader of Russian Orthodoxy, the Patriarch of Moscow, delivered an official condemnation to one of the most vocal proponents of Sophia, Sergei Bulgakov.

Bulgakov and other writers such as Vladimir Solovyov wrote of Sophia in conjunction with Mary as a figure that comes off to many readers as something akin to a Goddess, something equal to the Triune

God. Orthodox Christians refer to Mary as *Theotokos*, which means "God-bearer", a title similar to the Mother of God title given to Mary in Catholicism (*Mater Dei*). This union of Sophia with the Theotokos made more conservative Orthodox Christians uncomfortable as it veered into (in their mind) dangerous territory, territory where a divine woman was equal to God, participating in the act of creation and the sanctification and salvation of believers.

Regardless of whether the writers intended to birth the Mother in their works, the works themselves are potent examples of Mother-centered mysticism, particularly in a religion so devoid of the Goddess as Christianity. For any Christian seeker of Mother, or even someone who still feels rooted in their Christian past or family, I highly recommend diving into the mystical works of Sophiology.[12] The union of divine wisdom with the Trinity is a beautiful and deep tradition of Christian mysticism where I truly believe the face of Mother is present.

UNVEILING AND EXCAVATING

Sophia as the mind of Mother, the wisdom of creation, weaves throughout Christianity. To the devotee of Mother raised in churches where the position of women in authority stands at an absolute zero, this can be a doorway, a path, an unveiling of the Mother that provides succor to the soul and new ways of seeing the work of God alive in the world. She is present, even when we do not see her on the surface, a veiled Mother but a necessary one.

For many seekers, finding the ecstasy of belief and transformation requires an enormous amount of unlearning. We must unlearn the bad habits, linguistic tricks, and agenda-laden theologies of our upbringing and culture. Searching for Mother is excavation, at times. This has

---

[12] For starting points, see: *Divine Sophia: The Wisdom Writings of Vladimir Solovyov* (Cornell University Press, 2009) by Judith Deutsch Kornblatt, as well as *Sophia: The Wisdom of God* (Lindisfarne Books, 1993) by Sergei Bulgakov.

expressed itself in many ways throughout the work of theologians and devotees in traditions that deny Mother. There are historians and archaeologists finding the worship of Asherah in the history of the Hebrews, and Christians attempting to find the face of God the Mother in the work of salvation.[13]

Goddess figurine, 8th-7th c. BCE, which may represent a consort of Yahweh. (Met Museum)

---

[13] For an example of a seminal work in feminist theology, see: *Sexism and God-Talk: Toward a Feminist Theology* (Beacon Press, 1983), by Rosemary Ruether.

There will always be the accusations that the search for Mother in traditional religions implies that we are inventing her or putting her into systems that are not her own. These accusations can be correct, reminding us to check ourselves in our search. They are often, though, nothing more than misogynistic anger and staid traditionalism.

Marked efforts to deny the Mother drive many to purge her presence from their worship and their faith. There is also an insidious work at play when we are accused of "limiting God" by worshipping the Goddess. As Carol Christ writes, "Many state that the God they worship is neither female nor male…However, most people become flustered, upset, and even angry when it is suggested that the God they know as 'Lord' and 'Father' might also be called 'God the Mother' or 'Goddess.' This shows that they unconsciously accept the familiar image of God as male."[14]

We all come to the spiritual search with a bag of biases, learned mistrusts, and embedded agendas. This is unavoidable. Unlearning these biases is painful work at times, and we can be reticent or even oppositional to looking at what we think we know as true and opening it up to scrutiny, or new ways of thinking. Sometimes, we will carry with us the learned religious teachings of our childhood, or the dominant culture of our upbringing. Other times, we will convince ourselves that we are being "more spiritual" or "clearer" by "going beyond" traditional views of God, only to realize that we are in fact only parroting the very prejudices we are claiming to avoid. Carol Christ's quote above hits on this.

If the search for the divine can only happen under God the Father, or in a nebulous view of God that goes beyond all image and name, but never in God the Mother, then I challenge you to examine this more deeply. To call on the Goddess specifically is to invoke something unique. Starhawk once wrote, "The mystery, the paradox, is that the Goddess is not 'she' or 'he'—or she is both—but we call her 'she' because to name is not to limit or describe but to invoke. We call her in and a

---

[14] Carol P. Christ, *Rebirth of the Goddess: Finding Meaning in Feminist Spirituality* (New York, NY: Routledge, 1997), 23.

power comes who is different from what comes when we say 'he' or 'it.' Something happens, something that challenges the ways in which our minds have been shaped..."[15]

A humorous example of how this language of God the Father can dominate is found in the Catechism of the Catholic Church. The Catechism states that God is beyond all concepts of gender with a line that is worth looking at. It states: "**He** is neither man nor woman: **He** is God" (Emphasis mine).[16] Look at this sentence. Even in a paragraph that waxes on how God is so far beyond all of our petty human distinctions, God is still he, even in a sentence that is stating that God is beyond he or she. No matter what, we cannot escape it.

Sophia, and the other touchpoints mentioned in this chapter, are the tokens of Mother, reminding us that the story is incomplete without her mysteries. Even in the depth of Abrahamic religion, Mother is present. Everywhere she sings, everywhere she brings the work of her mysteries into the cycle of faith and the hunger for revelation. If you are called to the teachings and narrative power of Christianity, or other traditions, do not think that Mother cannot be found within your faith. She is found everywhere.

> *As a mother comforts her child,*
>
> *so will I comfort you;*
>
> *and you will be comforted over Jerusalem."*

-Isaiah 66:13

---

[15] Ibid, 24.

[16] *Catechism of the Catholic Church*. 2nd ed. Libreria Editrice Vaticana, 2000. Accessed January 4, 2023, https://www.vatican.va/archive/ENG0015/__P9M.HTM.

CHAPTER 14
GODDESS CIRCLES
SEEKING MOTHER IN GROUPS

 "I come pure from the pure, Queen of the Underworld…
for I too claim to belong to your blessed family…" [1]
– From an Orphic tablet

ONE TO MANY

For many seekers, finding a community opens up new and incredible pathways for development and fulfillment. There is no horror in solitary practice, but for many of us it simply does not provide the power and connection that worshipping and working rites in a group bring. For me, initiation was the most potent act I could've chosen to do on my path, and my spiritual development has hinged on the fellowship of initiates that I dance with, worship with, and carry on in my teaching and work.

Finding Mother in private devotion and ecstatic personal ritual is a beautiful thing, but to share that experience with others feels so different. There is an electric pulse behind group ritual, especially when it is done well. Continual return to a practice provides a framework, a system of discipline, and a world where you can expand your path and learn habits that affect you in transformative ways.

---

[1] Stephen Instone, *Greek Personal Religion: A Reader* (Liverpool, UK: Liverpool University Press, 2009), 76.

Much of this is central to spiritual development across lines of organized religions and traditions. The act of negotiating your own ego with other egos is a crucial task for any seeker. Echo chambers can be dangerous, where we are trapped in our own way of thinking, and we are never challenged to push up against the ideas and opinions of others. When our practice never extends beyond our own skin, we run the risk of limiting our magic, limiting our development.

There is also the connection to an egregore, or shared spiritual reality, in group work. United belief is a powerful thing, and it propels the soul forward. We can drink from a deeper well when many people are digging it and that well is less likely to run dry if many souls and minds are continually refilling it. Initiation is also a deep part of the traditions of Mother that I've examined in this work. I have continually drawn from the initiatory mystery cults of the Mother, and they are all unified in their belief in the transformative power of initiation. This is just as true in other lineages, such as African Diasporic Traditions, Tantra, and many others.

With that in mind, I want to address how you can go about evaluating a group, seeking initiation, or even working within a non-initiatory group to worship Mother and seek her mysteries. We all hunger for community, primed as we are by evolution to seek it. We may honor lone, hermit mystics, and individual magical practitioners working their rites in secret in locked towers and private rituals, but we also desire to extend our worship, to see it reflected back in the face of the metaphorical and psychological *Other*. Collective magic is potent.

CRAFT

Initiatory Craft, including Alexandrian and Gardnerian Witchcraft, is a religion devoted to the Goddess and her consort, the Horned God. I myself am an Alexandrian initiate, and these two systems are still alive and thriving at the time of writing, continually doing the work and providing doorways into the mysteries. If you seek initiation into this Craft, look for a lineaged coven and reach out to the High Priestess or High Priest of that coven. Covens that claim these lineages should be able to provide information on their lineage, and there are groups within social media and elsewhere that are available to help you. It is pretty easy to smell out a fraud, to be honest, and the community is present enough to provide a system of checks and balances for seekers.

Craft is a priesthood, and operates solely on an initiatory basis, with much of the religious beliefs and practices resting within an oathbound circle. If you feel drawn to seeking initiation, and are looking for resources, I recommend looking into the texts and works of the founding voices of the traditions, including Gerald Gardner, Alex and Maxine Sanders, Patricia Crowther, Lois Bourne, and Doreen Valiente. Alexandrian High Priest Brian Cain has also written a book specifically for seekers of initiatory Witchcraft.[2] For a Gardnerian perspective, High Priestess Thorn Mooney has written an introductory work as well.[3] There are also taped interviews, available online, with many of these founders and elders.

One important note is that charging for initiation in Craft is forbidden, so any group that demands money for initiating you is not operating in good faith within the traditions of Alexandrian or Gardnerian Witchcraft. Money may be used for festivals, or supplies, or other such things, but paying for the rite of initiation is not a part of these lineages.

OTHER PATHS: FLAGS, RED AND GREEN

There are many other groups that worship Mother available in the wide community of self-identified Witches, Pagans, magical practitioners, and spiritual seekers. I cannot speak to every incarnation of contemporary

---

[2] Brian Cain, *Initiation into Witchcraft* (New Orleans, LA: Warlock Press, 2019).

[3] Thorn Mooney, *Traditional Wicca: A Seeker's Guide* (Woodbury, MI: Llewellyn Publication, 2018).

Goddess worship, but I can provide what I believe to be healthy guidance to seeking out a group for spiritual development.

The first is to see if the group has a healthy dynamic between participants. Be leery of groups that feel domineering or engage in personality worship of a central figure. Look for dialogue among members of the group and watch out for signs of stifled opinion, or cruelty. Cult-like behavior should be a red flag to any spiritual tradition. Look to see if the people speaking for and living within the group are functioning well, growing, and embodying the values that matter to you.

And this also brings up a complex concept which is money. As stated above, my Craft (and the Gardnerian tradition as well) do not charge for initiation or education in the mysteries. This is not true for other traditions, such as many African Diasporic Traditions like Santeria, or Haitian Vodou. This can become a complex debate. I am not going to disparage any tradition that charges for initiation, but it is a practice unknown to me. My only real advice is to question anything that is going to be financially ruinous for you, or a serious drain on your resources. Spiritual knowledge should not put you in dire straits.

The New Age has also produced a lot of scams, to be frank, and I advise extreme caution with any group that continually goes for your wallet. I'm not talking about paying to attend a class, get a reading, participate in a festival, or similar situations. Spaces must be rented, food and refreshments purchased, and more. People have to eat. But when the constant pull at cash resources becomes a central issue, you're in dangerous territory and most likely falling prey to someone operating in bad faith.

I also want to provide a litmus test that I hold dear: look for shared leadership with women. If you step into a tradition that honors the Goddess, in theory, but there are no women around, then this is a problem. If the entirety of a tradition is men, with no women in any positions of authority, then it doesn't really matter how beautiful their liturgies to the Great Mother are, they're probably going to be hollow prayers. Shared opportunity for leadership is crucial. If the group you're seeking or looking into has a crowd in leadership that looks no different from a Roman Catholic seminary, then question that. And be leery of any group that treats feminism as a dirty word, or looks down their nose at feminist scholars, writers, artists, or spiritual teachers. Again, if a group gives lip service to the Goddess, but mocks or belittles feminist scholarship or feminist consciousness-raising, then they most likely are not worshipping the Goddess, but instead a patriarchal fantasy.

Also watch out for dangerous practices that uphold discriminatory practices, but often word them in careful and insidious ways. Within the world of Heathenry, or Asatru, which is a tradition formed in worship of Germanic deities such as the gods of the Norse, there is a history of racial ideologies that are exclusionary to people of color and even many that are based in outright white supremacy. Thankfully, many believers in this movement are speaking out adamantly against these movements and groups, but said groups are still present even though they are in the minority. Look out for those that describe their practice as "folkish" which is often the euphemism for racist used by these people. These ideologies are also present in certain reconstructionist movements, such as those that work within Slavic Paganism.

Finally, I want to speak a little about correspondence training and in-person worship and work. Correspondence groups have actually been a part of the magical community for some time, now. Major organizations that have helped to shape and teach within the world of "occultism" or magic and divination include Servants of the Light, Builders of the Adytum, the Ordo Aurum Solis, and more. These groups often teach through correspondence, but also include opportunities for in-person ritual work.

I am writing after the COVID-19 pandemic, and the experience of quarantines and distance learning and work-from-home culture that has developed because of that. This has propelled the idea of correspondence learning back into the central discussion of spiritual groups and seekers. I don't think there is anything wrong with correspondence-based learning, but I do believe it is a separate thing from worshipping and working ritual with other humans in the flesh.

As I've stated throughout writing, the Goddess is alive in our bodies. The Mother is spirit and body, working as one, animating our practice and enlivening our rituals. This experience is almost impossible to recreate digitally. That does not mean, in any way, that learning cannot happen at a distance. It very much can. But if you are hungry for something transformative, I encourage you to seek out practice with others, sharing space together. Even if you do decide to study through a correspondence system, try and look for opportunities for in-person ritual.

PARANOIA: THE MOTHER OF RED FLAGS

All of the above is meant to provide a little guidance to those who want to work within a group or seek a tradition. Many of these red and green flags hinge on the health and respect present within a spiritual organization, and I believe that perhaps the greatest concept I want to highlight is that of paranoia.

Any group that works from a place of paranoia is most likely unhealthy. What I mean by this is the unfortunate presence in our communities of those that prey on the nervous paranoia of seekers. It is an ugly little truth that many "practitioners" operate by convincing seekers that they are cursed, or maligned in some way, and that only a series of rituals, initiations, or costly exercises will save them from their fate. It is not uncommon, in circles of magical practitioners or psychics, to find those that tell you that you will need to be "cleansed" of a familial or generational curse to find healing or prosperity.

I want to be firm and clear: this is nonsense. The concept of a "generational curse" is a control mechanism and a fraud, used to bleed people of money. I do not believe in curses that carry through the bloodlines of innocent seekers that only some gifted guru or seer can remove for you, and only if you hand over gifts or large sums of cash. I say this all as someone who does readings for others, and as highlighted earlier in this book, believes in their potency.

To be specific, I am not talking about rituals of cleansing or grounding that exist in many traditions and can be enriching and transformative acts for believers and devotees. I am talking here of promises of healing you and fixing all the difficulties of your life with one ritual to remove some deep, dark, and ill-defined curse hanging over your head from the past. It gets even more ridiculous when the "curse" in question is from what some call "past life trauma." If someone tells you that they know your past lives, and that the challenges in your current situation come from one of these lives and only they can help you remove that negative karma (for a fee) …walk away. Walk fast.

I also want to speak of paranoia in a larger sense. If you are seeking for transformative religious and spiritual experiences, be wary of groups or leaders that seem to focus almost exclusively on vengeance and unending talk of enemies. I hope none of these warnings seem hyperbolic, because they come from my years in these communities, and I have seen their effects on so many seekers. I have lost count of how many seekers I've known who seek magic, or transformation, or mystical experiences, and end up obsessed with cursing, paranoid worries, and a laundry list of those they think are secretly working against them. If your entire spiritual life is made up of putting nails in jars to curse your neighbors, who you just *know* are working against you, then I do not think it is problematic to worry about what's really going on there.

None of this is meant to say that I don't believe in these forms of magic, or that they're always indicative of a problem. But the constant rhetoric of attacking enemies, protecting yourself from a host of negative influences, and cleansing your home and space of outside influence, is a recipe for paranoia and bitterness. Cleansings and ritual purifications make up the foundation of many approaches to spirituality, but they are one part of the mosaic, not the entire image.

And the deeper risk of these paranoid practices is that they can create a false sense in the seeker that all of your problems are outside of yourself. If many things are going wrong for you, it is a little too easy to state that all of them are the result of black magic or generational curses. It is a cliché bit of wisdom, but true nonetheless, to say *if you smell something vile everywhere you step, check the bottom of your own shoes.* Blaming something outside of yourself for every challenge you face means you will never take responsibility for your own actions, and you will never gather up the courage and resolve to work on yourself.

Spiritual development should not absolve you of the responsibility for seeking ways to improve your station and find contentment and fulfillment through your practice. The desire to avoid this responsibility is the major reason I believe the situations and beliefs I've highlighted here are so popular in the community. It is so tempting to believe that our failings, or difficulties, or missteps, are the fault of some force outside of ourselves. It is the black magic worker, or the past life trauma we carry, or the secret enemies we cannot see, or the spirit guides, or the ghosts and hauntings, or the demons. It's anything but us. Never us. We're blameless. This is not spirituality. It's cowardice. Sometimes, seeker, it's you. You're the problem. So fix it, as best you can.

And all of this often encourages seekers to forgo treatments and approaches to healthy living and well-being that are important. Any tradition that convinces you to forgo doctors, or therapists, is unhealthy. Magic, spirituality, transformation, ecstasy…none of these require you forgo mental or medical healthcare. Rituals of cleansing, empowerment, and devotion are transformative and healing. So is penicillin. So is cognitive behavioral therapy.

WAITING

If you make the decision to find a group, or to seek initiation, it can be a daunting task. Initiation into Craft in particular is a commitment to a living priesthood, a growing and breathing tradition of interconnected communities and lineage. It should not be taken lightly. The rise of unique spiritual communities that promise reward or enlightenment has continually grown in the modern world, many of them stemming from the 60's and from the countercultural movements that exploded onto the scene in that time. There has also been the growth in the Western world of traditions and religions that were once excluded from mainstream discourse. This explosion has led to the seeking of initiation, or a community, as something akin to picking up a new hobby, something quirky or fun that you can decorate your personality with or learn a few new tricks.

Nothing could be further from the truth. Initiation, regardless of the tradition, is a monumental experience when approached in its fullness. The very concept of initiation stems from traditions that involved the whole person, body and spirit, and came with oaths and responsibilities that pushed the seeker to transformation and revelation. They are fountains of power, and deep cisterns full of collected wisdom. To worship, grow, and commit to others is akin to a sacred marriage, or a love affair.

And there is nothing wrong with waiting for that experience. Take your time in deciding where your soul feels called in service to Mother. She is not going anywhere. Her mysteries flow from a source that cannot be depleted. Rushing into something meant to transform your life with little forethought is rarely a good idea.

And in the time of waiting, you are not closed off from the Goddess. This concept of waiting refers to commitment to initiation or group practice, not to service to the Mother. Continue in your prayers and rituals and honor the faces of Mother that are revealed to you. The deeper you explore the ecstasy of her devotion, the more you prepare yourself for whatever lies beyond the veil of your current experience. Allow yourself to fall in love, again and again, with Mother. Give in to the deepest call at the core of your being, the one that slips you from momentary time into the ocean of bliss, the endless sea of Mother. There, on the waves of that infinite moment, you will find the strength to go forward and seek her in the grotto, in the hollow mountain, in the circle of the Witches or the temples of the devotees.

INTO THE WORLD

The last thing I want to stress in this chapter is the importance of a lived faith existing *in the world*. The occult, Witchcraft, and Pagan communities do not have a strong track record of community service, or a shared and robust ethic of charity. Members of traditional religious institutions and their believers give far more to charity (both money and volunteer hours) than those people who either have no religious affiliation or perhaps only a personal, spiritual ethic. Traditional religious groups are, in the United States at least, the bulwark of non-governmental social services that benefit the poor, the oppressed, and those who are victims of the inequality and horrors of our world.

We, as devotees of the Great Mother, should not balk at charity, and think that the work of more traditional religions is negated because they espouse views we find hateful or bigoted. To be clear, we should absolutely call out those ignorant beliefs, but we should also make account for their charitable work and why we can't seem to equal it. We should put our money and time where our mouths are, frankly. I understand that we have not met Christian or Jewish institutions' levels of charitable giving and philanthropy because we have smaller numbers, but that is not the entire story.

Those seeking alternative religious or spiritual paths are often completely focused on self-betterment. Many who come to the Goddess, to Craft or Paganism, are victims themselves. They experience trauma from past bullying, much of it from religious fundamentalists, and many of us have always felt like outcasts. And so, the religious and spiritual groups that have grown in contemporary times around Paganism, Craft, etc. have all focused intently on our own healing, self-betterment, and personal empowerment. That's a wonderful thing, but it also can evolve over time into plain old-fashioned self-centeredness and selfishness. Sometimes, the greatest healing you can do for yourself is to be of service to others. Service only to yourself is a recipe for depression, detachment, and poor social skills.

We also tend to focus, I have noticed, on very large systemic issues, but rarely on the daily problems around us. Many Pagans, Witches, and Goddess devotees are deeply concerned about the environment and women's rights, for example. But wearing a button that says "Hex the Patriarchy!" is not the same thing as volunteering your time or money to the local shelter. A bumper sticker or social media post that says "The Earth is our MOTHER" is not as useful as donating your weekend to cleaning up a local area of pollution, or campaigning for political change (again…with actual time, or money, not just good vibes).

I am as guilty as anyone and I am not saying that I don't fall down the self-reflective trap myself. We all do. Our spirituality is so personal, and our groups so fractured and bickering, that it is often very difficult to find a path to actually helping our fellow humans. But I believe we must help our fellow humans. I believe in the Goddess. And that belief means that I must see the Goddess in all of Creation, including the poor, the abused, the asylum-seekers, the hungry, the imprisoned, and the ill.

The last pagan emperor of Rome, Julian (we met him earlier) once wrote a letter to an administrator bemoaning the fact that the old "Hellenic" (Pagan) religion did not provide enough charity and that Christians were far better at helping the disenfranchised.[4] I worry that nothing has really changed in our contemporary situation. So many

---

4   Julian, "Letter to Arsacius," In *The Works of the Emperor Julian*, vol. 3, edited by Wilmer Cave Wright (Cambridge, MA: Harvard University Press, 1923), 256.

solitary Pagans, Witches, and Goddess worshippers are so put off by groups and community, so monomaniacally focused on self-betterment, that they struggle to put their faith into action, to show the love of the Goddess to the world. We must fight this.

Finding a group is about religious experience, of course, but it also about your faith and practice becoming a real and tangible thing that you can work into the world. We need to reexamine our ethics and understand that if we believe in the love of the Mother, then we must be vehicles and embodiments of that love. If the only charity that our cities and communities have comes from Baptists or Pentecostals, then we have zero right to complain about why those churches are full and we feel so alone. Maybe you think that those churches hold views you find detestable, and your spiritual path is oh-so-more-enlightened than theirs. Is it really? If it's just a personal tool to make yourself feel better, superior, or cleverer than the people actually getting their hands dirty to help, well…that's a problem.

I know that I am being very strident here, but I find it the place I am most frequently disappointed in the wide net of believers in the Goddess, in magic, in Witchcraft or Pagan traditions. There is just so much hyper-individualist pop-psychology and so little community. So little charity. So little actual service. We are the living altars of the Mother, and our lives should bear out some level of service to her children. All her children. I worry that we fall short here.

I do want to put forward, however, that there are of course exceptions to this, exceptions that may serve as examples. The co-founder of my own tradition, Maxine Sanders, once led her coven in the care of the dying, often taking care of outcasts who had nowhere else to go at the end of their lives. Lilith Dorsey, whose books on African Diasporic Traditions I have recommended elsewhere in this work, has started a local community garden in my city and also is an active and vocal campaigner for justice and equality. There are many other examples, but they often struggle against resources, community in-fighting, and other hangups.

So, even if you do not wish to join a particular tradition or practicing group of fellow believers, please still consider how you can engage with your own community. Find opportunities to volunteer with others, religious or not, it doesn't matter. Find causes that you can donate to if you are able or give your time or skills.

All of this is a great offering, perhaps the sweetest offering, to the altar of the Mother. The Goddess is within us, and very much without us. She is everywhere, and we must seek her everywhere. We must find her in the places where we show our most deeply held beliefs: that all of life is the sacred theophany of the Goddess and that she is the great enemy of injustice, cruelty, and want.

CHAPTER 15
MOVING FORWARD (AND BACKWARD)
FINAL THOUGHTS

 Tell me, Moon Goddess, how my love began." [1]

– Theocritus, *The Idylls*

AT THE TEMPLE

I had the incredible experience of traveling, with my mother, through Egypt on a trip full of fellow teachers. We spanned the entire country in our travels, from Alexandria on the Mediterranean coast to Abu Simbel, near the border of Sudan where the temple of Ramesses II is carved into the stone. We did the normal tourist things, like climb into the Great Pyramid in Giza, and take boat rides on the Nile. I was an initiate at the time of this trip, so I was eager to explore the temples. Karnak is breathtaking, far larger than photographs lead you to believe, and the temple of Khom Ombo, with its museum of mummified crocodiles, is beautiful in the sunset. All of it was incredible.

But at the temple of Isis in Philae, I had an experience that I still hold onto, particularly when I am struggling. The temple was originally in a different location than it sits now, moved by the state for the construction of a major dam. I took a boat to the temple with my group and our

---

[1] Georg Luck, *Arcana Mundi: Magic and the Occult in the Greek and Roman Worlds* (Baltimore, MD: Johns Hopkins University Press, 2006), 105.

guide, gathering water from the Nile in little bottles that I still have. I sprinkle them during important rituals, a little token of my pilgrimage.

My mother and I at the famed temple of Ramesses II in Abu Simbel during our shared trip to Egypt. (Photo by Author)

When we got to the temple, I was feeling overwhelmed. The temperatures are brutal in Upper Egypt, and I was dealing with an illness at the time. The guide led us through the important landmarks around the temple, and I could not take my eyes off the carvings of Isis and the divine family. Something must have been written on my face, and the fact that I had religiously worn an ankh the entire time in Egypt, because I realized at some point that my guide, and the rest of the group, were all staring at me. It was an odd mix of concern and indulgence.

My guide asked the group, without my prodding or even asking, if we could wait to head back to the boat so that I could, in his words, "have a little extra time in the temple." No one even batted an eye. We had all sort of bonded on the trip. I felt a little guilty, but I couldn't say no. I slipped back into the temple, and into the holy of holies, where the stone altar still stands. There was a family taking pictures, but the room was largely deserted. The family asked me if I would take a picture of them, near the altar, and I did, before perhaps staring a little too awkwardly until they waved goodbye and left.

I was alone, standing in front of the altar of Isis. The walls in the room are etched with hieroglyphs and the room is cooler than the rest of the temple location, dark and comforting. I could hear the large crowd of tourists, just outside, shouting and laughing and moving through with their own tour guides. But for one blessed moment, I was alone. And I prayed. I prayed as hard I ever have and let it all flow out and around me. I spoke her name, there, at her altar, in the temple of her worship. It was a cathartic, incredible moment. But it is not the moment I am really talking about, the one I carry with me.

On the boat ride back, giddy with the experience of being in the temple of Isis, I relaxed with my mother, drinking overpriced canned sodas, and watching other boats sail down the enormous and muddy Nile. My father had died two years before our trip to Egypt. He had died from a long battle with a debilitating illness that had completely changed our lives and consumed us (my mother more so) with the incredibly daunting task of taking care of a dying person. The last years had been extremely painful for us. The trip to Egypt was the first major thing we had done after losing my father. And for my mother, it was her first major trip.

Truly. My mother had never even flown until that trip, and her son convinced her to fly from the Southeast US to Cairo for her first real vacation! And she climbed into the Great Pyramid. And she sailed on the Nile. And she ate shawarma near the Al Azhar Mosque and chatted with the church attendants in the Coptic district as if it were just any ole Tuesday.

And she loved it. My mother still talks about our trip to Egypt. She has a photobook of our journey and I find her flipping through it when I visit with her, still to this day. For almost three weeks, she had nothing to worry about but where our next stop was and whether they had cold bottled water or hibiscus tea to combat the crushing heat. I never expected her to love it as much as she did, but she still adamantly asserts it was the best time of her life.

And on that boat, tired from the sun and the walking, I felt the presence of the Goddess. I watched my mother's face relax in a way I had not seen in years, not since the long illness of my father had begun. I had prayed to the Goddess in the temple, a Ptolemaic temple from an era centuries before I was born and dedicated to a Mother worshipped millennia before that. And there she was too, in the face of my very real flesh and blood mother, beaming as she looked out over the Nile and experienced relief, peace, and joy after so much darkness had swallowed us up. God was on the boat, and she breathed across the longest river on earth, glinting off my mother's sunglasses and off my silver ankh.

That moment I remember when the darkness descends again, as it always does. I remember what it was like to feel connected to something that spanned so much time, so many people, so much hope and love worked into stone and worship and prayer. I remember the sense of conviction and magic, of glimpsing something beyond the veil of daily reality, something that burned bright as a star, radiating out everything that really mattered. I hold that with me, even now, and I hope that I will always hold it.

After that incredible experience, I had a conversation with a fellow seeker and devotee. They asked me if it didn't bother me that so many of our experiences as Witches, Pagans, or magical seekers, take place at ruins. Isn't it a little depressing, they asked, to only visit long-dead temples and historical monuments, not living places of worship? I've pondered this a lot. There are days when it feels so difficult to build community and connect to living faith. We do not have megachurches, or working cathedrals, it is true. But I am lucky to have a tradition. I am blessed to have found my own tribe of believers.

But it isn't just my initiation into Craft that comes to me when I ponder this question of ruins and "lost history." What comes to me is that...I prayed in that temple in Egypt. Me. I have consecrated sacred wine at Eleusis with a High Priestess, standing next to the "ruins" of the holy place of the Mysteries. I have prayed in Stonehenge, walking in long circles, singing with another High Priestess. I have a ring blessed by a fellow Witch with me on the Acropolis. Were they ruins then? Maybe. They did not feel like it, not while we worshiped and prayed together to the Mother in the face of Isis, Athena, Persephone, or the Earth herself.

When you take the leap into Mother, then the entire world is her shrine. And the temples that others pass through as "ruins" are anything but for you. Every touchpoint of her worship, even those that only few still practice in, are endlessly powerful. They still hold the spirit of place that animates and moves within them.

And we also build our own temples, carving them from the ether and standing within them, declaring her presence, calling her into flesh and spirit, dancing together while we sing her names. All those temples I mentioned visiting, being so fortunate to have made pilgrimages to them, were incredible. But I have also felt the living presence of Mother in the dining room-turned-temple of a beloved elder in a small town in England, and in the home of my own teacher, and in extra rooms and makeshift circles on both sides of the Atlantic. This still happens. It happens all over the wide and varied earth. What does it matter if the locale changes? What does it matter if one name has faded, or another has grown to prominence? The names rise and fall in endless song. The melody may evolve, but the music is eternal. Seek for her, and her believers, and you'll find how alive she truly is.

MOTHER-LIFE

I talk a lot about the Goddess. Giving a class at a festival in New Orleans, I once told a gathered group of spiritual speakers that I was a Pentecostal, Evangelical Goddess worshipper. I did it to get a chuckle and break the ice, but there was a modicum of truth in it, just like there is in most jokes. I have tried to use what little voice I have to elevate Mother and the path that has enriched my life so much that I cannot even enumerate a real list of what she's given me. Too much would be left out. Too much cannot be put down into words, concretized in ink.

My hope, though, is that I have concretized some it for you, or maybe even just provided entry points, or signposts on a path that I do not own. Nobody owns it. I hope that all those that look longingly into the face of the moon or feel the presence of the uncanny in the myth and lore of Mother can pull something from this book and use it as a springboard for further devotion and development. I hope, most of all, that you lose inhibitions and shake off fear and doubt.

So much of what holds us back is inhibition. We are tepid, afraid to commit to anything, afraid to actually admit our desires. We hunger for revelation but deny it when it comes. And we lovingly preserve myths and legends, but curate our language around them to ensure that we always have an escape hatch, a way to hold back and wait. *Well of course it's just a story. I'm really just exploring right now. I'm spiritual but not religious. I'm not sure what I believe.*

None of this is a bad thing, necessarily, but I hope that I can give some courage to those that want to move past the shore of waiting and dive into the water of experience. There is nothing wrong with commitment and devotion. We are all trying to get across a great and terrible river. And if we sit on the shore, constantly fiddling over which boat we are going to use to cross the river but never actually rowing, then we are never getting across the water.

What waits on the other side? What is looking out for you, waiting for you, across the waters of that great and terrible river? Everyone will name it differently. I name it Mother. I say it is the infinite and cosmic Goddess, creatrix of our reality, and the web of life. If that name sparks something in you, and you feel that presence waiting, too, then take the boat and begin rowing. There is no "right time" to seek and begin the quest. The time is always the moment. There is just the infinite moment. Get in the boat. Seek her face.

None of this is to say that I am advocating for dogmatic beliefs or rigid religious hierarchy. Those are exactly the things that Mother can obliterate in her great dance. Freedom is at the heart of the Goddess, liberation from the constraints of controlling doctrine and oppression. But there are different kinds of freedom. Sometimes freedom is the freedom to do whatever we want, a freedom from being squashed under bootheels and forces of control. At other times, though, true freedom can be the freedom to become what we were meant to be. Freedom can be the release of all those things that hold us back and stop us from progressing towards our fullest destiny. This, too, is freedom. Commitment is a form of freedom if it is chosen in liberty and joy. It is not dogmatic, nor controlling. It liberates within discipline. It frees within pointed devotion.

The choice to Mother-life, to the service and devotion of the Great Goddess, is a path of exactly what I subtitled this work: Ecstasy and Transformation. Worship and magic take us out of self (*ex stasis*) and transform the substance and trajectory of our life. When we take those first steps towards the altar, we are participating in the sacred act of countless believers before us, and countless more that will come after.

We are at Eleusis, tired and hungry, waiting for the revelation of the Goddess, learning the passwords that we will never forget. We are in the grottoes and caves of the mountains, listening to the terrifying cries and drumbeats of the worshippers outside, those who chant and scream the names of the Mother of the Gods. We are at Kalighat and Tarapith, at Samothrace and the temple of Hera in Argos. We are in Philae, listening to the story of a Mother who snatched her husband's mangled body from the maw of crocodiles and stitched him together with the breath of life itself. We are gathered around the Queen of Night, in defiance of the priest and the king, feasting at the sabbat of the Witches. We are even in the chapel and the convent, crowning statues of saints and virgins, naming them with titles older than the Christian scriptures.

We are all of these experiences. We look back and reach forward, multi-faced devotees, hands up in worship, voices loud in exalted prayer. We work magic to transform our lives and leave offerings on makeshift shrines and ornate altars alike. Is my language too big here? Is it too big everywhere in this book? No! It is not big enough. Nothing would be big enough to contain Mother. Nothing is beyond her, or outside of her. In an inversion of a famous Calvinist quote, I say there is not a single square inch in all of creation that the Mother does not cry: MINE! Our lives are the theophany of the Mother and we live as her breathing, bleeding, sweating, hoping, praying, loving icons. Turn your face to her. Sing her name. Ask her to part the veil, even if you are not ready. She will be there, just like she has always been there, waiting for you.

Let us always worship her, with prayer and adoration, to the ends of the Earth and even in the places beyond that. Let us pray:

Mother of Gods and mortals, from whom Earth and Sky are born; the winds of creation and the spreading sea both come from you. Come, in your blessings and attend to our holy work. Bring the abundance of your glories and drive out that which ails us. To the ends of the Earth, you are worshipped and adored. [2]

---

[2] Adapted from the Orphic Hymns

THE MOTHER'S BREVIARY
RITES, PRAYERS, AND OTHER HOLY THINGS

The prayers and rituals in this breviary can be used exactly as they are, but I also hope you use them as sources of inspiration to craft your own devotional practices.

PRAYERS, INVOCATIONS, AND CHANTS

7 SHORT PRAYERS FOR TIMES OF THANKSGIVING

THANKSGIVING FOR REVELATION

I have shaken the rattle of my bones and danced with the ones who carry the baskets. In the rushes, I saw the sacred things and underneath the linen did I spy your gifts. I drank the barley-water, Mother, and whispered the awful words. You are come, Mother, with your thumb and finger at my brow, to sing me off to sleep. Happy will I go, into those dark homes where the ashes blow, and the shades whisper their prayers. You have put the good name upon my heart, and I carry it as my password. Torch-Bearer, I am coming, coming on swift feet and the light breath of my prayer. I am coming, Mother, to you.

THANKSGIVING FOR JUSTICE

Happy are the children of the Great Mother, the ones who work justice on the earth and make right the twisted paths of mortal making. Glory! The river is a swift and terrible roar, but you are the bark of souls, Mother, and you have carried me across, showing me the blessed shores of your garden, there where the Truth echoes like the call of elephants and Justice illuminates like the midsummer Sun. Your wrath is corrective, Lioness, and your maw tears apart the wicked. Show us the way, Lawgiver, and set right the weighing stones.

THANKSGIVING FOR THE BOON OF WEALTH

The table of the Mother is overflowing, and her power echoes like the roll of storms. To you I sing my praise, Golden One, light of the ages. In your name I have drawn from the well, and I have tasted the sweet water there, the gift of your hands. My cup is filled with good wine. I have drawn from the lake of those that came before me. Priceless Jewel, Pearl of Wisdom, my voice rises in unending song, above the strife of living. Bountiful as the sea, wide as the milky star-path, All is underneath your feet, Mother, and happy are we to dine at your wedding feast.

THANKSGIVING FOR ARTISTIC INSPIRATION

The stars were born from your left eye, Mother, and in them are the crucibles of our being. From your first act, you wove together what would be. An offering, I brought, in thought and deed, to pour in love upon your sacred stones. There, in that holy place, I saw what new thing springs eternally from my soul. For you, shifting muse, I remake the day. I twist and grow, a hungry, drinking thing, and break the dark soil with my hands.

THANKSGIVING FOR DELIVERANCE FROM DISEASE

This body is the temple of you, O Mother, and every cell cries out to the web of creation that unfolds from between your eyes. I held your name behind my teeth when this temple was unrested. And there I sat with you in silence. And still, I felt you. I heard you. O Mother long were my nights and countless my worries, but still they were but pearls upon the string of your mercies. All life emanates from the heart of your wonders. Here, I offer thanks and praise for the continuation of life and the strength of my healing. Proud I walk before the temple of Mother. I am purified through the work of my hands, and no one may bar me from the sanctuary. Honor to you who is the medicine of souls.

THANKSGIVING FOR LOVE, PARTNERSHIP, OR MARRIAGE

You I saw, Mother, with the lapis face. You, I embraced, tracing the golden veins of your presence. Here we are, Mother, beneath the canopy of stars, heart wed to heart in the bliss of the new dawn. Sweet things I bring you, good to eat and pleasing to the nose. At this daybreak, I kiss the altar. When the sun is round and high, I am beneath the eyes of the Beloved. In the eventide, I worship, body and soul, the Fountain of the Undying One. Blessed is the Queen of Heaven, the Sea-formed Mother, who gives us joy on earth and hope beyond the veil of death.

THANKSGIVING FOR THE HARVEST AND THE RETURN OF LIFE

Mother, golden grain I have beaten, shelled from the stalks that come from you. Bread, I have eaten, toothsome in the mouth. All this I make from your wonders. To you, I sing, my voice a crawling vine, spread across the wide and green earth. From the roots of my devotion, I water the secrets of your mysteries. Under your hand, what I press into the mud of the valley is made alive and good. Grant that I may work for you still, that what I have is multiplied to the glory of your sunlit face. Take my prayer, as one fruit among the endless harvest of souls that make good sacrifice to you. Long is the bitter time when I rest with you, in mourning. But now, look! See, Mother, the return of your love! Let us rejoice in the reunion.

SEVEN SHORT PRAYERS FOR TIMES OF DARKNESS

A PRAYER WHILE FACING ANXIETY

Once I saw the face of Mother, rising from the edge of a great lake. Twice I saw her hands, pressing into the red mud of the southern reaches. Three times I saw her feet, walking on the surface of the sea. Mother, you are the balm that heals all burning things. My mind is on fire, Mother, and my dreams are unsettled. Take me to the well, Mother, where the black horse drinks, where the hare whispers to the moon. There, let me touch that cooling water and ease my mind. Be with me, Mother, in all your forms, and teach me to count the stars.

A PRAYER WHILE FACING ILLNESS

My body is the revelation of the Goddess. My heart is a beating fire at her altar. My breath is an invocation. My spittle is the endless sea. My blood is the first river. My right hand opens up to the stars. My left hand closes on the sun. Mother, pass the flowering branches over my skin, and let me taste the honeyed drink. Touch the root of the sacred tree and draw up the water of life so I may drink. Bring me the first bread, the promise of renewal. I am in the mountain, seeking you, knowing you await me. Make strong the body, Mother, that it may climb again.

A PRAYER IN TIMES OF LOSS OR DEATH

Mother, I am sitting with you, beside the cold hearth. You hold the soul in the rapture of your presence. Grant that I may come to know peace again, when the time of mourning has passed, and the dew lies fresh again in the daylight. Let me hold your strength, Mother, that I may pass through this dim land whole and upright. Grant me the knowledge, unshakeable, that we are reborn through your Love and that we will join again at your table, in the holy house of your gathering. Grant that I may see the eternal thread that spins from your wheel. Let me hold it tightly in my tired hands. It will lead me back, back to what is lost, back to you.

A PRAYER WHILE FACING DEPRESSION, SADNESS, OR WOE

At night I seek the shrine, knees aching, hands reaching into the dark. I feel you, Mother, walking near the break of trees, your feet among the leaves and stones. Bring me into the circle of those that heal. Bring me into the circle of those that do no harm. Bring me, Mother, into the well-lit path between the cities of the blessed. Let me borrow breath. Let me borrow a flint, a spark, a little light. Grant that I may steal a key, a token, a password, to the locked temple wherein dance the shining ones. Be with me, until I open that door, and hold me in your presence.

A PRAYER IN TIMES OF FINANCIAL BURDEN, POVERTY, OR STRAIN

Fortune is the Mother, and she holds the gold of earth, the shining stones that mortals have made living and hungry. Bring me to the storehouse, Mother, that I may fill my cup with comfort. Stretch out the wares before my hands. The hollow belly is a hateful god, Mother, and the deep lake is void of fatted fish. Let it be that I may pass into the golden grain. Let it be that I may pass into the fragrant orchard. Know that I love you, Great Mother, and know that I will rise, like you.

A PRAYER IN TIMES OF CONFUSION

Three paths unfold, Mother, from the center of my heart. Many more fork therefrom. Where are you? I look for you, eyes peering, hands outstretched, heart flayed open to your work. And I do not see you. I cannot feel you. Where is Mother? Come! Come again and walk with me. Light for me the lantern of your revelation and I will follow it through the gloaming. Be for me the clarity of daybreak. Be for me the burning tallow of my sacrifice. Guide me, Mother, and I will follow.

☽☉☾

A PRAYER WHEN FACING INJUSTICE

Dread Mother, come again, with the flecked scourge and the winnowing hook. Tie knucklebones into the whips, and fishhooks on the tails. Strike, Scorpion. Cackle. Howl. Tear down the walls of the tyrant and unmake the world if it be your will. At the gates of the holy places, cast down the unworthy. They are coming, Mother, with teeth bared, lips dripping in blasphemy, hands red with the blood of the innocent. Strike, Queen, with the edge of that awful flail. Cast into the outer night all those that would profane the gift of a life lived freely.

INVOCATIONS AND HONORING PRAYERS

THE WORDS OF MOTHER

In the first caves he painted me in red ochre and drew my image from his lover dying in childbirth, and from the face of his ailing mother—skin thin as a reed, eyes sunken, and teeth exposed. He drew me in fear and I responded in love and stretched out my hand to lift him into my Mystery that he may see in the rolls of my flesh the abundance of the Earth and the promise of the infant's squalling. I breathed language into the first of creation and taught the making of tools and the falling of great beasts. For me was the first seed planted.

In the Ganges River I stood knee-deep and have lived, unforgotten, even in an age of steel and Empire. I dance on the progenitors of your fathers, and I drip in the waters of sacrificial wonder. My call goes out like the breath of the universe even unto this day:

Om kreem Kalikaye namaha!

In the Schwarzwald, the Iberian lands, and the heath of England they sought me out and found me. Here they call me Queen of Elphame, Herodias, Habondea. Here I have a goat for a lover and a crescent crown. Here they stitch the Mysteries together with threads of the past—what has survived blind faith in desert books. Here they will whisper into the darkness and draw me down into their midst. They will burn for me, naked as baby birds, and on the pyre they will discover a Truth: they have always burned for me, for I am the white heat of the cosmos, the infinite burning of the stars that I birthed when I was young and the Earth was not but a dream in the grottoes of my mind. I am the crucible where the dross withers and the gold is purified to be beaten into my idols. I am brighter than the midday Sun and from the center of my chest the magnificence of creation spews out on the shining spindle of my radiance.

Once, I spread my wings over a fertile crescent and fed you bread and beer. They raised for me stone temples from Thebes to Rome and I snatched my husband from the maw of the crocodile so that you might see my names refracted one thousand times in the waters of life. I am the throne from which all kingship flows and no mortal flesh may claim the Earth without my blessing. My son is the sky and all sorceries are mine to teach. I know the secret names and may yet teach them to you after your heart has been weighed and you have not been found wanting.

They wrapped me in serpents and feathers in the heart of mountains and then cloaked me in propriety and mercy so that I might be smuggled into their chapels and convents. Yet even there I stand decked in stars, my foot upon the moon, and cast my eyes down at the children that sing my name. I am undying.

Sancta Maria, mater Dei, ora pro nobis...

Lo, I am the Mother of God.

I am the Venus of the poets, and they trace their loves in the curves of my flesh. All art is mine for I am beauty, and without me there is no Muse. In oil paints and India ink they carved out my worship unknowingly, breathing my heathen truths in the very hearts of Christendom. As Graces, as Aphrodite, as Diana of the Wild Hunt. They cannot forget me, for all lovers are mine. All blushing brides and handsome grooms are mine to heat and mold. I crown the worthy with laurel leaves. The first pluck of the harp and the last strike of the key are my offerings.

They put me in Hell only to burn brighter—as Adam's first wife, as Persephone, as Ishtar before her own sister. I am Queen not only of the stars but of the secret places under the Earth. I birth Typhon in brimstone and eat the red seeds of sin that remind you where you come from. Even the Reaper will kneel at my feet, for I am eternal. My kings all die in my arms, suckling at the full breasts of the promise of rebirth. I am the only medicine against the machinations of the grave and the cremation ground. Through me is Him, and through Us is eternity. I bear the pallor of the Moon and it is the same white as the shroud and the corpse. I consume all, create all, am all.

And I am ravenous.

TO THE QUEEN OF THE SECRET PLACES
AN INVOCATION IN RHYME

Her we call, with rattles and drums,

dread mother who comes, behold she comes!

Over the wide and terrible sea,

I scream the names of the wondrous three,

and carve your face on the monstrous mount

where your throne is etched, near the holy fount.

Our sacred rites they name profane,

in mute terror of your lion's mane,

but we still seek to part the night

and take to the stars, entranced in flight.

Queen of the River, and the blessed crown,

we give our bodies to call you down.

Come, ever anew, and touch the face,

to enliven the flesh in Mother's grace.

Now we dance, to quicken the spell,

like our sisters of old on their flights to Hell.

INVOCATION FOR THE GODDESS
AN INVOCATION IN RHYME

We dare to call your name into the dark,

etch your sigils in the sacred bark,

of that wide and deep-rooted tree,

which leads us down to the frothing sea.

You were the leaping doe, wondrous in the Spring,

and of your glories did the first fruits sing.

Plow and scythe, you bear them both,

to reap and cull, and still, you seed new growth.

You are born eternal, Queen, Mistress of the chase,

Diana's hand upon the earth—made holy by her grace.

Your beasts will answer, to the horns and drums,

oh, blessed Mother, you are the one who comes!

You are the hidden face, the Mistress in the night,

and from you come the stars, the birth of endless light.

In every shrine you are the fire. In
every hive you are the Queen.

You are Mother, in flesh before us, and
yet still you dance unseen.

You are the holy cavern; you are the endless stair.

You mount the skies, between your
thighs, and ride the starry mare.

Yours is life eternal, and yours the land of shades.

Yours is the wide green earth, its shores and hidden glades.

You lie curled within the moon.

You are the cup of gold.

You are the Promised One, whom
all prophets have foretold.

In your heart is the seed of life. In
your hand is an endless fire.

And you are with us, Mother, from the
cradle to the tomb to the pyre.

Come! Hear our prayers, mingled in the stinging smoke.

Step forth from ash and willow, from
beech and holly and oak.

You are come, dread Mother, to pull
us beyond the rosy thorn.

O there to see your face! O there to be reborn!

☽◯☾

INVOCATION FOR HERA

Come, Argive Queen of Heaven.

Akraia. Antheia. Zygia.

Juno Sospita. Savior.

She whose hand is above.

You are the atmosphere and the

first primordial elements of the heavens,

united in sacred marriage to the
crackling power of your equal.

You who are first of all Queens,

guide and tester of seekers, come!

Hera. Cow-eyed. Goat-eater of Laconia.

Yours were the first great temples of Hellas.

Yours are mortal lives to hold from above.

Olympian. Queen of the Deathless Ones.

To you! To you! I sing again, ever again.

Descend to bless us, golden-throned and mighty one.

INVOCATION FOR ISIS

Mother, I seek you in the reeds, praying for the gift of life.

Come again, on vulture wing, and breathe upon

the surface of the water. Enliven what is lost.

You who snatched love from the maw of the crocodile,

grant that I may see your face—the wide and cooling moon.

Teacher of sorcery, and keeper of the names of the sun,

answer to the sistrum once again and flood the blessed river.

Come, Great Throne, defender of the people, listen

to our prayers. Rise, Queen of the First Fruits, and

enrapture us in the dance of eternity.

INVOCATION FOR MORRIGAN

A raven call, screeching, heralds the end,

and you, phantom, are riding beneath the clouds.

Hear the call again, dread prophetess,

and mark the final moments of the world.

Come, come, on wing black as coal, slick

as a gutted fish, eyes drinking in the fields of green.

Crowmother, we clash the wheels and shields of time,

here to come into your presence. Lead us, Queen,

to that iron door, the door between loss and memory.

☽○☾

INVOCATION FOR INANNA
AN INVOCATION IN RHYME

Daughter of the alabaster moon,

come, come beyond the door.

The feast is laid on gilded trays,

for you whom we adore.

Shining Queen, you proved your love,

descended even unto death.

Now come, we pray, remove the veil;

we kneel with bated breath.

☽○☾

LITANY TO THE SAVIOR-MOTHER FOR TIMES OF CRISIS
CALL AND RESPONSE

We name you Sospita—savioress.
Juno, we send out the call.

Mother, hear our prayer.

We name you sign against evil, lady of the midwives. Taweret, we send out the call.

Mother, hear our prayer.

We name you guider of ships, safely to
port. Isis, we send out the call.

Mother, hear our prayer.

We name you Anesidora, the one who sends
forth gifts. Demeter, we send out the call.

Mother, hear our prayer.

We name you Phosphorus, Light-Bringer.
Hekate, we send out the call.

Mother, hear our prayer.

We name you guardian of the Night Bark.
Nephthys, we sound out the call.

Mother, hear our prayer.

We name you Symmachia—Ally.
Aphrodite, we send out the call.

Mother, hear our prayer.

We name you Eryma—defender.
Athena, we send out the call.

Mother, hear our prayer.

We name you the protectress and poetess.
Brigid, we send out the call.

Mother, hear our prayer.

We name you the one who snatches love from
death. Inanna, we send out the call.

Mother, hear our prayer.

We name you Malophorus—bearer of

fruit. Persephone, we send out the call.

Mother, hear our prayer.

We name you guardian of the storehouse. Bastet, we send out the call.

Mother, hear our prayer.

We name you Meter Theon—mother of all gods. Great One, we send out the call.

Mother, hear our prayer.

We name you the savior of all who seek your face, Mother. We send forth our calls and prayers in the valley of our fears, knowing that you carry us across the dread sea to the isle of the blessed. To you, above all, we send forth our Love.

Mother, hear our prayer.

5 INCANTATIONS IN VERSE

One of the most effective tools for magical practice is the chanting of simple, rhyming verses. I love complex, well thought out rituals, but sometimes a simple almost childlike rhyme can work its way into your brain and become a potent tool for ecstatic ritual and magical workings. Any of these examples can be used, as written, but I hope they also inspire you to create your own simple verses for your rites. It is easy to move to these kinds of verses, dancing alone or in a group. They are simple to learn and repeat, and in that simplicity, you can lose yourself and focus on the magic more than the words.

I

Bright Mother, Night Mother, the one we adore.
supplicant, touching it—one sacred door.
My will and her will in truth become one,
till all I desire on this earth be done.

II

I saw a woman, she was dressed in white,
dancing in the woods in the dead of night.
I called her forth with the secret names,
and we worked our magic at the midnight games.

III

Blackest night, the night we flew,
to tie the knots 'round the sacred yew.
We bind the cords that bind the will,
till all that troubles is calm and still.

IV

Diana, Night-Crier, lend me your light.
Send forth my fetch, into the night.

V

She-bear, black crow, tooth and claw.
Burn the tallow, weave the straw.
Mare within and sow beneath,
catch the snake between the teeth.

DEDICATION RITES TO THE GODDESS

The following are two rites of dedication. They are not self-initiations, as I do not believe there is such a thing as a self-initiation. Instead, these are meant to be transformative experiences that commit the soul to the worship of Mother, to the transformation and ecstasy given by the Great Goddess. There are two rites included here. The first is to an incarnation of the Mother as the Queen of Witches. The second is to an incarnation of the Mother as something more akin to the Earth. The former draws from more occult experiences and the latter is more like a contemporary pagan rite. Consider if you are ready for a dedication rite such as these before deciding that you really wish to enact one. Often, rites of dedication to deities can provoke intense reactions and emotional experiences.

A DEDICATION RITE TO THE QUEEN OF WITCHES

The day of the rite, you will wake at dawn and sit in a comfortable place to list your hopes. List everything you want from Mother in dedicating yourself to her worship. Burn this list when you are satisfied that it is complete. At noon, you will list all the things that hold you back from giving yourself over to the worship of Mother, or to the path of transformation that you desire. Burn this list just as the first. These lists are not meant to be mindless exercises. Take as much time as you need to complete them. Be ruthless and honest with yourself as to what holds you back. Do not be afraid to list everything, as you will consign it to fire anyway. They are useless if they are not true inventories of where you are at your current stage in life.

Spend time in meditation and prayer throughout your day. Focus on your desire, until it almost feels like anxiety somewhere inside of you, or a hunger. The thrust of this rite is the wonder behind deciding to worship at the altar of the Goddess. Before the rite, bathe in cool water with the following added to your bath: a single black stone of your choosing, dried rose petals, the root or seed from of a fruiting plant, and a bit of your own spit.

This rite is written to be performed on the new moon, at midnight, and out of doors at the base of a tree, preferably an older and sturdy tree with strong roots. If this is difficult, I recommend waiting until a time presents itself where you can work out of doors. There is no need to rush or cut corners. If you simply cannot find a space or time, then consider a different dedication rite or rework this one as needed. If possible, this rite is written to be performed skyclad, but that choice I leave to you as this is a deeply personal choice and may be constricted by time or other considerations around privacy.

Before the day of the rite, gather the following:

A small cauldron or receptacle containing the ashes from burned resin incense and used charcoal, long cooled

Two beeswax taper candles dressed with a mixture of olive oil, mugwort, and patchouli (very little is needed)

An offering cup

Honeyed wine, or mead

A handful of small sweets or candies

A rattle or sistrum

A single rose

Make your way to the tree. On your journey, focus your mind on an image of Mother, or use a repeating, simple prayer to hold your attention. When you arrive, bow to the four directions, then give a nod above you, and one towards the ground. Place the candles into the earth, if possible, or in holders—one to the left of where you will kneel before the tree, and one to the right. They will flank you. The spoken parts of the ritual are given in quotation marks.

Light the left candle.

> "Light of the hand of glories, heed the one who comes in the name of your Mistress. Illuminate the road, for thieves and brigands threaten me on every side."

Light the right candle.

> "Light of boons, heed the one who comes in the name of your Mistress. Illuminate the road, for the path is thorned and the hill is steep."

Kneel before the tree, between the two lights.

> "Mother, I am before the dread veil, the door of infinite space wherein stand the ones who bear your name upon their brow. In the crimson chamber I will pray, hands lifted to your eternal face. In three forms I have worshipped you. At break of dawn, I drank my hope. In the heat of noontide, I clasped my knowing self. Now, in the black cloak of night, I swallow the seed of my fear. In my belly, I make of it an offering. A toadstone is within me. Your hand is at my lips. Your scent is in the air."

Press your hands into the earth.

> "My witness is your body, the dark earth. Witness me then, roots. Witness me then, stones. All of this I claim as my testimony."

Dip your finger into the cool ashes and draw across your forehead a crescent.

> "Marked I am, between the eyes of faith and trust. I kneel at the altar of the Wondrous One, the Shining One. Light of the first stars, awaken upon my brow. Let me know you. Open is the home where I dwell, and unlocked is the door to my vision."

Dip your fingers into the cool ashes and draw across your chest a circle.

> "Feral and wild is the call of Mother. I hear it now, beating in the red chambers of my heart. Here is the High Altar. My flesh cries out for want of you. My body houses a soul aflame for the Night-Crier. Here I am, washed and ready."

Dip your fingers into the cool ashes and draw across each palm the approximation of an eye. Raise your palms high in worship.

> "Owl of Night, Silent One, I see from all sides the black square of your temple."

Bring your hands together before you, palms together.

> "I will not go by the white tree. The waters of memory are my right. In this life, I give the mind, the heart, the hands, to you. I see through the wide and luminous eye. I hear with the twitching shell. I touch the holy things."

Take up the wine and pour it out in libation onto the roots.

> "AH-OH-EE. AH-OH-EE. Balthasar! Lou! AS-IO-AH"

Repeat the call nine times.

Take up the sweets and bury them with your fingers, digging into the earth. Use no tools.

> "For your children, I bring gifts. I have not shown them to the eyes of the priest. Sweet is the worship of the Hidden One."

Rock the body in prayer.

> "Mother! Happy am I before the She-Wolf, the serpent-twined one, beneath the mounds of earth I have found you. In the silver valley, to the lowing of cattle and the rush of wind, I heard your name on the sea air and whispered it to the mountain. And in reply, the great rocks told me of your glories. I know your tales, Mother, and keep them locked in this cage of bones. There, with you, I sing eternal."

Bow your head to the earth and take up the rattle. Begin a slow, measured beat with the rattle.

> "AH-OH-EE. AH-OH-EE. Balthasar! Lou! AS-IO-AH!"

Repeat the chant with the rattle shaking. Grow your voice. Rock your body until you sweat. This is the heart of the rite. Do not stop until you feel her presence. You can rise, spin, dance, or move as you see fit. When she comes, at the height of your chanting, cry out the sacred name she has given to you and fall to the ground. Whoever comes is who you address. Take your time. Breathe. Rest in the knowledge when it comes.

Take up the rose, when ready, and place it between the lights.

"In the sepals and buds, I wind the thread of your name. This, I leave, a memory."

Extinguish the right candle.

"Eye of Night."

Extinguish the left candle.

"Eye of Day."

Nod to the four directions, then once above you and once towards the earth. Gather your things and leave the space. Leave the rose. Sleep with the markings still on your body.

A DEDICATION RITE TO THE QUEEN OF THE EARTH

Before the rite, spend time visualizing a journey into the earth. Review the Queen of Heaven chapter to look for examples of strong visualization meditation. Make sure to organize this rite during a time where you will not be disturbed. It is written to be performed out of doors if possible, and on the full moon. It can be performed skyclad or clothed, but if you do the rite clothed your clothing will get wet. Fasting is recommended if your situation allows for it safely, taking only water from dawn until the rite.

Before the day of the rite, gather the following:

An image of the Goddess

A bowl made of natural material

Gathered water (rainwater if possible)

Four beeswax tapers

Salt

Hops

A handful of dried grain or seeds

Flower petals

A selection of in-season fruits, nuts, bread, cheeses, or other foods that you enjoy, all on a single offering plate of natural material

Make your way to where you will perform your rite.

Draw into the soil a circle large enough to sit in and to hold all that you've brought and place an image of mother at the edge of the circle, within the drawn line.

Light the first beeswax taper and place it in the north. Continue until there is a burning candle at each of the cardinal directions. Give a small nod to each direction, once the candles are lit, saying at each point:

"Before me is the Mother. Behind me is the Mother. There is no place she does not claim."

When all candles are lit, kneel before the Goddess. Press your hands into the earth:

"First Mother of our mothers, living seed of the cosmos, long

have I loved you. Let me feel the presence of your breath."

Wash your hands with some of the water, letting the water soak into the earth. As you wash, say:

"Creature to creation, exalted in the blessing of my body, in you I bury the fear of my heart, giving over to the mud all that burns in my dreams. Mother of memory, keep the seeds of my faults, and water them to sprout anew, with sweeter fruit and greener leaf."

Fill the bowl with the rest of your gathered water. Sprinkle salt, hops, dried grains or seeds, and flower petals into the water. Swirl clockwise with your dominant hand, saying:

"One body, shared between the infinite incarnations of the Goddess. O Great Mother, I love you. I sing to you. You are the air that fills my chest. You are the cool rain in the summer. In the dreadful storm, I hear you. My soul will be with you, in the sacred cave where you teach me. I will meet you there when the light shines from the face of the pale moon, and I will see you in the realms of sleep and death. Holy Earth, witness this dedication to your worship."

Sprinkle the image of the Mother with the water, saying:

"Mother, your names are a chain of great mountains. Within each is a pit of fire. At the edge of that great chain is the first primordial sea. The wind bellows down to us from the craggy tops. You are the foundation of the elements."

Take up the bowl and pour the remaining water over your head. Say:

> "Here I devote myself, in the presence of the firstborn of creation, to your worship. Mother! Wash me in the sea of love and clear for me a path to your altar."

Take up your plate of offerings and hold them before the image of the Goddess. Say:

> "Earth beneath my feet, I know your name. You are the first one, the light that made the worlds. Accept this offering, Mother, and accept this sacrifice into the body that kneels within your Love."

Break your fast by eating in the presence of the Mother. If it is not distracting, you can play music. Meditate, pray, dance, or simply focus on what you have accomplished with your ritual. Once you feel the magic fading, dig your hands back into the earth, before the Mother, saying:

> "Holy one. All that is from you is good. You I worship, Bountiful One. You I adore. In you and with you, I work to tend the wonders of the Earth."

Extinguish the candles, saying with each:

> "First star of creation, you cannot be extinguished."

Leave nothing behind to tarnish or pollute the space. Return home.

THE MASS OF THE GREAT MOTHER

This is a Goddess-focused Mass, based on the text of the Tridentine Mass of Roman Catholicism. I know that for some readers, this ritual may seem blasphemous. It is not my intent to blaspheme a living religion, and I know that this particular ritual will not speak to all seekers. I am including it because, for me, I do believe there is power in finding the Mother in traditional liturgies that deny her, rewording the workings of faiths that cast the Goddess out of history and religion. If you do desire to perform this rite, it takes at least three participants: an officiant, an acolyte, and someone to stand in for the "congregation." The "congregation" can, of course, be as large as you desire. It is not expected that any of this rite be memorized, given its length, so printing out the order of the Mass or providing copies to participants is best practice.

To perform this Mass, you will need:

An altar

An image or statue of the Goddess

Two candles, in holders, preferably beeswax

A smaller votive candle or oil lamp

A chalice

An offering plate or paten

A bowl of water (for the aspergillum)

Salt

Fresh flowers

Apples

Honeyed wine (or mead)

A sacred knife

- Linen, or plain cloth to cover the offerings
- A censor, charcoal, and resin incense (I recommend frankincense)
- A sistrum or bell

PREPARATION OF THE ALTAR AND EUCHARISTIC ELEMENTS:

The altar is prepared before the Mass. It contains an image of the Great Mother, central on the space, flanked by two lit candles. A single votive light or oil lamp burns in front of the icon of the Mother. A sacred knife is present, as well as space for the Eucharistic elements that will be placed there. Fresh flowers, free from artificial colorants, should be present, as well as a bowl of water and a container of salt for the asperges. A sistrum or bell is on the altar. Before the Mass, wine is prepared with honey (mead may also be used or any other honey-based alcohol) and apples are placed on a serving plate, draped in white cloth.

☽◯☾

ORDER OF THE MASS

PROCESSION

The congregation is seated. Sacred music is used for the procession as the officiant and acolyte process in carrying the Eucharistic elements and censer. The officiant bears the chalice. They place the chalice on the altar, before the icon, and genuflect with head touching altar. Acolyte follows suit until all have offered and genuflected. Censer is placed on or near altar. The acolyte approaches and the sistrum is shaken or bell rang around the altar as an act of purifying and offering. After the music is ended, the officiant stands before the altar and faces the congregation.

ASPERGES

OFFICIANT [facing congregation, touching forehead, lips, and heart (the three-fold sign) as words are spoken]: In the name of the Great Mother, Queen of Heaven and Earth.

CONGREGATION: Amen.

OFFICIANT: Before we participate in the Sacred Rites, we purify with water and earth, for our Mother did first appear upon the wide and open sea and then trod her golden feet upon the land.

Officiant mingles salt and water in the aspergillum and kneels before the acolyte, who holds the mixture.

OFFICIANT: O Star of the Sea! Lady of Ten Thousand Names! You who tend the quickening of the womb and breathe the winds of life into the body, even unto death, come amongst us and bless this water that it may serve as a purifying balm and a preparation for those who approach your holy altar.

CONGREGATION: In the river did I see her. In the seas was she known.

Officiant makes a sign of consecration [1] over the water and salt, rises, and then takes the aspergillum into the congregation. All are asperged (sprinkled). The instruments are returned to the altar and the officiant faces the congregation.

---

[1] Any token or symbolic gesture of the Great Goddess can be used as the sign of consecration. Some simple suggestions: a triangle, a circle, an equilateral cross.

CONFITEOR

OFFICIANT (making three-fold sign): In the name of the Great Mother, Queen of Heaven and Earth.

CONGREGATION: Amen.

OFFICIANT: I will go unto the altar of the Goddess.

CONGREGATION: To her, the joy of all that live.

OFFICIANT: In the worship offered by those outside the Mother, they confess their sins before a throne of judgment and beg for release.

CONGREGATION: Her throne is merciful. Shame, she does not know.

OFFICIANT: Then let us acknowledge that though our shortcomings be as numerous as the uncounted stars, we bow to none but her and acknowledge only the progression of our souls towards the Great Work.

CONGREGATION: I confess I seek the mysteries and walk the lead path that turns to gold. I confess that I am soul and flesh, united in one, with neither greater than the other. I do not recognize the authority of the tyrant, nor believe that my soul can be broken for it is of her, and thus eternal. I am purified before the Great Mother.

OFFICIANT: For she is the fount of rebirth, and even her severity is tempered with wisdom.

CONGREGATION: Amen.

GLORIA AND PRAYER OF INTERCESSION

OFFICIANT: Glory to the Great Mother, she who reigns in the sacred places, whose throne encircles the stars and whose crown shines like the midday sun.

CONGREGATION: Glory to the Great Mother, and peace to her children on earth. We praise you. We bless you. We worship you. We glorify you. Two-horned Queen of Heaven, bright Morningstar, eternally begotten begetter, lead us into your mercies and deliver us unto the rapturous love of your mysteries. You alone are the keeper of the names, and you alone are the circle of light from which life springs eternal. You who guard the cradle of creation and tend the graveyard at night, move amongst us as it was in the beginning, is now, and ever shall be. Amen.

OFFICIANT: May the Great Mother be with you always.

CONGREGATION: And with your spirit.

OFFICIANT: Let us pray.

Here the officiant kneels and prays a short prayer appropriate for the season of the year, the needs of the congregation, or the inspiration in their heart. This should be a natural outpouring from the person conducting the rite. Officiant ends with "Amen" and rises.

CONGREGATION: Amen.

OFFICIANT: And let us pray in her many names for the good of her people, and for all the Earth.

(Note: the litany here is a standard litany. It is advisable to change the litany based on the needs of the congregation or the season. All names of the divine may be used as long as they are incarnations of the Goddess. The officiant's section to Isis remains the same, regardless of changes to the litany.)

ACOLYTE: In the name of Inanna, Queen of Heaven, we pray that the reign of earthly leaders works towards justice, freedom, and peace. We pray to her.

CONGREGATION: Mother, hear our prayer.

ACOLYTE: In the name of Diana, Lady of the Wild Hunt, we pray that we tend the Earth with respect and dignity, treating all creatures as they deserve to be treated. We pray to her.

CONGREGATION: Mother, hear our prayer.

ACOLYTE: In the name of Ma'at, who knows our hearts, we pray for strength to fight against injustice and cruelty. We pray to her.

CONGREGATION: Mother, hear our prayer.

ACOLYTE: In the name of Nephthys, tender of the jars, we pray for healing for all those amongst us with afflictions of mind and body. We pray to her.

CONGREGATION: Mother, hear our prayer.

ACOLYTE: In the name of Sophia, first of creation, we pray for wisdom in times of ignorance. We pray to her.

CONGREGATION: Mother, hear our prayer.

OFFICIANT: In the name of Isis, Supreme of All Incarnations, bearer of her many names, we pray for these and all the desires of our heart. Amen.

CONGREGATION: Amen.

LITURGY OF THE WORD AND CREDO

OFFICIANT: O Great Mother, throughout the ages your children have poured a river of ink to sing your praises. With our voices we praise you and with our bodies we exalt you. In dance, song, and poetry do we unite our souls to you. Let us hear from those who have sung your praises.

(Acolyte approaches with reading.[2])

ACOLYTE: A reading from [name of the reading, or name of the author].

CONGREGATION: Glory to her.

Acolyte gives reading with a slight pause after for contemplation.

ACOLYTE: May we never cease to praise her.

OFFICIANT: May she reign upon our lips, in the work of our hands, and above all within our hearts.

CONGREGATION: Amen.

OFFICIANT: Let us proclaim the heart of her faith.

---

[2] In lieu of Biblical texts, the reading may come from hymns to the Mother, historical prayers, personal writings, or sacred texts that speak of the Great Goddess.

CONGREGATION:

I believe in one Goddess, the Great Mother, Queen of Heaven and Earth.
I believe in one God, the first dawn, born of the Goddess before all ages: God from Goddess,
   light from light, true God from true Goddess—Love.
I believe, from this Love, all things were created in her reflection.
I believe in her many names, both known and secret.
I believe in the soul of nature and the eternal circle of rebirth.
I believe in initiation passed down through the ages and manifested in many incarnations.
I believe every soul is a star.
I believe in the Great Work.
Amen. [3]

OFFERTORY AND INCENSE

Officiant arranges Eucharistic elements on the altar, then kneels.

OFFICIANT: Accept, O Holy Mother, almighty and eternal Goddess, these spotless offerings which I your humble servant offer to you, my living and true light, to prepare the way of the Great Work within our souls and enshroud us in the rapture of our service to you.

CONGREGATION: Amen.

OFFICIANT: O Goddess, who created the world in wondrous dignity and more admirably sustains and protects it, grant that by the mystery

---

[3] Credo from Brian Cain

of these offerings we may come to share in your divinity, one spirit, as it was in the beginning, is now, and ever shall be, throughout the cycles of rebirth and unto the end of the eons. Amen. (Officiant rises).

CONGREGATION: Amen.

Acolyte brings forth the censer and the officiant makes a sign of consecration over it.

OFFICIANT: May those that stand at the right hand of her power vouchsafe to bless and consecrate this incense and receive its wondrous odors upon the altar of her glories. Amen.

CONGREGATION: Amen.

Officiant censes the altar.

OFFICIANT (while censing): May this incense, blessed by you, arise before you, O Mother, and may your mercy come down amongst us. Let my prayer, O Queen, come like this incense before you, my hands lifted as the evening sacrifice. O Mother, set a watch before my mouth, a guard at the door of my lips. Let not my heart incline to the evil of profaning your mysteries.

Officiant returns censer to the Acolyte.

OFFICIANT: May the Mother enkindle in us the fire of her love and the flame of everlasting charity. Amen.

CONGREGATION: Amen.

LITURGY OF THE EUCHARIST AND ENDING

The officiant washes their hands with water from the aspergillum.

OFFICIANT: I wash my hands in innocence as I approach your altar, O Mother, giving voice to my thanks and recounting all your wondrous deeds. O Goddess, I love the house in which you dwell, the tenting place of your glory. Gather not my soul with the ignorant, nor with the unworthy and profane. I walk in integrity and my foot stands on level ground for I will bless you in all the assemblies of the Earth. Glory be to the Mother, Queen of Heaven and Earth, as it was in the beginning, is now, and ever shall be. Amen.

CONGREGATION: Amen.

OFFICIANT: Pray, my sisters and brothers, that these offerings may be acceptable to her, the Mistress of all creation.

CONGREGATION: May the Mother accept these offerings, at your hands, for our good and for the good of all the Earth.

OFFICIANT: May the Great Mother be with you always.

CONGREGATION: And with your spirit.

OFFICIANT: Lift up your hearts.

CONGREGATION: We lift them to her.

OFFICIANT: Let us give thanks and praise.

CONGREGATION: It is right to give her thanks and praise.

OFFICIANT: It is truly right and just to give her thanks and praise, at all times and in all places. We sing her many names with the strings of our hearts and our lips never cease to recount her wonders.

CONGREGATION: Holy, holy, holy! Queen of the Heavenly Host! The heavens and the Earth are full of your glories. Blessed are those that come in the knowledge of her.

The officiant takes up the chalice.

OFFICIANT: When the world was young, the fathers of our fathers and the mothers of our mothers drew out the golden light from within the Earth and tasted the sweet ecstasy of the Goddess.

CONGREGATION: The knowledge of her is sweet indeed.

OFFICIANT (raising chalice high): This is the royal jelly of the Queen of Every Hive!

Officiant turns, places chalice on the altar, and genuflects with head touching altar. Acolyte shakes the sistrum or rings the bell and there is silence. Officiant rises and takes up the offering plate of veiled apples.

OFFICIANT: In the beginning, the first of our mothers did look upon the bitter sea and say to the coiled dragon within, "I choose wisdom over paradise." (Officiant unveils apples.) And lo, she ate of the fruit and the great serpent coiled around her, flesh and spirit united as one.

CONGREGATION: The serpent beguiled me, and I did eat.

Officiant turns and takes up the sacred knife. They slice one apple in half and turn to the congregation, holding up the two halves which show the star design hidden within.

OFFICIANT: And within the sacred flesh is the crucible of stars, the seed of all life, death, and rebirth: the wonder of creation.

CONGREGATION: Amen.

Officiant turns, places apples on altar and genuflects, head touching altar. The Acolyte shakes the sistrum or rings the bell and there is silence. Officiant rises and they take up the Eucharistic elements.

OFFICIANT: Let us pray.

CONGREGATION: Our Mother, Queen of Heaven, secret be thy names. Thy reign endures. Thy will be done above, upon, and under the Earth. Give us this day the fruits of thy harvest and teach us thy Mysteries, as they have been taught through the ages. And lead us not into ignorance but deliver us unto thy wisdom.

OFFICIANT: Deliver us, Mother, into that eternal wisdom which is revealed by you. Through your bountiful mercies may we continue to work your rites upon the Earth and unite our souls with your eternal light. Amen.

CONGREGATION: Amen.

OFFICIANT: May the Great Mother be with you always.

CONGREGATION: And with your Spirit.

OFFICIANT: Come to the altar, all who find their heart's desire in her.

Congregation may come to take communion, wine first, then apple. The acolyte or officiant who bears the apples stands by the altar, slicing off each piece with the sacred knife to offer. The acolyte or officiant who bears the chalice offers it to each communicant then wipes it with a cloth.

OFFICIANT/ACOLYTE (while offering wine or apples): Flesh and Spirit.

CONGREGANT (receiving wine or apple): Amen.

After all communicants are finished, the acolyte and officiant take their portion and reset the altar.

OFFICIANT (facing congregation): May the spirit of the Eternal Mother reside within your hearts and keep you in life everlasting, through this life and all lives, through the cycle of death and rebirth and unto the endless ages to come.

CONGREGATION: Amen.

OFFICIANT: The Mass is ended, let we her children go forth in peace.

CONGREGATION: Thanks be to her.

Officiant and acolyte take up the censer and chalice. Sacred music. Procession out.

RITE FOR THE BLESSING OF AN ICON

As stated earlier in this book, it was a common practice in some Hellenistic religious communities to "enliven" or awaken a statue, to see it as a living vessel for the deity. This is similar to the treatment given to Egyptian statues and oracles as well, and in rituals enacted in Hindu traditions. This rite is for the blessing or "enlivening" of a statue or other representation of Mother that will be used in ritual, magic, or worship of the Great Goddess.

> **Gather:**
>
> The image or statue
>
> A small bowl of water, sprinkled with rosemary, hyssop, and rue
>
> A small bowl of soil
>
> A votive beeswax candle or a small oil lamp (the light)
>
> A censer or small cauldron of incense (recommendations: frankincense, copal, or benzoin)
>
> A veil or piece of cloth large enough to cover the image or statue
>
> Flowers and other offerings you wish to leave (libations, fruits, other foods)
>
> A sweet anointing oil with a pinch of mugwort (recommendations: almond oil, grapeseed, olive)

Clean and adorn the image how you desire (jewels, offerings, drapery)

Sprinkle the image with the herbal water, saying:

> *"Mother you are the waters of life."*

Touch your finger to the soil and then press against the base or bottom of the image, saying:

"Mother you are the soil and the root of all living things."

Take up the light and walk three times around the image, saying:

"Mother, you are the World Soul, the fire within the cosmos."

Breathe onto the image, slowly, exhaling fully. Say:

"Mother, every being within creation breathes out your song."

Take the incense and cense the image repeatedly, saying: "Sweet and precious is the Love of the Great Goddess. Carry our prayers, mingled in this smoke, to the hidden palace within the sea, to the pearl throne where she waits for us."

Take up the anointing oil.

Anoint the eyes of the image, saying:

"Open your eyes, Mother, that I might see through them."

Anoint the ears of the image, saying:

"Open your ears, Mother, that you might hear the shouted prayers."

Anoint the mouth of the image, saying:

"Open your mouth, Mother, that you might whisper the

passwords to eternal life."

Anoint the hands, feet, or outer part of the image, saying:

"Flesh and spirit, Mother, twined in one. All life proceeds from your hand."

Place the flowers and other offerings around the image. Say:

"Let it be that I may sit at that great feast, beneath the mound of earth, in the halls of the blessed, with you, Eternal Goddess."

Draw the veil or cloth over the image, saying:

"Beyond the fruiting tree, I will find you Mother. Within the hollow mountain, I will seek your face. Come to me, Goddess, in dreams and revelations, that I may know you and work your wonders upon the earth."

Shake the sistrum and cense the veiled image a final time. Offer any personal prayers you wish to say. Leave the image veiled throughout the night. Unveil before your next devotion, working, or rite. You may wish to continually veil the image until you go for devotional or magical work, but this is not necessary unless it becomes part of your regular practice. It can become a powerful part of ritual practice to tend to an image of the Goddess, veiling it in the evening, "waking her up" with unveiling, offerings, and morning prayers. All of this depends on the time and flow of your practice.

AFTERWORD
AFTERLIFE

I debated adding this afterword, but I believe that it is necessary, so I am trusting in the Great Goddess to help me convey what I believe must be said.

While writing this book I was the primary caretaker for my mother as she dealt with the brutal and often debilitating treatments used to combat advanced cancer. Between writing chapters, I was helping to bathe, feed, and continue to bond with my mother as her illness advanced and her body changed rapidly. The mother who had carried me and held me became a mother that I had to carry, like a child in my arms. Eventually, we made the decision to move into home-based hospice care as her disease progressed.

I finished the first draft not long before my mother passed away. She died on June 19th of 2023 in our living room, surrounded by myself and her son-in-law—my loving husband Patrick. Her last conscious words, uttered not long before passing, were "I love you so much."

I cannot put into words what this loss has meant for me. Even as I write, I find myself struggling not to disassociate from the experiences of this year. I am writing these words not three months after her death. And I would be dishonest to anyone reading this if I did not admit that her loss struck my faith, my sense of being, and my life to the very core. My father passed years before my mother, and I have no living grandparents. I am also an only child. There is an incredible loneliness in this.

My mother was my best friend. She was the light of my life for my entire life up to this point. Having grown up in a somewhat difficult area and situation, my mother and I bonded in a way that I am sure many people would label "codependent." I would never use that language, because I know that we shared a closeness that, to me, is a rare and precious thing.

So, why am I sharing this? I share this story because this book is dedicated to my mother. This book is the explanation, on some small level, of what allows me to move through this grief in a way that leaves the parts of me that matter whole and functional. And I believe that the Goddess can be that for anyone.

The "magical community" (a term I don't fully trust) is opening pathways for many people who are seeking some form of contact or communication with the numinous. Frequently, I find, these paths are careful to—as I say in this book—distance themselves from religious faith, firmly stated belief, or tradition. I think this is a tragedy.

When we leave the confines of the church-house, mosque, or synagogue, we do not need to leave behind the experience, language, and comfort of religious faith.

I do not worship the Goddess because she is a useful tool for political change. I do not worship the Goddess because I am "experimenting" with being "spiritual but not religious." I do not worship the Goddess because I am angry at Christianity. I do not worship the Goddess because I had a childhood fascination with sixth-grade Greek mythology lessons.

I worship the Goddess because in her worship I have felt the infinite and ever-changing presence of that ground of all being that gives meaning to my life. I worship the Goddess because I was able to hold my dying mother's hand and believe, with a diamond clarity, that human consciousness participates in something greater than synaptic firing and neurological complexity. I worship the Goddess because when I cry out in rage and despair, in those nights when the utter bleakness of existence digs into my chest like an icepick…it is the face of the Great Goddess that comes burning through the evening gloom like a comet.

I worship the Goddess because, in my twenties, kneeling on a hardwood floor in the Treme in New Orleans, initiated, I heard her voice like the call of my own heartbeat, echoing through the channels of my body. And that song still hums louder than my grief. It still hums louder than my despair. It still hums louder than my failings, petty missteps, and attempts to leave her worship. Even when the temptation to leave the Goddess came to me, while holding my mother's ashes, I couldn't. I could not bring myself to let go of that thread that weaves my being into being itself. Despite my anger and sadness, I could no more deny the song of the Goddess than I could deny that water is wet or fire burns.

And I write this to hopefully give voice to anyone that wishes to sing in that choir. To hear her song. To keep the faith alive, even in the face of oblivion.

My mother was an incredibly compassionate woman who never let the difficult circumstances of her upbringing change her into something bitter or cruel. Her loss is devastating, and yet, a reaffirmation that what we seek, as devotees of Mother, is return. We seek return to the fountain of pure consciousness. The fountain of love. The fountain and foundation of existence. We are not just creating new ways of finding the divine…we are remembering. Worship is an act of remembrance.

And so, I hope never to forget. I hope to always remember. In this life. In all lives. Until I dwell reunited with what is lost in the ecstasy of the Great Goddess. In that place where nothing is ever lost.

– New Orleans, September 2023

Paula Raye Rowland (née Conley) in Aswan, Egypt
April 1964 – June 2023. (Photo by Author)

BIBLIOGRAPHY

Administration for Community Living. "2020 Profile of Older Americans," May 2021. https://acl.gov/sites/default/files/Profile%20of%20OA/2020ProfileOlderAmericans_RevisedFinal.pdf.

Adamson, Peter, and Jonardon Ganeri. *Classical Indian Philosophy*. New York, NY: Oxford University Press, 2020.

Apuleius. *The Metamorphosis or Golden Ass of Apuleius*. Translated by Thomas Taylor. London, UK: Universal Press, 1822.

Ashcroft-Nowicki, Dolores. *The Shining Paths: An Experiential Journey Through the Tree of Life*. Loughborough, UK: Thoth Publications, 1997.

Athanassakis, Apostolos N. *The Orphic Hymns: Text, Translation, and Notes*. 2nd ed. Baltimore, MD: Johns Hopkins University Press, 2013.

Attar. *The Conference of the Birds*. Translated by Sholeh Wolpe. New York, NY: W.W. Norton & Company, 2017.

Augustine. *City of God*. London, UK: Penguin UK, 2003.

Avila, Teresa de. *The Life of St. Teresa of Jesus, of the Order of Our Lady of Carmel*. Translated by David Lewis. New York, NY: Benziger Bros., 1904. https://www.gutenberg.org/files/8120/8120-h/8120-h.htm.

Ballard, H. Byron. *Earth Works: Ceremonies in Tower Time*. Asheville, NC: Smith Bridge Press, 2018.

Barnes, Jonathan. *The Presocratic Philosophers*. London, UK: Routledge, 1996.

Beard, Mary, John North, and Simon Price. *Religions of Rome: Volume 2, A Sourcebook*. Cambridge, UK: Cambridge University Press, 1998.

Betz, Hans Dieter. *The Greek Magical Papyri in Translation, Including the Demotic Spells, Volume 1*. Chicago, IL: University of Chicago Press, 1992.

Bhikkhu Sujato. "MN 115: Bahudhātukasutta." SuttaCentral. Accessed June 9, 2023. https://suttacentral.net/mn115/en/sujato

Billinghurst, Frances. *Encountering the Dark Goddess: A Journey into the Shadow Realms*. Winchester, UK: Moon Books, 2021.

Bingen, Hildegard von. *Scivias*. Translated by Columba Hart, Jane Bishop, Barbara J. Newman, and Caroline Walker Bynum. New York, NY: Paulist Press, 1990.

Blundell, Sue, and Margaret Williamson. *The Sacred and the Feminine in Ancient Greece*. London, UK: Routledge, 1998.

Brakke, David. *The Gnostics: Myth, Ritual, and Diversity in Early Christianity*. Cambridge, MA: Harvard University Press, 2012.

Braude, Ann. *Radical Spirits: Spiritualism and Women's Rights in Nineteenth-Century America*. Bloomington, IN: Indiana University Press, 1989.

Brown, C. Mackenzie. *The Devī Gītā: The Song of the Goddess, A Translation, Annotation, and Commentary*. Albany, NY: State University of New York Press, 1998.

Bryant, Edwin F. *Bhakti Yoga: Tales and Teaching from the Bhagavata Purana, An Exploration of the Philosophy and Practices of Krishna Devotion*. New York, NY: North Point Press, 2017.

———. *Yoga Sutras of Patanjali: A New Edition, Translation, and Commentary*. New York, NY: North Point Press, 2009.

Bulgakov, Sergei. *Sophia: The Wisdom of God*. Great Barrington, MA: Lindisfarne Books, 1993.

Burkett, Walter. *Greek Religion*. Cambridge, MA: Harvard University Press, 1985.

Cain, Brian. *Initiation into Witchcraft*. New Orleans, LA: Warlock Press, 2019.

Vatican Digital Library. "Catechism of the Catholic Church." Internet Office of the Holy See. Accessed May 29, 2023. https://www.vatican.va/archive/ENG0015/__P9M.HTM.

Chinnaiyan, Kavitha. *Fractals of Reality: Living the Śrīcakra*. Northville, MI: Sfaim Press, 2022.

———. *Glorious Alchemy: Living the Lalitā Sahasranāma*. San Francisco, CA: New Sarum Press, 2019.

Chlup, Radek. *Proclus: An Introduction*. Cambridge, UK: Cambridge University Press, 2016.

Christ, Carol P. *Rebirth of the Goddess: Finding Meaning in Feminist Spirituality*. New York, NY: Routledge, 1997.

Cicero. *The Treatises of M.T. Cicero*. Translated by C.D. Younge. London, UK: Henry G. Bohne, 1853.

Cooney, Kara. *When Women Ruled the World: Six Queens of Egypt*. Washington, D.C.: National Geographic Books, 2018.

Crowther, Patricia. *The Zodiac Experience: Initiation Through the Twelve Signs*. Nottingham, UK: Fenix Flames Publishing, 2020.

Doniger, Wendy, and Jack Miles. *Norton Anthology of World Religions: Hinduism*. New York, NY: W. W. Norton & Company, 2015.

Dorsey, Lilith. *Orishas, Goddesses, and Voodoo Queens: The Divine Feminine in the African Religious Traditions*. Newburyport, MA: Weiser, 2020.

———. *Voodoo and African Traditional Religion*. New Orleans, LA: Warlock Press, 2021.

Eisler, Riane. *The Chalice and the Blade*. New York, NY: Harper Collins, 2011.

Este, Sorita d'. *Circle for Hekate, Volume I: History & Mythology*. Glastonbury, UK: Avalonia, 2017.

Este, Sorita d', and David Rankine. *Visions of the Cailleach: Exploring the Myths, Folklore and Legends of the Pre-Eminent Celtic Hag Goddess*. Glastonbury, UK: Avalonia, 2009.

Fortune, Dion. *The Winged Bull*. York Beach, ME: Weiser, 1999.

Freud, Sigmund. *The Standard Edition of the Complete Psychological Works of Sigmund Freud*. Edited by James Strachey. Vol. 22. London, UK: Hogarth Press, 1964.

PubMed Central (PMC). "Gender Differences in Caregiving at End of Life: Implications for Hospice Teams." Accessed June 9, 2023. https://www.ncbi.nlm.nih.gov/pmc/articles/PMC4677542/.

George, Demetra. *Mysteries of the Dark Moon: The Healing Power of the Dark Goddess.* New York, NY: Harper Collins, 1992.

Gimbutas, Marija. *The Civilization of the Goddess.* New York, NY: Harper Collins, 1993.

———. *The Goddesses and Gods of Old Europe.* Oakland, CA: University of California Press, 2007.

———. *The Living Goddesses.* Oakland, CA: University of California Press, 2001.

Ginzburg, Carlo. *Ecstasies: Deciphering the Witches' Sabbath.* Chicago, IL: University of Chicago Press, 2004.

———. *The Night Battles: Witchcraft and Agrarian Cults in the Sixteenth and Seventeenth Centuries.* Baltimore, MD: Johns Hopkins University Press, 1983.

Graves, Robert. *The White Goddess: A Historical Grammar of Poetic Myth.* New York, NY: Farrar, Straus and Girous, 1948.

Hardacre, Helen. *Shinto: A History.* Oxford, UK: Oxford University Press, 2016.

Harding, Elizabeth U. *Kali: The Black Goddess of Dakshineswar.* Berwich, ME: Nicolas- Hays, Inc., 1993.

Hart, David Bentley. *Kenogaia (A Gnostic Tale).* New York, NY: Angelico Press, 2021.

Hield, Fay. *Hare Spell.* Folk. Wrackline. USA, 2020. https://audio-ssl.itunes.apple.com/itunes- assets/AudioPreview124/v4/51/e5/ce/51e5cea3-4408-baae-ef09- a4c23f70706e/mzaf_28739382333338631474.plus.aac.p.m4a.

Homer. *The Iliad.* Translated by Richmond Lattimore. Chicago, IL: Chicago University Press, 2011.

Huson, Paul. *Mastering Witchcraft: A Practical Guide for Witches, Warlocks, and Covens.* Lincoln, NE: iUniverse, 2006.

Iamblichus. *Iamblichus: De Mysteriis.* Translated by Emma C. Clarke, John M. Dillon, and Jackson P. Hershbell. Atlanta, GA: Society of Biblical Literature, 2003.

Instone, Stephen. *Greek Personal Religion: A Reader.* Liverpool, UK:

Liverpool University Press, 2009.

Johnston, Sarah Iles. *Hekate Soteira: A Study of Hekate's Roles in the Chaldean Oracles and Related Literature.* New York, NY: The American Philological Association, 1990.

Jones, Charles B. *Pure Land: History, Tradition, and Practice.* Boulder, CO: Shambhala Publications, 2021.

Julian. *The Works of the Emperor Julian.* Translated by Wilmer Cave Wright. Cambridge, MA: Harvard University Press, 1913. https://www.gutenberg.org/files/48664/48664-h/48664-h.html#toc23.

Jung, Carl. *Jung on Synchronicity and the Paranormal.* Edited by Roderick Main. Princeton, NJ: Princeton University Press, 1997.

———. *The Collected Works of C. G. Jung.* Edited by Herbert Read, Michael Fordham, and Gerhard Adler. Translated by R.F.C. Hull. Princeton, NJ: Princeton University Press, 1968.

Kali, Devadatta. *In Praise of the Goddess: The Devimahatmya and Its Meaning.* Berwick, ME: Nicolas-Hays, Inc., 2003.

Kitaiskaia, Taisia. *Ask Baba Yaga: Otherworldly Advice for Everyday Troubles.* Kansas City, MO: Andrews McMeel Publishing, 2017.

Kugle, Scott. *Sufi Meditation and Contemplation: Timeless Wisdom from Mughal India.* Translated by Carl Ernst. New Lebanon, NY: Omega Publications, 2012.

Laozi. *Tao Te Ching.* Translated by Stephen Mitchell. New York, NY: HarperCollins, 2006.

Layton, Bentley. *The Gnostic Scriptures: A New Translation with Annotations and Introductions.* 2nd ed. New Haven, CT: Yale University Press, 2007.

Leland, Charles Godfrey. *Aradia: Gospel of the Witches.* Custer, WA: Phoenix Publishing, 1996.

———. *Aradia: Gospel of the Witches.* Providence, RI: The Witches' Almanac, 2010.

Lerner, Gerda. *The Creation of Feminist Consciousness: From the Middle Ages to Eighteen-Seventy.* New York, NY: Oxford

University Press, 1993.

Levack, Brian P. *The Witchcraft Sourcebook*. New York, NY: Routledge, 2015.

Lovelock, James. *Gaia: A New Look at Life on Earth*. New York, NY: Oxford University Press, USA, 1987.

Luck, Georg. *Arcana Mundi: Magic and the Occult in the Greek and Roman Worlds*. Baltimore, MD: Johns Hopkins University Press, 2006.

Lucretius. *On the Nature of Things*. Translated by William E. Leonard. MIT: Classics Archive, n.d. http://classics.mit.edu/Carus/nature_things.2.ii.html.

Majercik, Ruth Dorothy. *The Chaldean Oracles: Text, Translation and Commentary*. Wiltshire, UK: The Promethean Trust, 2013.

McDaniel, June. *Offering Flowers, Feeding Skulls: Popular Goddess Worship in West Bengal*. New York, NY: Oxford University Press, 2004.

———. *The Madness of the Saints: Ecstatic Religion in Bengal*. Chicago, IL: University of Chicago Press, 1989.

McDermott, Rachel Fell, and Jeffrey John Kripal. *Encountering Kali: In the Margins, at the Center, in the West*. Oakland, CA: University of California Press, 2005.

Meyer, Marvin W. *The Ancient Mysteries: A Sourcebook of Ancient Texts*. Philadelphia, PA: University of Pennsylvania Press, 1999.

Midgley, Mary. *The Myths We Live By*. New York, NY: Routledge, 2003.

Mooney, Thorn. *Traditional Wicca: A Seeker's Guide*. Woodbury, MI: LLewellyn Publications, 2018.

Murray, Margaret. *The God of the Witches*. London, UK: Sampson Low, Marston & Co. Ltd., 1931.

———. *The Witch-Cult in Western Europe: A Study in Anthropology*. Oxford, UK: Oxford University Press, 1921.

Pew Research Center. "'New Age' Beliefs Common among Religious, Nonreligious Americans | Pew Research Center." Pew Research

Center. Accessed June 8, 2023. https://www.pewresearch.org/fact-tank/2018/10/01/new-age-beliefs-common-among-both-religious-and-nonreligious-americans/.

Nietzsche, Friedrich. *Nietzsche: The Gay Science.* Cambridge, UK: Cambridge University Press, 2001.

Nikhilananda, trans. *The Gospel of Sri Ramakrishna.* New York, NY: Ramakrishna- Vivekananda Center, 1942.

Novick, Leah. *Shekhinah: Rediscovering Judaism's Divine Feminine.* Wheaton, IL: Quest Books, 2008.

Oleszkiewicz-Peralba, Małgorzata. *The Black Madonna in Latin America and Europe: Tradition and Transformation.* Santa Fe, NM: University of New Mexico Press, 2007.

O'Neill Jr., Eugene, trans. *The Complete Greek Drama.* Vol. 2. New York, NY: Random House, 1938. https://www.perseus.tufts.edu/hopper/text?doc=Perseus%3Atext%3A1999.01.0026%3Acard%3D1737.

Padoux, André. *The Hindu Tantric World: An Overview.* Chicago, IL: University of Chicago Press, 2017.

Pausanias. *Pausanias Descriptions of Greece.* Translated by W.H.S. Jones and H.A. Ormerod. Tufts University: Perseus Digital Library, n.d. http://www.perseus.tufts.edu/hopper/text?doc=urn:cts:greekLit:tlg0525.tlg001.perseus-eng1:3.16.

Pinch, Geraldine. *Magic in Ancient Egypt.* London, UK: British Museum Press, 1994.

Plato. *Plato in Twelve Volumes.* Translated by Harold N. Fowler. Tufts University: Perseus Digital Library, n.d. http://www.perseus.tufts.edu/hopper/text?doc=urn:cts:greekLit:tlg0059.tlg004.perseus-eng1:69c.

———. *The Collected Dialogues of Plato.* Edited by Edith Hamilton and Huntington Cairns. Princeton, NJ: Princeton University Press, 1989.

Powell, Barry B. *Greek Poems to the Gods: Hymns from Homer to Proclus.* Oakland, CA: University of California Press, 2021.

Proclus, and Dirk Baltzly. *Proclus: Commentary on Plato's Timaeus.*

Cambridge, UK: Cambridge University Press, 2007.

Rangos, Spyridon. "Proclus and Artemis: On the Relevance of Neoplatonism to the Modern Study of Ancient Religion." *Kernos*, 2000. https://doi.org/10.4000/kernos.1293.

Rodrigues, Hillary. *Ritual Worship of the Great Goddess: The Liturgy of the Durga Puja with Interpretations*. Albany, NY: State University of New York Press, 2003.

Rogers, Guy MacLean. *The Mysteries of Artemis of Ephesos: Cult, Polis, and Change in the Graeco-Roman World*. New Haven, CT: Yale University Press, 2012.

Roller, Lynn E. *In Search of God the Mother: The Cult of Anatolian Cybele*. Oakland, CA: University of California Press, 1999.

Rowland, Levi. *The Art Cosmic: The Magic of Traditional Astrology*. New Orleans, LA: Warlock Press, 2021.

Ruether, Rosemary. *Sexism and God-Talk: Toward a Feminist Theology*. Boston, MA: Beacon Press, 1983.

Sanders, Maxine. *Firechild*. Mandrake, 2007.

Scholem, Gershom. *Major Trends in Jewish Mysticism*. New York, NY: Schocken Books, 1961.

———. *On the Mystical Shape of the Godhead: Basic Concepts in the Kabbalah*. New York, NY: Schocken Books, 1991.

Scott, Michael. *Delphi: A History of the Center of the Ancient World*. Princeton, NJ: Princeton University Press, 2014.

Sherab, Palden, and Tsewang Dongyal. *Tara's Enlightened Activity: Commentary on The Praises to the Twenty-One Taras*. Ithaca, NY: Snow Lion, 2007.

Solovyov, Vladimir. *Divine Sophia: The Wisdom Writings of Vladimir Solovyov*. Translated by Judith Deutsch Kornblatt. Ithaca, NY: Cornell University Press, 2009.

Starhawk. *The Spiral Dance: A Rebirth of the Ancient Religion of the Great Goddess*. San Francisco, CA: HarperOne, 1999.

"Supreme Court Questions Jyotir Vigyan." *The Times of India*, September 3, 2001.

Tapasyananda, trans. *Sri Lalita Sahasranama: Text, Transliteration and English Translation*. Chennai, India: Sri Ramakrishna Math Printing Press, 1988.

Tartt, Donna. *The Secret History*. New York, NY: Vintage Books, 1992.

Tertullian. *Ante-Nicene Church Fathers*. Edited by Alexander Roberts, James Donaldson, A. Cleveland Coxe, and Kevin Knight. Vol. 4. Buffalo, NY: Christian Literature Publishing Co., 1885. https://www.newadvent.org/fathers/0402.htm.

ETCSL. "The Electronic Text Corpus of Sumerian Literature." Accessed June 8, 2023. https://etcsl.orinst.ox.ac.uk/cgi-bin/etcsl.cgi?text=t.4.07.6#.

Access to Insight. "The Round of Rebirth: Samsara." Accessed June 9, 2023. http://www.accesstoinsight.org/ptf/dhamma/sacca/sacca1/samsara.html.

Townsend, Richard F. *The Aztecs*. London, UK: Thames & Hudson, 2009.

Turcan, Robert. *The Cults of the Roman Empire*. Cambridge, MA: Blackwell Publishers, 1996.

Uždavinys, Algis. *Philosophy & Theurgy in Late Antiquity*. Kettering, OH: Sophia Perennis, 2010.

———. *Philosophy as a Rite of Rebirth: From Ancient Egypt to Neoplatonism*. Wiltshire, UK: The Promethean Trust, 2008.

Versluis, Arthur. *Entering the Mysteries: The Secret Traditions of Indigenous Europe*. Minneapolis, MI: New Cultures Press, 2016.

Watson, Lindsay. *Magic in Ancient Greece and Rome*. London, UK: Bloomsbury Publishing, 2019.

Wilby, Emma. *Cunning-Folk and Familiar Spirits: Shamanistic Visionary Traditions in Early Modern British Witchcraft and Magic*. Chicago, IL: Sussex Academic Press, 2005.

———. *The Visions of Isobel Gowdie: Magic, Witchcraft and Dark Shamanism in Seventeenth-Century Scotland*. Chicago, IL: Sussex Academic Press, 2010.

Williams, Mark. *The Celtic Myths That Shape the Way We Think*.

London, UK: Thames & Hudson, 2021.

Witt, R. E. *Isis in the Ancient World*. Baltimore, MD: Johns Hopkins University Press, 1971.

Wolkstein, Diane, and Samuel Noah Kramer. *Inanna Queen of Heaven and Earth: Her Stories and Hymns from Sumer*. New York, NY: Harper & Row Publishers, 1983.

Wooten, Rachael. *Tara: The Liberating Power of the Female Buddha*. Boulder, CO: Sounds True, 2020.

INDEX

Abrahamic Faiths: 12, 66

Adam: 151, 221, 265

Addiction: 2, 143

Advaita Vedanta (SEE: Vedanta)

Aeneid: 102

Afterlife: 209-210

Aging: 145-146

Agriculture: 112, 211

Alchemy: 172

Amitabha: 50

Ancestors: 65, 67, 168

Angels: 63, 128

Anubis: 207

Aphrodite: 8, 12, 18, 102, 109, 160, 265, 271

Apollo: 184, 186-189

Apuleius: 10-11, 18, 21

Aradia: 120

Ares: 109

Argos: 104, 106, 109-110, 112, 255, 268

Aristotle: 63, 151-152

Asatru: 240

Asherah: 233

Astrology: 5-6, 35, 63, 70, 151, 182, 184-186, 191, 197-198

Asura: 87

Atheism: 3, 80, 172

Athena: 109, 112, 160, 253, 271

Athens: 19, 25, 109

Atman: 89, 151

Attar: 51

Attis: 25

Avalokitesvara: 170

Ayahuasca: 39

Aztec: 165, 206

Baba Yaga: 148

Barbelo: 227

Bhakti: 91-92, 94, 107

Blavatsky, H.P.: 5, 15

Bodhisattva: 170-171, 173

Brahman: 89, 151

Buddhism: 7-8, 12, 49-50, 56, 62, 64, 84, 153, 156-157, 170-174, 205, 213, 217, 223-225

Bulgakov, Sergei: 231

Cailleach: 147-148

Carthage: 104-105, 111

Catabasis: 161

Catechism: 37, 49, 66, 235

Catholicism: 2-3, 40, 49, 51, 63-66, 120, 142, 145, 169, 172, 182-183, 214, 218-219, 221, 232, 235, 240, 283

Cauldron: 73, 142, 155, 160, 178, 275, 296

Celts: 48, 80, 124, 127, 166-167, 169, 179, 207

Ceres: 19

Cerridwen: 138, 154, 160, 167-168, 173-174, 178-179

Chaldean Oracles: 14, 47, 75, 189, 197

Chalice: 58, 73-74, 155, 283-284, 293, 295

Chamunda: 86-88, 108

Childbirth: 71, 105, 108, 206, 208, 221, 263

China: 50, 170, 173-174, 225

Christianity: 3, 7, 12-15, 18, 20-22, 27-28, 31, 41, 47-48, 52, 55, 64-65, 73, 82, 88, 94, 96, 99, 103, 116, 118-119, 122-123, 125, 142-143, 167-168, 172-174, 177, 179-180, 194, 203, 212, 215, 217-218, 220-222, 226, 228-233, 235, 245-246, 256, 265, 300

Clio: 181

Crone: 146

Crowley, Aleister: 5, 15, 129

Cults: 15, 17-19, 22-24, 32, 43, 46, 55-57, 69-70, 80-81, 104, 112, 120, 123, 127, 166, 169, 172, 174-176, 209, 226, 237, 239

Cybele: 15, 17, 42, 46, 56, 58, 60, 72, 127
Daoism: 150, 171-172, 184, 206, 225
Death: 72, 138-139, 169, 207-210, 214
Delphi: 186-188
Demeter: 16-17, 72, 77, 127, 139, 271
Demiurge: 227-228
Demons: 67, 83, 87-88, 96, 101, 112, 117, 128, 146, 169, 188, 243
Devi: 83, 85, 89-90, 96, 200
Devil: 116-117, 124, 194
Diana: 6, 19, 23, 69, 72, 117-122, 124-127, 265, 267, 273, 288
Dionysus: 25, 57
Divination: 6, 11, 36-37, 63, 143, 172, 182-186, 189, 191-193, 197-199, 240
Durga: 81-83, 85, 88, 92, 95, 108, 148
Egypt: 8, 14, 17, 19, 28, 48, 54, 59, 80, 169, 206-208, 249-253, 296
Eleusis: 15
Elysium: 20, 24, 96, 209
Entheogens: 39-40
Ephesus: 14, 17, 23, 72, 119
Epistemology: 35
Epona: 80
Ethics: 9, 138, 157, 172, 213, 247
Eucharist: 3, 49, 64, 284, 290, 292, 294
Eve: 194, 221-222
Fairies: 124, 127, 148, 215
Feminism: 184, 240
Festivals: 13, 57, 76, 81, 85, 88, 92, 96, 104, 110, 202, 211, 214, 238-239, 254
Folklore: 124
Freud, Sigmund: 142-143
Freyja: 208
Gaia: 60, 212-213, 215
Gardner, Gerald: 174, 177, 185, 210, 238
Gardnerian Witchcraft: 125, 177, 237-239
Ginzburg, Carlo: 123-124
Gnosticism: 63, 217, 226-229, 231

Gorgon: 144, 169, 176
Gowdie, Isobel: 123
Grail: 154, 160
Greek: 99-100, 102-105, 173, 186, 209, 229
Greek Magical Papyri: 53-54, 131
Grimoires: 48, 63, 128-129, 175
Hades: 139, 207, 209
Halloween: 124, 214
Hallucinogens: 39-40, 214
Hekate: 19, 47, 69, 71, 118-119, 127, 132, 189, 197-198, 271
Hel: 208
Hellenism: 15, 20, 56, 67, 69, 80, 92, 104, 111, 118, 173, 189, 217, 295
Hephaestus: 102
Hera: 69-70, 99-113, 138, 160, 166, 188, 206, 255, 268
Hermeticism: 15, 28, 62, 67, 151, 154, 201
Herodias: 120-122, 264
Hildegard of Bingen: 195-197, 225
Hinduism: 12, 31, 39, 49, 56, 63-66, 75, 81-85, 91-92, 94, 96-97, 127, 148, 152-153, 175, 180, 185, 213, 225, 296
Homer: 101-102, 112
Iamblichus: 24-25, 50, 189
Idolatry: 31, 65-67
Immortality: 132, 209, 225
Inanna: 59, 73, 136, 150, 270-271, 288
Incense: 43, 54, 58-59, 158-159, 162, 198, 275, 284, 290-291, 296-297
India: 92
Indigenous: 19, 28-29, 39, 213
Initiation: 3, 10, 15-16, 18-19, 22, 24, 32, 37, 39, 43, 70, 73, 81, 115, 127, 153, 160, 177, 184-186, 209, 211, 236-239, 244, 249, 253, 274, 290
Ishtar: 18, 59, 160, 207, 265
Isis: 8, 14-15, 17-20, 45, 54, 56, 58-59, 77, 80-81, 90, 112, 127, 160, 169, 175, 206-207, 249-251, 253, 269, 271, 288-289
Islam: 7, 31-32, 49, 51-52, 56-57, 64-65, 103, 172, 203, 214
Jainism: 8

Japan: 50, 157, 225
Jesus Christ: 7, 12, 15, 64-65, 124, 166, 179, 219-220, 226-227, 230, 234
Judaism: 7, 31-32, 49, 81, 146, 169, 222-223, 245
Jung, Carl: 142-143
Juno: 19, 72, 99, 101, 104-105, 108, 110-111, 268, 270
Jupiter: 63, 104-105, 108
Justice: 9, 131, 133, 141, 178, 247, 260, 288
Kabbalah: 31, 151, 222-223
Kali: 12, 82-83, 85-88, 91-94, 96-98, 108, 136, 148, 215, 225
Karma: 97, 136, 242
Kore (SEE: Persephone)
Krishna: 85, 89, 91
Laveau, Marie: 178
Leland, Charles Godfrey: 120-121
Lilith: 169-170, 247
Liturgy: 49, 177, 231, 239, 283, 289, 292
Lotus: 77, 157, 159
Magic: 10-14, 24, 32, 36, 47-48, 63, 124, 126-130, 151, 175, 200, 237, 242-243
Magna Mater: 14, 24, 42, 46, 56, 218
Marriage: 109
Medudsa: 169-170, 176
Moon: 68-71, 200
Mountain: 1, 38, 52, 60, 71, 89, 102, 105, 111, 133, 138, 155, 160, 179, 196, 213, 215, 245, 255, 261, 264, 278, 281, 298
Mudra: 62
Murray, Margaret: 125
Muslim (SEE: Islam)
Mystery Cults: 15, 17-18, 22-24, 43, 70, 81, 166, 209, 237
Mysticism: 30-34, 39-41, 219, 232
Neoplatonism: 14, 21, 24, 50, 62, 64, 67, 105, 107, 126, 151-152, 189, 194
Nephthys: 59, 112, 207, 271, 288
Nile: 77, 249-252
Nuns: 38, 155, 157, 177, 223
Oaths: 125, 198, 238, 244

Occultism: 3, 5-6, 10, 12, 15, 27-28, 48, 63, 108, 117, 143, 151, 154, 158, 174-175, 240, 245, 274

Ocean: 38, 75, 109, 160, 214, 245

Oracles: 14, 47, 67, 75, 172, 182-184, 186-190, 192, 197-198, 296

Orthia: 24, 41-42, 109

Orthodoxy: 229-231

Osiris: 160, 207

Paganism: 14-15, 18, 48, 70, 96, 117-118, 173-174, 180, 191, 200, 245-247

Paranoia: 192, 241-242

Pathworking: 154, 159-160, 162

Patriarchy: 5, 10, 27, 37, 59, 80, 103, 112-113, 125, 170, 194, 215, 217, 229, 240, 246

Persephone: 16-17, 131-132, 137, 139-140, 160-161, 207, 253, 265, 272

Polytheism: 18, 21-22, 48, 173

Poseidon: 109

Potnia Theron: 55, 72

Prayer: 10, 14, 19, 43-44, 47-60, 91, 104-105, 126, 159, 176, 219, 222, 256-257, 260-263, 270-272, 287-288, 297-298

Proclus: 106-107, 126, 189

Psychoanalysis: 141-143

Pythia: 188

Python: 188

Qabalah (SEE: Kabbalah)

Quran: 12, 64

Ramakrishna: 92-94, 96

Ramprasad Sen: 92, 94, 96

Reincarnation: 20, 22, 24-25, 44, 73, 76-77, 84, 92, 96, 151, 171, 173, 202, 204-205, 209-211, 265, 286, 290-291, 294-295

Religious Witchcraft: 4, 14, 27, 65, 125, 127, 173-174, 179-180, 185, 200, 211, 216

Rome: 2-3, 8, 14, 17-18, 22, 24-25, 33, 42, 45, 56-57, 63, 80-81, 99-100, 102-104, 109, 116, 118-119, 121, 134, 152, 160, 167, 169, 174-175, 206, 212, 218, 229, 231, 240, 246, 264, 283

Sabbats: 6, 39, 45, 115-116, 120, 211, 256

Sacraments: 64, 231

Saivism: 39, 85, 89
Salome: 120, 122
Selene: 69, 118, 131-132
Serpents: 83, 90, 120, 131, 133, 176, 188, 218, 222, 264, 278, 293
Sex: 84-85, 121, 143, 194
Shakti: 83-84, 86-87, 89, 96-97
Shekinah: 223
Shinto: 225
Sibyls: 183-184, 186, 198
Sistrum: 58, 269, 275, 284, 293-294, 298
Siva: 85-87, 89
Sophia: 198, 216-218, 222, 226-232, 235, 288
Spiritualism: 5, 184-185, 187-188, 193
Starhawk: 211, 234
Sufism (SEE: Islam)
Sunthemata: 62, 162
Symbolism: 26, 61, 63-64, 68, 70, 79, 162, 198
Taboo: 34, 44, 85, 124, 126-127, 139
Tantra: 31-32, 56, 83-85, 91, 93, 97, 126-128, 153, 175, 180, 224, 237
Tara: 224
Tarot (SEE: Divination)
Taweret: 206, 208, 270
Teresa of Avila: 32-33, 40-41, 51, 225
Theosophy: 5, 12, 151
Therapy: 144, 243
Theurgy: 14, 21, 24-25, 45, 50, 67, 92, 105, 107, 109, 130, 189
Tiamat: 138, 178, 215
Triple Goddess: 69-70, 146
Typhon: 112, 188, 265
Underworld: 19-20, 102, 135, 137, 140, 155, 158, 160-161, 207, 209, 236
Vedanta: 89, 93-94, 151-152
Vedas: 61, 93, 185
Venus: 19, 96, 108, 112, 160, 265
Virgin Mary: 65, 68, 169, 218-220

Vishnua: 89
Vodou: 80, 239
Wilby, Emma: 123-124
Witch Trials: 116, 118, 120-121, 123-125
Witchcraft: 6, 25, 27-28, 47, 69-70, 114-118, 120-121, 123-127, 147, 173-174, 177-180, 185, 200, 238, 245, 247, 274
Wrath: 13, 260
Yahweh: 233
Yaldabaoth: 227
Yantra: 64, 153, 200
Yoga: 93
Zeus: 21, 25, 99, 101-102, 104-107, 109, 133, 139, 184

ABOUT THE AUTHOR

Levi Rowland is an Alexandrian Witch and High Priest leading the Pontchartrain Coven in New Orleans, Louisiana. He also co-hosts Covendom, a podcast dedicated to the practice and spirituality of Initiatory Witchcraft. His service to the Great Goddess has led to teaching classes and workshops both online and in person, opening up pathways and systems of magic for seekers across traditions and backgrounds. His book, The Art Cosmic: The Magic of Traditional Astrology, explores the rich history of traditional astrological techniques and magic. In his teaching, Levi strives to be a voice for the transformative power of both magic and Goddess religion.

Warlock Press™
WarlockPress.com

Warlock Press is an independent occult publisher that is driven to provide unequalled content written by a diverse roster of today's magical adepts. Our authors hail from a spectrum of magical traditions, but share crucial things in common: authentic practice, established credentials, thorough research, and genuine devotion. This means that you can trust that you are getting the very capstone of the pyramid of occult wisdom.

INITIATION INTO WITCHCRAFT
Brian Cain
Foreword by Maxine Sanders

This is a book about the religion of Witchcraft. It honors the old Gods, the ancient mysteries, and the secrets of magic. It is an exploration of the timeless traditions, essential ethics, and the awe-inspiring power of our Craft and provides basic practices that will help the reader to embrace the deeper ways of the Witch. It is a signpost for those seeking the path that begins the journey of initiation into Witchcraft and primer of occult techniques and rituals to prepare for that journey.

THE WITCHES' BOOK OF THE DEAD
Christian Day
Foreword by Laurie Cabot

The revised and expanded tenth-anniversary edition of this genre changing classic is available August, 2021. Readers will learn to summon and honor the spirits of the dead to bring blessings in their everyday lives, discover Witches of legend who raised the dead, and explore methods of spirit contact, necromancy, potent rituals, recipes, and exercises, and features two new chapters, new foreword, and a new preface!

LIVING THE ELEMENTS: EXTREME ADVENTURES FOR WITCHES
Fiona Horne

Join world traveling rockstar Witch, Fiona Horne and experience the sacred elements of Witchcraft in an action-packed, dynamic way that enlivens every fiber of your being and supercharges your spell casting. Air, Earth, Fire, Water, and Spirit are at the core of magickal work and in this unique book, Fiona gives you the advice you need to invoke your most empowered self. Fiona's personal stories entertain, enchant, and educate. She gives you the tools to get out of your comfort zones, stretch your boundaries and let go of limitations. Fiona offers three activity levels, Transcendent, Potent and Passionate—choose one or work through all three—from visiting waterfalls to freediving, kite flying to skydiving, firedancing to volcano climbing, dark retreats to stargazing. Whatever your physical or financial conditions, Living the Elements will change your life!

MAGICK WITHOUT TOOLS
Sean Wilde
Foreword by Lilith Dorsey

This book is designed for everyone from absolute beginners to experienced practitioners, giving a solid foundation of background and practices for the former and new ways of looking at magic for the latter. Through the practices and rituals in this book, you will be able to start your path using magic or develop it further, possibly transforming it entirely. This book is intended for everyone. It doesn't matter your background, where your family comes from, where you live, or any other type of status. What I teach and share with you is accessible to all and is your birthright.

VOODOO AND AFRICAN TRADITIONAL RELIGION
Lilith Dorsey

Journey beyond the basic tenets of the faiths of the African diaspora to the vibrant, living spirit world of their peoples. This seminal guide to African spirituality has been revised and expanded to include tools for activists to empower their work for social change with the wisdom of their ancestors, as well as never-before-published recipes, personal spells and charms, such as root magick for protection and protest, and devotional rituals readers can perform themselves.

THE ART COSMIC: THE MAGIC OF TRADITIONAL ASTROLOGY
Levi Rowland
Foreword by Sorita d'Este

A detailed guide to the fundamentals of planetary magic using the seven sacred spheres of the ancients, including a system of celestial correspondences to use as a basis for meaningful spells, rituals, and workings. Readers will learn how to interpret natal charts using timeless methods of traditional astrology, use horary astrology for divination, incorporate the planetary hours for more successful spell work, and perform potent magical rites for each planet.

www.ingramcontent.com/pod-product-compliance
Lightning Source LLC
Chambersburg PA
CBHW072147070526
44585CB00015B/1034